Marxism and
Native Americans

Marxism
and
Native Americans

edited by
Ward Churchill

SOUTH END PRESS BOSTON

Library of Congress Number: 83-060182
ISBN 0-89608-177-X Paperback
ISBN 0-89608-178-8 Hardcover

Cover Design and Production by Carl Conetta

South End Press
302 Columbus Ave.
Boston MA 02116

Acknowledgements

The editor would like to thank the following individuals for their assistance, both direct and indirect, in the completion of this project: Charlie Cambridge, Dan Debo, Reyes Garcia, Demetries Stevies, Tom Holm, Roxanne Dunbar Ortiz, Nick Meinhardt, Bertell Ollman, Bill Means, Susi Schneider, Jesse Hiroaka and Gonzalo Santos, for offering constructive criticism of the idea and/or various aspects of the manuscript. Grace and Wallace Black Elk, Charles Fast Horse, John Trudell, Chris Westerman, Rick Williams, Charlie Hill, Cate Gilles and others too numerous to mention provided hours upon hours of conversation affording insight to a portion of the subject matter. And a *very* special thanks is due to Faye Brown who provided all of the above freely and unstintingly.

I'd also like to thank Bernardine Dohrn and Jeff Jones, whose postulations provided my first crash-course into the world of Marxist Leninist theory; Walter and Roseanne Kimmel, teachers who put a new perspective on my understanding of the Marxist paragigm; Kwame Ture, Bob Brown and Macheo Shabaka, brothers who are to an important extent broadening that perspective; Sarah Sneed, who has seen fit to challenge virtually ever resultant position I hold; Norbert S. Hill Jr., who has allowed me a certain amount of job flexibility in pursuing a project which failed to particularly interest him; Michael Albert and Sheila Walsh, whose letters, calls and advice from South End Press provided a vital editorial assistance; and Alice Englebretsen, Janet Shotwell and Carol Moor, whose skills at proofing and typing saved me a demoralizing portion of the one-finger method through which I ordinarily complete final copy.

Also: Dakota AIM, Women of All Red Nations, Yellow Thunder Tiospaye, Black Hills Alliance, Akesasne, and—of course—the contributors from the Preface to the Postscript, as well as all the others I've missed mentioning—thanks for everything.

CONTENTS

PREFACE
Natural To Synthetic And Back Again
Winona Laduke

This America has been a burden
of steel and mud
and death,
But look now,
there are flowers
and new grass
and a spring wind
Rising
from Sand Creek.
                    Simon J. Ortiz
                    From Sand Creek

I would argue that Americans of "foreign" descent must become Americans. That is not to become a patriot of the United States, a patriot to the flag, but a patriot to the land of this continent, these continents. You were born here, you will not likely go away, or live anywhere else, and there are simply no more frontiers to follow. We must all relearn a way of thinking, a state of mind that is from this common ground. North America is not Europe, and this is the 1980s—those are two "facts" that we must remember when we begin to relearn and rebuild. And, if we are in this together, we must rebuild, redevelop, and reclaim an understanding/analysis which is uniquely ours. Within the essays which follow, I believe that some of the questions are beginning to be asked which we need answer if we are to move towards a new understanding.

There are many histories of North America. The experiences of successive waves of immigrants are distinct, as are—to a large degree—the histories of the different classes comprising the immigrant waves. The histories of the various peoples native to the continent are also quite distinct within themselves. The story of each of these groups holds a rightful claim to its own integrity, to its own place and fullness of meaning within the whole. To deny this is to distort.

1

Yet there is another history, one which is most frequently overlooked or ignored in attempts at understanding "America": the history of the land itself, the land and its relationship to all the peoples who live, have lived, or will live here. It is within this aspect of reality, a reality common to us all, that the key to understanding lies. Without addressing the history marked indelibly in the land, a history neither to be refuted nor "interpreted" thru ideological sophistry, no theory can be anchored. Since an unanchored theory must inevitably result in misunderstanding, it is to the history of the land that we must turn.

Before the European penetration of North America, thousands of generations of peoples indigenous to this hemisphere lived out their lives, practiced their cultures and extended their societies through time. The societies these people developed were highly rich and diversified but, in general, they were universally marked by being "natural" in the sense that they functioned in accord with, literally as a part of, nature and the natural environs.

But with the arrival of the Europeans a break was made such that every seeming step forward into greater "development" could be measured simultaneously by the degree of divorce of society from the natural environs. It is no accident that felling natives as a means to expropriate land represented little more within the operative mentality than felling trees to clear a field. The American Indian was rightly, if unwittingly, considered as part and parcel of the natural order, a *thing* to be profitably surmounted.

While proclaiming the land a wilderness to be brought under human control, the settlers relied upon the primieval richness of its soil to provide the basis of their agriculture; the pristine quality of its lakes and rivers to provide fish and fur; and its teeming wildlife to provide protein. In like fashion, while pronouncing the Indian as "savage," they lifted the form of the Iroquois Confederacy to organize their government and the crops of the Pequot and Pennobscott, Passamaquoddy and Wampano as the basis of their agriculture. Never once in their arrogance did they stumble upon the single fact that in subsuming the wilderness and the Indian within their synthesis they were irrevocably cutting themselves off from the very substanc of the new life they were forging in North America.

The long history of colonization by Europeans changed the face of the land—for a new economic order was forged *on* the land, not *with* the land. Across the country, forests retreated steadily before the ax, the wildlife disappeared and, with them, the indigenous peoples. Land was sacrificed to the need for iron, and then steel. In West Virginia it was coal. In Pennsylvania, oil. As the land bled its wealth into the pockets of the newly rich in the East, the eyes of empire turned west toward gold, silver, and oil; Bauxite and manganese; copper and zeelites, natural gas, coal and uranium. And thus the developing technological society became ever more divorced from nature, ever more "synthetic." Eden is "tamed," man is master of the universe; that is the essence of the American synthesis, the foundation of American power.

Two Canadian authors, Robert Davis and Mark Zannis, in their book *The Genocide Machine in Canada,* have succinctly described the result:

> Simply stated, the difference between the economics of the "old colonialism" with its reliance on territorial conquest and manpower and the "new colonialism," with its reliance on technologically oriented resource extraction and transportation to the metropolitan centers, is the expendable relationship of the subject peoples to multinational corporations.

This "new colonialism" was, to a certain extent, predicted by Karl Marx in his observation that industrialization would necessitate the expropriation of the general masses of people from the soil, their means of subsistence. And, in his view, this fearful and painful expropriation of the peasant formed the prelude to the history of capitalism.

We would argue that while Marx was correct, not only the expropriation and its immediate social aftermath are important. Rather, the sort of permanent society which not only emerges, but which is *possible* under such circumstances must be brought into serious consideration. Is it enough to mitigate the physical suffering of the people thus dislocated, or must one also look to the psychic or spiritual damage suffered, and *to the land as well?* Is it possible to heal the wounds of the people, of whatever sort, caused by the process of separating them from the land, while *keeping* them separated by virtue of a process which literally consumes the land itself? In other words, can the synthetic *ever* adequately replace the organic, the natural? These are questions which must be asked as the result of any reasonable examination of North American history.

It is widely recognized that something is drastically wrong. The topsoil of America has washed away, agriculture can only be accomplished through massive applications of chemical "enrichments." This "better living through chemistry" seeps into our aquifirs, lacing our groundwater with lethal toxins and, as acid rain produced by the fly-ash of our steel mills and coal-fired power plants renders our surface water equally lethal, so bottled water becomes the fastest growing "foodstuff" item in the nation.

The United States thrashes about seeking technological "fixes" to technological catastrophes, and entire regions of the west are written off as "National Sacrifice Areas." In search of a long-term solution to an array of crises, reliance is placed upon "the friendly atom," and we find increasing expanses of our environment contaminated beyond habitation for the next quarter million years. The synthetic system threatens to implode in radioactive chaos. It is no longer able to fend for itself, but the momentum of its existence refuses to allow it to stop.

It is the land, always the land, which suffers first and most. As the cities, those ultimate manifestations of synthetic culture decay, so increasingly is the produce of the earth ripped loose to shore up their continuation. Steel, the stuff of the girders comprising bridges and skyscrapers, becomes exhausted with age and must be replaced. The earth yields iron ore to processes which require mushrooming quantities of energy, and so coal is stripped away from the yawning craters at Black Mesa, WyoDak and elsewhere to fuel the generators of electrical currents which now litter the map. The land will yield until the land can yield no more. But the need for its offerings will remain. And then?

As the land suffers, so suffer the people. Whether they are the citizens of the natural or the synthetic order, in the end there is no escaping this basic link. It is an aspect—indeed, the imperative—of the synthetic order to forget or ignore such facts. Nor could it be otherwise. To face the facts would have led inevitably to a retreat from synthetic procedures and ideologies, to a withdrawal from a way of life busily consuming the basis of life itself. The facts were not faced and, as Malcolm X once put it, "The chickens are coming home to roost."

The spiraling costs of continuously refitting cities has exceeded the social ability to pay. This is particularly true in relation to the current moment, when the bulk of social wealth and resources are being diverted to tools of conquest, an overt return to notions that an expansion of landbase can in itself create the substance of a "vital" and "growing" synthetic reality. Meanwhile, the citizens of the inner cities discover themselves subsisting on a government dole of dogfood and rice, much the same as the citizens of traditionally colonized peoples, both within and without the United States. As the land has become utterly expendable, so too have the people—*all* the people—in the name of "progress" and "the system." Once again, perversely, the land and the people are fused; the logic of synthesis.

How do we turn such a nightmare to positive ends? How to turn from the synthetic reality of consumption and expendability to the natural reality of conservation and harmony? How *not* to perpetuate the cycle of self-destruction within which we are currently engaged? These are questions which not only need to be, but must be answered—and soon—if we are not to have passed the point of no return as a species, possibly as a planet.

We can agree with Marxists that the point is not only to understand the problem, but also to solve it. There are undoubtedly many routes to the answers. Throughout the United States people are moving into resistance to many of the more covert forms of synthetic oppression. The draft has met with massive rejection even before it could be fully implemented. A relatively broad anti-nuclear war movement has taken root across geographic, class, sex, and ethnic lines. Much the same can be said of a movement to oppose utilization of nuclear power in any form at all. A number of environmentalist groups are engaged in extending many of the anti-nuclear rationales to encompass much of the industrial process itself. Elsewhere, others have targeted issues of the most disenfranchised social strata—mostly within urban centers—as their focus.

The common denominator of all these is direct action, action directed against the status-quo. If there is a unifying theme, it would seem to be a firm rejection of the status quo, of "business as usual." The synthetic order is thus being questioned and, in some areas, truly challenged. This is certainly to the good. But something more is needed. No movement or group of related movements can succeed in offsetting present circumstances merely through a shared rejection. Not only must they struggle against something, but they must also struggle *toward* something. Action alone can never provide the required answers. Only a unifying theory, a unifying *vision* of the alternatives can fulfill this task. Only such a vision can bind together the fragmentary streams of action and resistance currently at large in America into a single multi-faceted whole capable of transforming the synthetic reality of a death culture into the natural reality of a culture of life.

This need should come as no revelation. It seems well known within most sectors of the active resistance. The quest for a unifying vision has been going on for some time. By and large, it seems to have gravitated steadily towards one or another of the Marxist or neo-Marxist ideologies with the result that there is currently in print the widest array of Marxian literature in the United States since, perhaps, the 1930s. This is a logical enough development. Marxism, it must be said, offers a coherent and unifying system of critical analysis within which to "peg" a wide variety of lines of action. Further, it offers at least an implicit range of plausible options and alternatives to the status-quo. The details of a Marxist society may be forged in the struggle to overthrow the existing order.

The Marxian scenario is rather neat. It seems all but ready-made for applicaton to our current dilemma. Of course, it will require certain alterations, modifications intended to keep it ahead of the development of its opposition, and of those among its adherents as well, but such adjustment is not impossible. Habermas, Althusser, Marcuse, Gramsci, and others have demonstrated that. In effect, this is part of Marxism's neatness.

This book questions that very neatness. Without denying that Marxism is (or can be) a unifying system, it steps outside the Marxist paradigm to ask new questions. What is Marxism's understanding of the land? What is or will be the relationship of a Marxist society to the land? Is Marxist thought other than a part of the synthetic order which is at issue? If Marxism is now inadequate to dealing with such issues, can it be altered in such a way as to make it adequate? If it is to be altered in such ways, will the result remain Marxist, or will it become something else? Is Marxism as it is now structured, *or could be structured*, a part of the solution or a part of the problem? And finally, is it, or what is appropriate to North America? These are not questions springing from the Marxist tradition. Nor do they come from *any* European or neo-European context. They are not the sort of questions posed by "First World" (capitalist) polemicists, by those of the "Second (socialist) World" or "Third (industrializing) World." Instead, they come from the realm of the remaining landbased peoples of the North American continent, the remaining representatives of the natural order which preceded the advent of synthetic reality. In some quarters, this has come to be called the "Fourth World;" we prefer to term it the "Host World." In answering such questions, Marxism goes far in defining its true allegiance and place in the world. It begins to explain "what must be done" in overcoming the synthetic by returning it to the natural.

We say the questions posed by this book come from the perspective of the North American Host World, the truly landbased peoples. As Kwame Toure has stated, "When you speak of liberation, true liberation, you are speaking of land. And when you speak of land in this hemisphere, you are speaking of American Indians." The questions, then, come specifically from the perspective of the Native American. The Host World, however, is not so confined. The questions asked in the text which follows could well have been posed by the tribal peoples of South or Central America, of Africa, the Kurds and others of the Middle East, the tribes of the Scandinavian arctic, the mountain peoples of Southeast Asia, the Einuet of Greenland, the Pacific Islanders, and many others across the planet. In responding to the American Indian critique, Marxism responds in some way to the questions of all these peoples. We have a common ground and it is not only that which lies beneath our feet. Rather, it lies within a shared understanding of the correctness of Simon Ortiz' assessment of what America has become, and what it must become if we are to survive. The massacre of the Cheyenne people at Sand Creek in 1864 was not theirs alone; it was representative of the massacre of us all. Such a legacy *must* be turned into its opposite. We must "negate the negation" which is stained by blood that forever seeps into the *land* of Colorado and everywhere else the synthetic order has reigned. This is the vision, the dream which will allow us to free ourselves of the death culture.

As Simon put it elsewhere in his epic poem:

> That dream shall have a name,
> After all,
> And it will not be vengeful
> But wealthy in life
> And compassion
> And knowledge
> And it will rise
> In this heart
> Which is our America

On this continent we have come from the natural to the synthetic. We must find our way back again. We must turn the common ground of our agony into the common ground of our vision. This book is an important step in such a process, not because it provides the necessary answers, but because it asks many of the right questions. Only through the asking of such questions can the answers emerge. They must be answers which include the land as well as the people, which perceive and project land and people as being one and the same, which understand that until alternatives are found which prevent the destruction of the land, the destruction of the people cannot be stayed: the movement back from the synthetic to the natural.

Within such a movement Marxism, or aspects of Marxism, may well have a role and function. What and how remains to be seen. What better direction to turn for clarification than to those who have no particular question as to their relationship to the land, those who have all along retained their affinity to the natural order rather than "progressing" into the synthetic one? Let Marxism explain its utility to its hosts. Let it differentiate itself clearly from synthetic reality. And let the hosts for the first time take an active role in assisting in this process, denying what is false, supporting that which is true.

Such an interchange cannot help but assist in establishing a strategy, a vision through which to reclaim the natural order. We must all participate in the process of completing the cycle: natural to synthetic and back again.

INTRODUCTION
Journeying Toward A Debate
Ward Churchill

This book was born of a sense of frustration. It began in earnest nearly ten years ago at a place called Sangamon State University, with a guest lecture by Karl Hess, former Goldwater speechwriter, sometime SDS theoretician and at the time a sort of avant garde urban anarchist. For me it was an evening marked by an almost crystalline clarification.

Hess' talk covered what was (for him) tried and proven ground: growing trout under high density conditions in tenement cellars, roof-top gardening techniques, solar power in the slums, neighborhood self-police forces and block governing committees, collective small-shop production of "appropriate" technology, the needlessness of federal income tax. The upshot of his vision was that the federal government is a worse than useless social oppression which should be dissolved so the United States can be taken over by a self-sufficient citizenry at each local level.

After the customary polite applause, the session was thrown open to questions from the audience. The question I had to ask was: "How, in the plan you describe, do you propose to continue guarantees to the various Native American tribes that their landbase and other treaty rights will be continued?"

1

2   Marxism and Native Americans

Hess seemed truly flabbergasted. Rather than address the question, he pivoted neatly into the time-honored polemicist's tactic of discrediting the "opposition" by imputing to it subversive or (in this case) reactionary intentions: "Well, I have to admit that that's the *weirdest* defense of the federal government I've ever heard." The debate was joined.

I countered that I had no interest in protecting the federal government, but since Hess was proposing to do away with it, I was curious to know the nature of the mechanism he advocated to keep the Indian's rather more numerous white neighbors from stealing the last dregs of Indian land—and anything else they could get their hands on. After all, such a scenario of wanton expropriation hardly lacks historical basis.

Perplexed by my insistence and a growing tension in the room, Hess replied that the federal government seemed something of a poor risk for Native Americans to place their faith in. Perhaps, he suggested, it was time Indians tried "putting their faith in their *fellow man* rather than in bureaucracies." Now it was my turn to be stunned.

A bit feebly, I rejoined that I wasn't aware that anyone was making an argument in favor of the federal bureaucracy, but I was still waiting to hear what his *replacement* for federal guarantees would be in the new anarchist society, or in a Marxist state if he wished to address that. But I couldn't grasp his notion that elimination of the feds would do anything positive for Native people if it threw them upon the goodwill of their non-Indian neighbors. What, I asked, was it that whites had ever done to warrant the sort of faith in their collective intentions that Hess was recommending?

Clearly disgusted with my "racism," Hess answered abruptly, "I hope at least *you're* a Native American, given your line of questioning." I gave up before asking why one needed to be Indian in order to consider issues relevant to them; somehow, I already knew the answer. This was in 1973.

*   *   *   *   *

As I said, the experience had a certain crystallizing effect for me. I had been active for years in that vague and amorphous configuration generally termed the "New Left." It was a time when, it was commonly understood, a generation was in the process of hacking and hewing an "American Radical Vision" out of the living fabric of US society, an alternative to imported dogmas which had led to intellectual bankruptcy and disaster for the left in the not so distant past. Yet I had witnessed the dissipation of SDS at Chicago's Amphitheater in 1969 amidst choreographed wavings of Mao Tse Tung's *Little Red Book* by ranks of factionalized automatons chanting prearranged Chinese slogans in unison. I had been confused by this, to say the least.

I had investigated the Young Socialist Alliance, the youth wing of the Socialist Worker's Party and erstwhile sponsor of the Student Mobilization to End the War in Vietnam, as a prospective member. The "American Radical Vision" I encountered was a watered-down version of Leon Trotsky's doctrines. In the San Francisco area, I found the Free Speech Movement had been transformed into the "Bay Area Radical Union," an amalgamation of various left groups sporting portraits of Joseph Stalin on the covers of their publications. Returning to Chicago, I explored the legendary Industrial Workers of the World (Wobblies), and found the publication of songbooks to be its main contemporary stock in trade; that, and the rehashing of factional disputes more than half a century old. (The original protagonists had had the good graces to die off in the interim, but their descendants didn't seem overly conscious of that fact.)

On the Boston/New York circuit, the Progressive Labor Faction of what had been SDS held the Maoist monopoly, calling on non-whites to join its version of "Third World Revolution." Elsewhere, tiny splinter groups advanced the various theses of Euro-communism, Albanian Revolutionary Principles, Kim el Sung's Maoist variations, and so on, and on; and Karl Hess' and Murray Bookchin's contemporary anarchism were also available commodities. Of course there were also grass roots activism, the growing women's movement, New Leftish projects, support groups, community organizations and the like. But the sects were the most visible remnants of the organized New Left in the early 1970s.

It certainly occurred to me that the *white* left might not really be "the wave of the future" in terms of an *American* version of radical social change. But a survey of non-white groups revealed essentially the same pattern: an overwhelming reliance on Lenin, Mao, Castro/Guevarra; ultimately reliance on adaptations of theories advanced by Karl Marx well over a century earlier, in Europe. The Black Panther Party, the Young Lords Organization, and the Brown Berets; each group possessed an imported ideology, which, as far as I could see, they were attempting to rhetorically adapt to the American context in the same way as their white counterparts.

Nowhere could I see anything which remotely resembled the called-for "American Radical Vision" which had so often and so loudly been promoted in both the New Left and mainstream press. But, while I could raise considered objections to these particular developments, I could not define what was lacking to establish a theoretical vision that could match the realities of the American context. The whole situation was most discouraging.

Of course, there were flickerings in my own experiences that were indicative, but I was unable to put them together into anything like a coherent framework. Very briefly, in 1970, left attention had been captured by the "Indians of All Tribes" Occupation of Alcatraz Island; there was a flurry of non-Indian interest, but no more. Locally, in Chicago, Indians occupied an abandoned Nike Missile base; it caused scarcely a ripple of left attention. The Bureau of Indian Affairs Building in Washington, DC, was occupied by a group of Indians for nearly a week, but still left attention was minimal. Then there was Wounded Knee in 1973. . .

It was during the American Indian Movement occupation of Wounded Knee that Karl Hess made his appearance at Sangamon State University. The drama unfolding in South Dakota was riveting the attention of most of the country, the left included, as it had become a National Media Event. The American left was finally being made aware of Native Americans, and it was being made aware in precisely the same manner as the rest of the population—through the spectacles offered by CBS/NBC/ABC. In short, it dawned on me that the American left's awareness of the situation of Native Americans was not particularly better informed than that demonstrated by the rest of America outside of "Indian Country."

The occupation of Wounded Knee was undertaken primarily as a stand concerning issues of treaty rights, sovereignty and self-determination for Native people. These were precisely the issues I was attempting to address through my questions to Karl Hess in a public (overwhelmingly white) forum; they were and are serious issues to any Native American. His replies, and indeed his entire attitude, suddenly clarified the whole range of confusions I had experienced relative to the American left for several years.

In the first place, he did not seem to wish to deal with Native American issues *at all*; he obviously had not considered Indians in the construction of his utopian scenario and the mere introduction of such considerations was so threatening and disturbing as to prompt innuendos of "reaction" from him. Second, he considered this particular form of reactionary question to be in some way *weird*, not a topic for intelligent discussion. Then there was the pitch to the "greater common good": there are clearly more invaders than Indians in this country so Indian interests must be subordinate; in fact, given population ratios, a "democratic" assessment of Indian interests must conclude they are almost non-existent, irrelevant in terms of revolutionary consideration. And finally, there was his assertion that to be preoccupied with Native American issues, one has to be Native, an apt summation of the posture of the American left; non-Indians simply have more important things to think about.

Perhaps perversely, Hess' position (if it may be called that) solidified a notion which had been implicit in my ambiguous affiliations with the American left for a long while. This was simply that the touted American Radical Vision was a failed promise; "American" radicalism was fundamentally and completely an intellectual import. Conversely, there could be no American Vision, radical or otherwise, which did not *begin* with the original "American," the Native American. Unless and until this population is addressed on its own terms and in accordance with its own definition of its human needs, *any* conceivable revolutionary theory can only amount to a continuation of "the invasion of America." So much seemed and still seems academic to me.

Unfortunately, the matter seems a bit less obvious to many of my opposition-minded colleagues. There are, of course, a number of arguments to be made, but one of the more basic relates to the question of landbase. There can be no question that the entirety of the continental United States has been expropriated from its original, indigenous inhabitants, with incalculably harmful consequences accruing to them in the process. From a moral perspective, it should be equally clear that no humane solution to the overall issues confronting any American radical can reasonably be said to exist, should it exclude mechanisms through which to safeguard the residual landbase and cultural identities of these people.

This presents something of a dilemma in that the land currently occupied by Indian tribal groups contains something on the order of two-thirds of all readily extractable US energy resource deposits, as well as quite substantial inventories of other critical raw materials. Such resources are as necessary to a left-oriented industrialized society as they are to one with a right-wing philosophy. Unless the left acknowledges this, there is potentially no difference between the left and the right in their impact on Native Americans. On the face of it, matters will be essentially the same: the Indians will be divested of control over their last remaining resources by all factions of the Euro-American political spectrum, unless the left can articulate a coherent formulation of priorities and values allowing for (at the very least) maintenance of the Indian/white status quo in terms of landbase. This is not an unimportant consideration, given the direct linkage of indigenous cultures to various geographical areas and conditions. The alternative to a satisfactory solution in this instance is genocide.

And yet an examination of the dissident literature reveals an outright void regarding the Native American. There is a vast literature generated by non-leftists concerning the Indian, and sometimes selections from it are read by the left, but nowhere is there an analytical work, never mind a *body* of literature, considering the Native American, both historically and in contemporary terms, as a fundamental ingredient which would make any left vision truly American. As Russell Means so aptly expressed it to me in late 1980, "Indians just don't fit in anywhere."

Oddly, the same cannot be said for the colonized peoples of China, Cuba, Vietnam, Zimbabwe, Algeria, Palestine, South

Africa, and elsewhere. Concerning them, the American left has often devoted itself to analysis and theory. Nor can it be said that the thoughts and writings of other Third World revolutionary leaders—Mao, Fanon, Che, Lumumba, Arafat, Ho, Kim el Sung, Memmi, Castro, among others—have been ignored to anything like the extent to which the American left has ignored the voices of its own indigenous population.

*   *   *   *   *

In this context I effectively disengaged from active participation on the left per se. I wasn't disinterested—the problem was what I perceived as a none too subtle shift from the 1960s New Left rejection of Marxist tradition as sole political foundation, to a formal acceptance of Marxism as *the* guiding American alternative vision. At least prior to 1968 there seemed to have been widespread acceptance of the idea that something other than, or in addition to, Marxism was necessary to create a truly American alternative. By 1975 it seemed such an idea had been defeated. To my eyes Marxism possessed—in one or another combination of its variants—a literal hegemony over the American radical consciousness. To paraphrase songwriter Pete Townshend, "Meet the New Left, same as the Old Left."

From the new stations I took up, first in South Dakota, then in Wyoming and finally in Colorado, I considered this development. Perhaps it was for the best, I thought. Marxism at least offered a coherent analytical framework into which new data might be fed, a vast intellectual improvement over the emotive radicalism of the 1960s. Perhaps the means of synthesizing an American Radical Vision was becoming available through the unlikeliest of sources: an often dogmatic and utterly alien critical philosophical structure. Perhaps the theoretical and analytical insights offered by Marxism could provide the foundation from which to launch a new perspective for future social forms.

I reread the works of Marx, Lenin, Lukacs, and others in this light. I ventured into Habermas, Marcuse, Adorno, and Benjamin. I slogged through Sartre, Gramsci, Luxemburg and Mao. I paid special attention to Fanon and Memmi. And I tried something novel and unique. I combined the reading with dialogue and discussion with other Indian people from various tribal and geographic backgrounds, various stations in life, and various political perspectives (in the Euro sense of the term). I then carried the results of such dialogue back into my reading and on into discussions with non-Indian friends I'd made on the left over the years.

Ultimately, a pattern of fundamental objections began to emerge on the part of the Indian people I talked with. Similarly, a pattern of defensive positions emerged on the part of my Marxist friends. Eventually, the Marxist position could be summed up as identical to Hess': Native Americans are irrelevant to the course of World History, they constitute a minor sideshow on the stage of World Revolution, they are a retrospective consideration. One astute "advanced" Marxist theorist even took time to inform me that it would really be pointless to become too involved in such issues because "all hunting and gathering societies will have ceased to exist before the year 2000." The "iron laws of historical development" are at work.

My protest that such an attitude was as genocidal in its implications as anything espoused by Manifest Destiny imperialism or heathen-crushing Christianity, met with a shrug. My assertions that Native peoples were hardly "hunting and gathering societies" these days met with mild interest on occasion, but more often with amused commentary on my "romanticism." American Indians, as people and as whole cultures, had been effectively written out of serious Marxist consideration.

Still, I could not bring myself to discount all Marxian rhetoric concerning "the liberation of humanity." Marxism, for better or worse, had come to represent the primary "liberatory" alternative within the United States. Naively, I supposed that I must be talking to the wrong people, that among the broader spectrum of US Marxism there must be significant schools of thought which would be quick to pick up on the intrinsic centrality of Native American issues if only the facts and the context were presented in a forum taken seriously by them. Such a process of exposition seemed simple enough.

From early 1978 onward, I began to write—and to solicit writing by other Native Americans—on Indian issues as these might relate to existing Marxist analyses of American conditions. I contacted several "serious" left publications about their willingness to receive such material. All expressed interest, observing that they had never before been offered the opportunity to publish the "inside story on Indian Affairs." Manuscripts were duly submitted, but *nothing* ever saw print. Instead, each publication's editorial board saw fit to "correct" the political perspectives presented by Indian activists and return the writings for "revision." What was meant in each case (and on the part of titles as seemingly diverse as *Marxist Perspectives, The Insurgent Sociologist,* and *Socialist Revolution/Review)* was that Native American submissions were desirable, but only insofar as they reinforced preexisting Marxist notions of what and how Indians should think. Marxism was presuming to externally assess the internal validity of the American Indian perspective and was rejecting it as unacceptable at every turn.

The form the manuscripts took followed a peculiar line of development. Initially, they consisted primarily of observations and analysis of the internal colonial status of the US geographic tribes, resource distribution within US reservation areas, juridical analysis based on treaties, etc. As these were returned with comments like ". . . very useful data, *but* . . ." the content shifted to a more theoretical level, in order to articulate *why* given political conclusions had been drawn from previously submitted data studies. As the more theoretical pieces were submitted, their return became much more prompt, the commentary more detailed and negative. This, in turn, prompted a series of submissions flatly challenging Marxist cultural assumptions which had surfaced in the rejection commentaries; the absolute *a priori* validity of Marxism itself was brought into question. These last submissions caused abrupt and permanent rupture in communication between the various journals and authors.

What had been intended as the initiation of an informed dialogue between two groups vitally interested in social change ended in hostile silence. Organized Marxism indicated no willingness to entertain the viewpoints of Native America unless such views turned out to be rubberstamps for Marxism. No dialogue was possible either way: divergent or countering analysis was simply rejected out of hand while rubberstamp material—had it been submitted—would have provided a reinforcement for Marxism rather then a dialogue concerning its merits. What the Marxist publications sought were essentially "wooden Indians" for their ethnic stables.

The results were multiple. In a personal sense it made for a rather chastizing lesson; the AIM people with whom I associate simply smiled knowingly as if to say, "we told you so." And indeed they had. On another level, I found the conclusions I had been reaching concerning the relationship between Marxism and Native Americans catapulted into a world context. If, as it seemed, Marxism was unwilling to consider possible cultural differentiation between its tradition and those of Native peoples in the Americas, what was the Marxist stance *vis a vis* other non-European traditions? If Marxism *universally* chose to disregard cultural perspectives outside its own preconceived paradigm, what were the global implications?

These questions had been there all along, but it was the icy rejection by Marxist publications themselves which provoked this clear formulation. Once confronted in such a fashion, there was no way to back off from the questions raised.

*   *   *   *   *

Hence, this book. I lay out the preceding historical sketch not because I consider my strange odyssey across the landscape of American leftism to be especially noteworthy, but because of the precise opposite. I hold the bumps and jolts and frozen moments I've experienced to be grimly reflective of the experiences of a large and growing number of activists, both Native American and otherwise. And, although it seems to have gone sadly out of fashion in radical circles, I believe there remain a significant number of us out here still committed to the idea that a uniquely *American* radical vision is a transcendent requirement to effecting positive social change in America. Imports, in and of themselves, without critique and careful adaptation, can only worsen an already intolerable situation.

Marxism is no doubt a quite useful tool within American theory, but first things first. And the Indian was first by any criterion which can be designed for evaluative measurement. This is an objective condition with which Marxism, in its present configuration, has flatly refused to deal. No American theory can write the Indian off as irrelevant; the Indian's is the first vision in this hemisphere, not only as a matter of chronological fact, but because the Indian experience was and remains formative to this society's psychological and material character. In addition, Indian cultures adapted to, and where they have not been destroyed continue to respect, local and regional conditions rather than treating them purely as resources to exploit. Until theory comes to grips with these consistently evaded facts, it can never adequately deal with the realities of the American situation.

No one can speak *for* the Native American. For any non-Indian to assume a superiority in expressing the "correct" Indian perspective is arrogant folly at best, intentional and self-serving distortion at worst. The culturally generated political consciousness of Native people must enter into the effective formulation of any alternative American politics. The only valid question is how to effect this.

The nature and structure of this book were dictated by such considerations. It had seemed to me quite necessary to understand the deficiencies of the prevailing Marxist vision in order to go beyond them. It had also seemed necessary to articulate the theoretical principles of the Marxist vision in their own right as the critique proceeded; one cannot necessarily assume they are known in their particulars. I felt Native Americans were in an ideal position to test the limits and pretentions of the Marxist vision, to challenge its most basic assumptions: to provide the critique and thus one pole of the debate.

A natural juxtaposition suggested itself. On the one hand, Marxists could articulate whatever multi-cultural validity they perceived in their theory. On the other hand, Native American writers could explain what they perceived to be the defects and inadequacies of Marxism. Such a point/counterpoint would constitute a dialogue that might allow mutual learning.

I assumed that each side possessed roughly equal opportunity to know the other. Therefore, I "assigned" each author a given subject to elaborate. I expected each to have a grasp on his/her subject matter sufficient to make the case at hand *without* reference to one another's manuscripts. This was intended to insure presentation of each point as it might be generally understood rather than interpersonal polemics between authors. The resulting manuscripts were to be edited and arranged within two basic sections: Part I was to be the Marxist Theory of Culture, while Part II was to be the Native American Critique.

However, for a variety of reasons, virtually all preconceived notions of the book's structure broke down during the process of its assembly. First, the authors changed. Several "big name" Marxists initially expressed definite interest in contributing but then backed out for reasons such as "lack of time." Then, as replacement authors came forward I discovered that direct manuscript juxtapositions were necessary to maintain continuity between the pros and cons of each point covered. The original two-part scenario had to be abandoned in favor of a different sequencing. Finally, predictably enough, certain writers fractured every conceivable timetable in submitting their material. The delay was not critical, however, as the book could be published whenever it was completed.

Political realities, however, entered by the side door. The entire package was originally scheduled to be be submitted to South End Press by the end of June 1980; that is, prior to the Black Hills Survival Gathering at Rapid City, South Dakota. Late arrivals caused postponements, and Russell Means, as was also scheduled, read his contribution as a major speech on the second day of that event.* Of course, at that point the idea of each author not being made privy to the content of any other's essay became impractical, to say the least. Indeed, Means' Black Hills presentation provoked a quite lengthy and vituperative polemical reply from the Revolutionary Communist Party, USA, in its political organ, *The Revolutionary Worker.*

---

*Means' presentation has since appeared in print in several variations: under the original title used in this book, in the September, 1980 edition of *Lakota Eyapaha* (Pine Ridge, SD); as "Marxism is a European Tradition" in the Fall 1980 edition of *Akwasasne Notes* (Mohawk Nation): and as "For the World to Live, Europe Must Die" in the December, 1980 edition of *Mother Jones.*

This ultimately proved an unanticipated boon. Certain difficulties with the Leninist section of the book had become apparent. Despite repeated and sometimes quite detailed descriptions of the sort of focus needed for this project, literally every Leninist submission had fallen considerably wide of the mark. One manuscript was an informative treatment of "socialist realist" aesthetics. Another attempted to cope with the role of Third World literature in the coming global revolution. A third became opaquely mired in attempting to unravel the distinctions between early Soviet artistic experimentation and the standards for "cultural deployment" established during China's mid-60s "Cultural Revolution."

I was extremely perplexed as there seemed little I could say which would convince the Leninist writers that when I solicited an analytical elaboration of "Leninist Theory of Culture," I was not referring to arts and letters, dance, folk forms or any other of the aesthetic expressions implied by the popular use of the term tossed about so casually in contemporary conversation. Indeed, I'd expressly requested an *anthropological* treatment of the ingredients of Leninist theory which allow it to function as a liberatory doctrine in a multi-cultural world. I specifically referred to "linguistic matrix," "socio-religious symbology," "kinship patterns," etc., as being indicative of the sense in which the book would be employing the term "culture."

Means, it seemed to me, had hit squarely at the implicit cultural content of the Leninist tradition in his statement. Yet I had nothing of equal substance to juxtapose as a Leninist articulation. The *Revolutionary Worker* polemic actually salvaged a bad situation, at the expense of forcing a direct interchange between authors (or authorial groups, in this case). The two pieces, together with a response to certain points raised by the RCP but not addressed initially by Means (jointly written by Dora-Lee Larson and myself), created a strong section covering the contemporary Leninist ethos. No doubt many Leninists will disagree, feeling the RCP's views fail to represent "real Leninism." In this connection, it should be noted that the RCP has subjected itself to a public "self-criticism" relative to its rejoinder to Means. This occurred after the section was assembled, but would have had little bearing in any event. The

Party found itself guilty of no substantive errors, other than having acted inappropriately in including the material reflected by the title of its piece (a matter apparently now considered accurate but unnecessarily "impolite" by RCP propagandists). However, the interchange on Leninism was certainly not enough. Marxism today holds too many facets, possesses too many streams of thinking to be readily confronted through an exchange with the mechanistic charicature offered by the RCP. Hence, Elisabeth Lloyd offers her view of a comprehensive Marxism, rich in formulation and potential for genuine cross-cultural understanding through application of dialectical methodology. Bob Sipe presents a Marxism emphasizing both material and psychological relations as its route to universally useful and appropriate knowledge.

Vine Deloria, Jr. and Frank Black Elk follow by contending that Marxism, for all its possible good intentions and grandiloquent pronouncements on behalf of humanity, remains as it has always been: an ethnocentric dogma expressing eternal variations upon a given theme and possessing little conceptual utility beyond its original European cultural paradigm. At worst, these contributors contend, Marxism can only serve to exacerbate the contemporary problems facing Native America; at best, Marxism can employ its own methodology to transcend its ethnocentrism and thus *become* useful to peoples of non-European heritage. In either event, Marxism is currently no particular bargain for Indians.

Bill Tabb closes out the dialogue with an essay written after having read all other contributions in the volume to that point. His is the perspective of the committed Marxist activist who has, from time to time, engaged directly in Indian struggles for land and sovereignty. He is prepared to argue the points raised by the Indian critiques of the Marxist tradition, and in what might be best described as an accessible down to earth fashion.

With this material in hand, I began two projects. First, I began to reassemble the manuscript, abandoning the distinctions between critical theory, phenomenological Marxism and post-Marxism I had once intended. Second, I began to make an effort to bring some of the protagonists together for purposes of verbal debate in a public forum. The latter occurred at the Western Social Science Association Conference, in San Diego, in the spring of 1981. Three contributors were present, as well as Phil Heiple, a post-Marxist scholar from Santa Barbara. The results are incorporated into Heiple's excellent "postscript" contained in the last section of this collection, which also includes my own comments on a number of issues raised in the course of the book. Since the point at which the last of these contributions were received, things have gone rather slowly. I have been preoccupied with the establishment of Yellow Thunder Tiospaye, an effort led by Russell and Bill Means to reoccupy a portion of the Lakota territory guaranteed in perpetuity by the Fort Laramie Treaty of 1868, and since usurped by the United States. The occupation began April 4, 1981, and continues as a rallying point of the struggle for sovereignty and self-determination by American Indian peoples. It seems almost redundant to observe that this watershed action has received scant attention and support from the non-Indian left "opposition."

Even now, I am unsatisfied with the book which follows. I always will be. Like any collection or anthology, it is incomplete, unbalanced, and anything but definitive. Still, nothing similar has gone into print. As an indication of the reasons for this, let me mention that Vine Deloria, Jr., probably the best-known American Indian author to this point, was informed flatly by his erstwhile publisher (Harper and Row) when he delivered up the manuscript to his *Metaphysics of Modern Existence*, that "Indians don't write books on philosophy." For all the thousands of books on Marxism in print and available in the contemporary United States, not one clearly attempts to assess the Native American relationship to Marxism.

And so the book is somewhat fragmentary. It has holes. Pieces of the equation, both real and potential, remain unaddressed. It nonetheless moves into a vacuum of left consideration, and such incompleteness is unavoidable. One must begin somewhere. Indians *do* write books on philosophy and possess a knowledge of its intricacies the "white man" has never acknowledged. Such books just fail to see print, for the most part. Perhaps this collective effort can do something to change that.

Hopefully, this book will anger people. If, like the RCP, a number of Marxist groups and Marxist individuals are provoked into addressing rather than ignoring the issues raised, perhaps they will articulate their positions in concrete rather than rhetorical fashion. At long last, for better or worse, their true colors will be flown. Nearly a century into the history of US Marxism, this seems little enough to ask. As it is, concrete positions are taken in some rather important connections. The subject at hand has been broached in depth and by a variety of individuals. One hopes that this represents at least a tenuous beginning, a basis from which similarly focused work may emerge, so omissions in this particular treatment may be addressed and other perspectives added. There are certainly other Native Americans who have much to contribute to such an exchange and no doubt there are also numerous Marxists with pieces to add. Perhaps in a cauldron of intercultural dialogue concerning theoretical issues of significance to social change, a uniquely *American* Radical Vision may at last be born.

Ward Churchill
Boulder, Colorado
1982

PART ONE

Spread the word of your religion,
Convert the whole world if you can,
Kill and slaughter those who oppose you
It's worth it if you save one man.
Take the land to build your churches,
A sin to tax the house of God,
Take the child while she is supple,
Spoil the mind and spare the rod.
Go and tell the savage native
That he must be Christianized.
Tell him, end his heathen worship
And you will make him civilized.
Shove your gospel, force your values,
Down her throat until its raw,
And after she is crippled,
Turn your back and lock the door.
Like an ever circling vulture,
You descend upon your prey,
Then you pick the soul to pieces
And you watch while it decays.
Missionaries, missionaries, go leave us all alone.
Take your white God to your white man,
We've a God of our own.

From a Sung Song by
Floyd Westerman

1
The Same Old Song
Russell Means

The only possible opening for a statement of this kind is that I detest writing. The process itself epitomizes the European concept of "legitimate" thinking; what is written has an importance that is denied the spoken. My culture, the Lakota culture, has an oral tradition and so I ordinarily reject writing. It is one of the white world's ways of destroying the cultures of non-European peoples, the imposing of an abstraction over the spoken relationship of a people.

So what you read here is not what I've written. It's what I've said and someone else has written down. I will allow this, because it seems that the only way to communicate with the white world is through the dead, dry leaves of a book. I don't really care whether my words reach whites or not. They've already demonstrated through their history that they can't hear, can't see, they can only read (of course, there are exceptions, but the exceptions only prove the rule). I'm more concerned with American Indian people, students and others, who've begun to be absorbed into the white world through universities and other institutions. But even then it's a marginal sort of concern. It's very possible to grow into a red face with a white mind and if that's a person's individual choice, so be it, but I have no use for them. This is part of the process of cultural genocide being waged by Europeans against American Indian peoples today. My concern is with those American Indians who choose to resist this genocide, but who may be confused as to how to proceed.

It takes a strong effort on the part of each American Indian *not* to become Europeanized. The strength for this effort can only come from the traditional ways, the traditional values that our elders retain. It must come from the hoop, the four directions, the relations; it cannot come from the pages of a book or a thousand books; no European can ever teach a Lakota to be Lakota, a Hopi to be a Hopi. A master's degree in "Indian Studies" or in "education" or anything else cannot make a person into a human being or provide knowledge into the traditional ways. It can only make you into a mental European, an outsider.

I should be clear about something here, because there seems to be some confusion about it. When I speak of Europeans or mental Europeans, I'm not allowing for false distinctions. I'm not saying that on the one hand there are the byproducts of a few thousand years of genocidal, reactionary European intellectual development which is bad, and on the other hand there is some new revolutionary intellectual development which is good. I'm referring here to the so-called theories of Marxism and anarchism and "leftism" in general. I don't believe these theories can be separated from the rest of the European intellectual tradition. It's really just the same old song.

Take Christianity as an historical example. In its day Christianity was revolutionary. It changed European power relations for all time; that is, unless you happen to think the Roman Empire is still a dominant military force. But European culture, of which Christianity became a part, acted on the religion in such a way as to use it as a tool for the destruction of non-European peoples, for the expansion of European military and economic power across the planet, for the consolidation of the European nation-states, for the formation of the capitalist economic system. The Christian revolution or revolutions were an important part of the development of European culture in directions it was *already* headed; it changed nothing other than to speed up Europe's genocide outside Europe, and maybe inside Europe too.

The same holds true for the capitalist and other European "revolutions." They changed power relations within Europe around a bit, but only to meet the needs of the white world at the expense of everyone and everything else.

Newton "revolutionized" physics and the so-called natural sciences by reducing the physical universe to a linear mathematical equation. Descartes did the same thing with culture. John Locke did it with politics and Adam Smith did it with economics. Each one of these "thinkers" took a piece of the spirituality of human existance and converted it into a code, an abstraction. They were picking up where Christianity ended, they "secularized" Christian religion as the "scholars" like to say—and in doing this they made Europe more able and ready to act as an expansionist culture. Each of these intellectual revolutions served to abstract the European mentality even further, to remove the wonderful complexity and spirituality from the universe and replace it with a "logical sequence"; one-two-three-ANSWER. This is what's come to be termed as "efficiency" in the European mind. Whatever is mechanical is perfect, whatever seems to work at the moment—that is, proves the mechanical model is the right one—is considered correct even when it is clearly untrue. This is why "truth" changes so fast in the European mind; the answers which result from such a process are only stop-gaps, only temporary, and must be continuously discarded in favor of new stop-gaps which support the mathematical models; which keep them (the models) alive.

Hegel and then Marx were heirs to the thinking of Newton, Descartes, Locke and Smith. Hegel finished the process of secularizing theology—and that is put in his *own* terms; he secularized the religious thinking through which Europe understood the universe. Then Marx put Hegel's philosophy into terms of "materialism." That is to say that Marx despiritualized Hegel's work altogether. Again, this is in Marx's own terms. And this is now seen as the future revolutionary potential of Europe. Europeans may see this as revolutionary, but American Indians see it simply as still more of that same old European conflict between *being* and *gaining*. The intellectual roots for a new Marxist form of European imperialism lies in Marx's—and his followers'—links to the tradition of Newton, Hegel, etc.

Being is a spiritual proposition. Gaining is a material act. Traditionally, American Indians have always attempted to *be* the best people they could. Part of that spiritual process was and is to give away wealth, to discard wealth in order *not* to gain. Material gain is an indicator of false status among traditional people while it is "proof that the system works" to Europeans. Clearly, there are two completely opposing views at issue here, and Marxism is very far over to the other side from the American Indian view. But let's look at a major implication of this; it is not merely an intellectual debate.

The European materialist tradition of despiritualizing the universe is very similar to the mental process which goes into dehumanizing another person. And who seems most expert at dehumanizing other people? And why? Soldiers who have seen a lot of combat learn to do this to the enemy before going back into combat. Murderers do it before going out to commit murder. SS guards did it to concentration camp inmates. Cops do it. Corporation leaders do it to workers they send into uranium mines and to work in steel mills. Politicians do it to everyone in sight. And what each process of dehumanization has in common for each group doing the dehumanizing is that it makes it alright to kill and otherwise destroy other people. One of the Christian commandments says "thou shall not kill," at least not humans, so the trick is to mentally convert the victims into non-humans. Then you can proclaim violation of your own commandment as a virtue.

In terms of the despiritualization of the universe, the mental process works so that it becomes virtuous to destroy the planet. Terms like "progress" and "development" are used as cover words here the way "victory" and "freedom" are used to justify butchery in the dehumanization process. For example, a real-estate speculator may refer to "developing" a parcel of ground by opening a gravel quarry there; "development" really means total, permanent destruction with the earth itself removed. But European logic has *gained* a few tons of gravel with which more land can be "developed" in the construction of road beds. Ultimately, the whole universe is open—in the European view—to this sort of insanity.

Most important here, perhaps, is the fact that Europeans feel no sense of loss in all this. After all, their philosophers have despiritualized reality, so there is no satisfaction (for them) to be gained in simply observing the wonder of a mountain or a lake or a people *in being*. No, satisfaction is measured in terms of gaining material—so the mountain becomes gravel and the lake becomes coolant for a factory and the people are rounded up for processing through the indoctrination mills Europeans like to call schools. This is all very "rational" and to the good, so no sense of loss is experienced. And it's very difficult, or impossible, to convince a person there's something wrong with the process of gaining when they lack the spiritual wisdom to feel a loss for what is being destroyed along the way.

Each new European abstraction is born of a direct need. Each time an abstraction begins to wear out, each time the costs involved become obvious—even obvious to some Europeans—a new abstraction is created which staves off the inevitable. For a while. Newton, Locke, Descartes, and Smith lead to Hegel and Marx and to Darwin, then there's Einstein and Niels Bohr, etc. Each one abstracted reality even further and contributed to continuing the system of science/materialism when the old "answers" were wearing out. But each new abstraction, each stop-gap, upped the ante out in the real world. Take fuel for the industrial machine as an example. Little more than two centuries ago, nearly everyone used wood—a replenishable, natural item— as fuel for the very human needs of cooking and staying warm. Along came the industrial revolution and coal became the dominant fuel as production became the social imperative for Europe. Pollution began to become a problem in the cities and the earth was ripped open to provide coal where wood was always simply gathered or harvested at no great expense to the environment. Later, oil became the major fuel as the technology of production was perfected through a series of scientific "revolutions." Pollution increased dramatically and nobody yet knows what the environmental costs of pumping all that oil out of the ground will really be in the long run. Now there's an "energy crisis" and uranium is becoming the dominant fuel—still in the name of the same system of materialist values which set up the crises, both of energy and of the environment.

Capitalists, at least, can be relied upon only to develop uranium as fuel at a rate at which they can show a good profit. That's their ethic, and maybe that will buy some time. Marxists, on the other hand, can be relied upon to develop uranium fuel as rapidly as possible simply because it's the most "efficient" production fuel available. That's *their* ethic, and I fail to see where it's preferable. Like I said, Marxism is right smack in the middle of the European tradition. It's the same old song.

The missionaries spearheaded Europe's drive to destroy the continents of this hemisphere; not just the people who are indigenous here, but the continents themselves. The missionaries are still here and they're still active, and traditional people recognize them as the enemy. But they've mainly been replaced in importance by capitalists whose mission it is to "efficiently" exploit what the missionaries opened up. This change from church to capitalism has no doubt made some superficial differences in the structure of European society—they've even gone to great lengths to "separate church and state" in their laws (to reduce the power of the church)—but, the point is, this "revolution" only made things worse for non-Europeans. Capitalism *is* more destructive and efficient than the missionary version of Europe we encountered a few hundred years ago.

There's a rule of thumb which can be applied here. You can't judge the real nature of a European revolutionary doctrine on the basis of the changes it proposes to make within the European power structure and society. You can only judge it by the effects it will have on non-European peoples. This is because every revolution in European history has served to reinforce Europe's tendencies and abilities to export destruction to other peoples, other cultures and the environment itself. I defy anyone to point out an example where this isn't true.

So now we, as American Indian people, are asked to believe that a "new" European revolutionary doctrine such as Marxism will reverse the negative effects of European history on us. European power relations are to be adjusted once again, and that's supposed to make things better for all of us. But what does this really mean?

Right now, today, we who live on the Pine Ridge Reservation are living in what white society has designated a "national sacrifice area." What this means is that we have a lot of uranium deposits here and white culture (not us) needs this uranium as energy production material. The cheapest, most efficient way for industry to extract and deal with the processing of this uranium is to dump the waste byproducts right here at the digging sites.

Right here where we live. This waste is radioactive and will make the entire region uninhabitable forever. This is considered by industry, and the white society which created this industry, to be an "acceptable" price to pay for energy resource development. Along the way they also plan to drain the water-table under this part of South Dakota as part of the industrial process, so the region becomes doubly uninhabitable. The same sort of thing is happening down in the land of the Navajo and Hopi, up in the land of the Northern Cheyenne and Crow, and elsewhere. Over 60 percent of all U.S. energy resources have been found to lie under reservation land, so there's no way this can be called a minor issue. For American Indians it's a question of survival in the purest sense of the term. For white society and its industry it's a question of being able to continue to exist in their present form.

We are resisting being turned into a national sacrifice area. We're resisting being turned into a national sacrifice people. The costs of this industrial process are not acceptable to us. It is genocide to dig the uranium here and to drain the water-table, no more, no less. So the reasons for our resistance are obvious enough and shouldn't have to be explained further. To anyone.

Now let's suppose that in our resistance to extermination we begin to seek allies (we have). Let's suppose further that we were to take revolutionary Marxism at its word: that it intends nothing less than the complete overthrow of the European capitalist order which has presented this threat to our very existence. This would seem to be a natural alliance for American Indian people to make. After all, as the Marxists say, it is the capitalists who set us up to be a national sacrifice. This is true as far as it goes.

But, as I've tried to point out, this "truth" is very deceptive. Look beneath the surface of revolutionary Marxism and what do you find? A commitment to reversing the industrial system which created the need of white society for uranium? No. A commitment to guaranteeing the Lakota and other American Indian peoples real control over the land and resources they have left? No, not unless the industrial process is to be reversed as part of their doctrine. A commitment to our rights, as peoples, to maintaining our values and traditions? No, not as long as they need the uranium within our land to feed the industrial system of the society, the culture of which the Marxists *are still a part.*

Revolutionary Marxism is committed to even further perpetuation and perfection of the very industrial process which is destroying us all. It is offering only to "redistribute" the results, the money maybe, of this industrialization to a wider section of the population. It offers to take wealth from the capitalist and pass it around, but in order to do so, Marxism must maintain the industrial system. Once again, the power relations within European society will have to be altered, but once again the effects upon American Indian peoples here and non-Europeans elsewhere will remain the same. This is much the same as when power was redistributed from the church to private business during the so-called "bourgeois revolution." European society changed a bit, at least superficially, but its conduct toward non-Europeans continued as before. You can see what the American Revolution of 1776 did for American Indians. It's the same old song.

Revolutionary Marxism, as with industrial society in other forms, seeks to "rationalize" all people in relation to industry, maximum industry, maximum production. It is a materialist doctrine which despises the American Indian spiritual tradition, our cultures, our lifeways. Marx himself called us "precapitalists" and "primitive." Precapitalist simply means that, in his view, we would eventually discover capitalism and become capitalists; we have always been economically retarded in Marxist terms. The only manner in which American Indian people could participate in a Marxist revolution would be to *join* the industrial system, to become factory workers or "proletarians" as Marx called them. The man was very clear about the fact that his revolution could occur only through the struggle of the proletariat, that the existence of a massive industrial system is a precondition of a successful Marxist society.

I think there's a problem with language here. Christians, capitalists, Marxists, all of them have been revolutionary in their own minds. But none of them really mean revolution. What they really mean is a *continuation*. They do what they do in order that European culture can continue to exist and develop according to its needs. Like germs, European culture goes through occasional convulsions, even divisions within itself, in order to go on living and growing. This isn't a revolution we're talking about, but a means to continuing what already exists. An amoeba is still an amoeba after it reproduces. But maybe comparing European culture to an amoeba isn't really fair to the amoeba. Maybe cancer cells are a more accurate comparison because European culture has historically destroyed everything around it; and it will eventually destroy itself.

So, in order for us to *really* join forces with Marxism, we Indians would have to accept the national sacrifice of our homeland; we'd have to commit cultural suicide and become industrialized, Europeanized, maybe even sanforized. We would have to totally defeat ourselves. Only the insane could consider this to be desirable to us.

At this point, I've got to stop and ask myself whether I'm being to harsh. Marxism has something of a history. Does this history bear out my observations? I look to the process of industrialization in the Soviet Union since 1920 and I see that these Marxists have done what it took the English "industrial revolution" three hundred years to do; and the Marxists did it in sixty years. I see that the territory of the USSR used to contain a number of tribal peoples and that they have been crushed to make way for the factories. The Soviets refer to this as "The National Question," the question of whether the tribal peoples had the right to exist as peoples; and they decided the tribal peoples were an acceptable sacrifice to industrial needs. I look to China and I see the same thing. I look to Vietnam and I see Marxists imposing an industrial order and rooting out the indigenous tribal mountain peoples.

I hear a leading Soviet scientist saying that when uranium is exhausted *then* alternatives will be found. I see the Vietnamese taking over a nuclear power plant abandoned by the U.S. military. Have they dismantled and destroyed it? No, they are using it. I see China explode nuclear bombs, developing uranium reactors, preparing a space program in order to colonize and exploit the planets the same as the Europeans colonized and exploited this hemisphere. It's the same old song, but maybe with a faster tempo this time.

The statement of the Soviet scientist is very interesting. Does he know what this alternative energy source will be? No, he simply has faith. Science will find a way. I hear revolutionary Marxists saying that the destruction of the environment, pollution, radiation, all these things will be controlled. And I see them act upon their words. Do they know *how* these things will be controlled? No, they simply have faith. Science will find a way. Industrialization is fine and necessary. How do they know this? Faith. Science will find a way. Faith of this sort has always been known in Europe as religion. Science has become the new European religion for both capitalists and Marxists; they are truly inseparable; they are part and parcel of the same culture. So, in both theory and practice, Marxism demands that non-European peoples give up their values, their traditions, their cultural existence altogether. We will all be industrialized science addicts in a Marxist society.

I do not believe that capitalism itself is really responsible for the situation in which we have been declared a national sacrifice. No, it is the European tradition; European culture itself is responsible. Marxism is just the latest continuation of this tradition, not a solution to it. To ally with Marxism is to ally with the very same forces which declare us an acceptable "cost."

There is another way. There is the traditional Lakota way and the ways of the other American Indian peoples. It is the way that knows that humans do *not* have the right to degrade Mother Earth, that there are forces beyond anything the European mind has conceived, that humans must be in harmony with *all* relations or the relations will eventually eliminate the disharmony. A lopsided emphasis on humans by humans, the European arrogance of acting as though they were beyond the nature of all related things, can only result in a total disharmony and a readjustment which cuts arrogant humans down to size, gives them a taste of that reality beyond their grasp or control and restores the harmony. There is no need for a revolutionary theory to bring this about, it's beyond human control. The natural peoples of this planet know this and so they do not theorize about it. Theory is an abstraction; our knowledge is real.

Distilled to its basic terms, European faith—including the new faith in science—equals a belief that man is god. Europe has always sought a messiah, whether that be the man Jesus Christ or the man Karl Marx or the man Albert Einstein. American Indians know this to be totally absurd. Humans are the weakest of all creatures, so weak that other creatures are willing to give up their flesh so that we may live. Humans are only able to survive through the exercise of rationality since they lack the abilities of other creatures to gain food through the use of fang and claw. But rationality is a curse since it can cause humans to forget the natural order of things in ways other creatures do not. A wolf never forgets his/her place in the natural order. American Indians can. Europeans almost always do. We pray our thanks to the deer, our relations, for allowing us their flesh to eat. Europeans simply take the flesh for granted and consider the deer inferior. After all, Europeans consider themselves godlike in their rationalism and science; god is the supreme being; all else *must* be inferior. Thus, the ability of Europe to create disharmony knows no limits.

All European tradition, Marxism included, has conspired to defy the natural order of all things. Mother Earth has been abused, the powers have been abused, and this cannot go on for ever. No theory can alter that simple fact. Mother Earth will retaliate, the whole environment will retaliate, and the abusers will be eliminated. Things come full circle. Back to where they started. *That's* revolution. And that's a prophecy of my people, of the Hopi people and other correct peoples.

American Indians have been trying to explain this to Europeans for centuries. But, as I said earlier, they have proven themselves unable to hear. The natural order will win out and the offenders will die back, the way deer die when they offend the harmony by overpopulating a given region. It's only a matter of time until what Europeans call "a major catastrophe of global proportions" will occur. It is the role of American Indian peoples, the role of all natural beings to survive. A part of our survival is to resist. We resist, not to overthrow a government or to take political power, but because it is natural to resist extermination, to survive. We don't want power over white institutions; we want white institutions to disappear. *That's* revolution.

American Indians are still in touch with these realities, the prophecies, the traditions of our ancestors. We learn from the elders, from nature, from the powers. And when the catastrophe is over, we American Indian peoples will still be here to inhabit the hemisphere. I don't care if it's only a handful of red people living high in the Andes, American Indian people will survive and harmony will be reestablished. *That's* revolution.

Now, at this point perhaps I should be very clear about another matter, one which *should* already be clear as a result of what I've said in the past few minutes. But confusion breeds easily these days, so I want to hammer home this point. When I use the term "European," I'm not referring to a skin color or a particular genetic structure. What I'm referring to is a mind-set, a world view which is a product of the development of European culture. People are not genetically encoded to hold this outlook, they are *acculturated* to hold it. The same holds true for American Indians or for the members of any other culture.

It is possible for an American Indian to share European values, a European world-view. We have a term for these people; we call them "apples"—red on the outside (genetics) and white on the inside (their minds). Other groups have similar terms; Blacks have their "oreos," Hispanos have "coconuts," etc. And, as I said at the beginning of this talk, there *are* exceptions to the white norm; people who are white on the outside, but not white inside. I'm not sure what term should be applied to them other than "human beings."

What I'm putting out here is not a racial proposition, but a cultural proposition. Those who ultimately advocate and defend the realities of European culture and its industrialism are my enemies. Those who resist it, who struggle against it, are my allies, the allies of American Indian people. And I don't give a damn what their skin color happens to be. Caucasian is the white term for the white race; *European* is an outlook I oppose.

The "Vietnamese Communists" are not exactly what you might consider as genetic Caucasians, but they are functioning as ing as mental Europeans. The same hold true for "Chinese Communists," for "Japanese Capitalists" or "Bantu Catholics" or Peter McDollar down at Navajo or Dickie Wilson up here at Pine Ridge. There is no racism involved in my position, just an acknowledgment of the mind and spirit which make up culture.

In Marxist terms I suppose I'm a "cultural nationalist." I work first with my people, the traditional Lakota people, because we hold a common world view and share an immediate struggle. Beyond this I work with other traditional American Indian peoples, against because of a certain commonality in world view and form of struggle. Beyond that I work with anyone who has experienced the colonial oppression of Europe and who resists Europe as a cultural/industrial totality. Obviously, this includes genetic Caucasians who struggle to resist the dominant norms of

European culture; the Irish and the Basques come immediately to mind, but there are many others.

I work primarily with my own people, with my own community. Other people who hold non-European perspectives should do the same. I do not proclaim myself able to effectively deal with the struggles of the Black community in Watts or Newark. And I don't expect a Black activist from those communities to be particularly effective in the day-to-day struggles of the Lakota people. Each cultural group can and must build upon the basis of its own cultural integrity. This is our strength and the source of our vision, a vision which compells us to resist the industrialization of European culture. It is this sort of vision which allows us to come together, to ally with one another, to pool our strength and resources to resist Europe's death culture while retaining our own identities as human beings.

I do believe in the slogan, "Trust your brother's vision," although I'd like to add sisters into the bargain. I trust the community/culturally based vision of all the races which naturally resist industrialization and human extinction. Clearly, individual whites can share in this, given only that they have reached the awareness that continuation of the industrial imperatives of Europe is not a vision, but species suicide. White is one of the sacred colors of the Lakota people; red, yellow, white, and black. The four directions. The four seasons. The four periods of life and aging. Four races of humanity. Mix red, yellow, white, and black together and you get brown, the color of the fifth race. This is a natural ordering of things. And so it seems natural to me to work with all races, each with its own special meaning, identity, and message.

But there is a peculiar behavior among most Caucasians. As soon as I become critical of Europe and its impact on other cultures, they become defensive. They begin to defend themselves. But I'm not attacking *them* personally. I'm attacking Europe. In personalizing my observations on Europe they are personalizing European culture, identifying themselves with it; in defending themselves in *this* context they are ultimately defending the death culture. This is a confusion which must be overcome, and it must be overcome in a hurry. None of us have energy to waste in such false struggles.

Caucasians have a more positive vision to offer humanity than European culture. I believe this. But in order to attain this vision it is necessary for Caucasians to step outside of European culture—alongside the rest of humanity—to see Europe for what it is and what it does. To cling to capitalism and Marxism and all the other "isms" is simply to remain within European culture. There is no avoiding this basic fact. As a fact this constitutes a choice. Understand that the choice is based on culture, not race. Understand that to choose European culture and industrialism is to choose to be my enemy. And understand the choice is yours, not mine.

This leads me back to those American Indians who are drifting through the universities, the city slums and other European institutions. If you are there to learn to resist the oppressor in accordance with your traditional ways, so be it. I don't know how you manage to combine the two, but perhaps you will succeed. But retain your sense of reality. Beware of coming to believe the white world now offers solutions to the problems it confronts us with. Beware too of allowing the words of Native people to be twisted to the advantage of our enemies. Europe invented the practice of turning words around on themselves. You need only look to the treaties between American Indian peoples and various European governments to know that this is true. Draw your strength from who you are.

The twisting of words goes on today; it has never stopped. This is why when I spoke in Geneva, Switzerland, about the colonization of indigenous peoples in this hemisphere, I was misrepresented as a "leftist" by some white radicals. This is why certain idiots are believed by a few empty heads when they label American Indian activists as being "Marxist-Leninists." This is why certain groups in the white "left" believe they share our values while rejecting the same values at every practical turn. A culture which regularly confuses revolution with continuation, which confuses science and religion, which confuses revolt with resistence has nothing helpful to teach you, has nothing to offer you as a way of life. Europeans have long since lost all touch with reality, if ever they were in touch with it. Feel sorry for them if you need to, but be comfortable with who you are as American Indians.

So, I suppose to conclude this, I should state clearly that leading anyone toward Marxism is the last thing on my mind. Marxism is as alien to my culture as capitalism and Christianity. In fact, I can say I don't think I'm trying to lead anyone toward anything. To some extent I tried to be a "leader" in the sense that the white media likes to use that term when the American Indian Movement was a young organization. This was a result of a confusion I no longer have. You cannot be everything to everyone. I do not propose to be used in such fashion by my enemies; I am not a "leader." I *am* an Oglala Lakota patriot. That's all I want or need to be. And I am very comfortable with who I am . . .

2
Searching for a Second Harvest
The RCP

It is a sign of both the advances and the still remaining backwardness of the developing revolutionary movement in the U.S. that we are forced to reply to a recent speech made by Russell Means, for some time a well-known figure in the struggle of Native Americans. The occasion for his tirade was the 1980 Black Hills International Survival Gathering held from July 18-27 on a ranch outside the Black Hills of South Dakota which drew and estimated 10,000 people. Participants were mostly vists from the anti-nuke movement, but the event also drew some Indians and some local ranchers. This area, the location of the Lakota Pine Ridge Reservation, has been the focus of a great deal of struggle as reported in the *RW* in the past. It is a key source in the U.S. of uranium, the mining of which has left behind a lethal legacy of contaminated water, a rate of miscarriages on the reservation 6½ times the national average, and an abominably high rate of birth defects, cancer and other causes of death and disease to the Indian people.

Means spoke on behalf of the Lakota American Indian Movement and his speech was billed as the keynote address. It disgusted literally hundreds, left thousands with a sour taste in their mouths, and in addition to certain strong-arm tactics pursued by some forces gathered around Means at the gathering, has been the source of widespread controversy within the Indian movement and more broadly since the event concluded.

35

The heart of Means' speech is an attack on revolution in general and revolutionary Marxism in particular. He attempts to trade on his reputation as an "American Indian *leader*" (despite the obligatory false disclaimers of "humility" to the contrary) to advocate a program of capitulation to the enemy for both the struggle of the American Indians—a struggle which is gaining in intensity and has been the object of vicious government reprisals— as well as the movement more broadly.

But beyond this, Means' speech is a sort of inadvertent admission of the truth time and again noted in various ways by the great leaders of communism, from Karl Marx to Mao Tsetung: that for there to be a revolutionary movement, there must be revolutionary theory. Therefore, Means' speech is principally *ideological.* He is well aware that political activists from various spheres of social life are searching for answers, searching for a way out of this mad-dog capitalist system. He at least senses the renewal of revolutionary ripples in the social fabric of this country and sense that these may well develop into mighty waves in the not too distant future. But rather than welcoming these developments for the promise they hold, he fears getting washed away— like beach debris in the tides. He has thus assigned himself the task (and we are not yet prepared to say that he has *been assigned* the task) of concentrating the *most backward* ideas which have arisen particularly among some anti-nuke and Indian activists into a worked out polemic against the *most advanced* ideas represented in the political struggle in this and other countries, ideas which are today gaining a beginning but significant influence in the struggle of American Indians—the ideas of revolutionary Marxism.

To accomplish this task, Means adopts the pose of the "noble savage," fighting to resist the corruption of "European" or "industrial" society. His thesis is that the enemy of Native Americans is the *industrialization* to which Indians have been subjected by European civilization and culture. Industrialization—even material progress itself—is the enemy, independent of what class commands it. Means sees white everywhere, warning Indian youth to reject "European culture" and return to the "natural ways" of the Indians. He says: "It takes a strong effort on the part of each American Indian *not* to become Europeanized. The strength of this effort can only come from their traditional ways, the traditional values that our elders retained. It must come from the hoop, the four directions, the relations; it cannot come from the pages of a book or a thousand books; no European can ever teach a Lakota to be a Lakota, a Hopi to be a Hopi.

And further, notes Means, when we say European we mean *all* whites. In fact, his speech might appropriately be entitled "it's the same old song," a phrase he uses throughout. "I should be clear about something here, because there seems to be some confusion about it. When I speak of Europeans or mental Europeans, I'm not allowing for false distinctions. I'm not saying that on the one hand there are the byproducts of a few thousand years of genocidal, reactionary European intellectual development which is bad, and on the other hand there is some new revolutionary intellectual development which is good. I'm referring here to the so-called theories of Marxism and anarchism and 'leftism' in general. I don't believe these theories can be separated from the rest of the European intellectual tradition. It's really just the same old song."

Indeed there is nothing all that new in a "song" which attacks Marxism, even in the ever-so-slightly adapted "natural" garb in which it is dressed here. And could the "confusion" noted by Means indicate that the general intent of his speech is a feeble but very "theoretical" attempt to drum revolutionary Marxist ideas out of the heads of any young activist, or for that matter, any other ideas with a revolutionary thrust? Evidently, this is his intent, because what follows these introductory comments is a tirade which insidiously tries to *lump together* capitalism and communism, the bourgeoisie and the proletariat, reaction and revolution. And this is combined with demagogic but almost laughable appeals to quit fucking with mother nature. And while all this may well had had some influence among people who view the atom as the enemy, a fact that we certainly take into account, it is also important to note the widespread sentiment of many concerning Means' speech, concentrated in the words of one young activist in the Indian movement: "The fool is trying to take us back 250 years."

Actually, there is even more truth in that comment than this comrade may have realized. For this idea of the "noble savage," the supposedly *natural* man who has not been corrupted by the artificialities, hypocrisy and destructive spiritual emptiness of civilization—this idea is not the original creation of Russell Means or of the American Indians or of "primitive man," but rather has its origins in Europe some 250-300 years ago. The expanding bourgeoisie and their ideologists of that time idealized the American Indians and other indigenous peoples with whom they were aggressively coming in contact, purporting to find in them all the virtues which their own burgeoning civilization so obviously lacked. And as Marx pointed out, this particular ideological creation was not just accidental, nor was it what it appeared to be on the surface, but rather it had definite roots in the growing *bourgeois* relations of production.

> The individual and isolated hunter or fisherman, with whom Smith and Ricardo begin, is one of the unimaginative fantasies of eighteenth-century romances *a la* Robinson Crusoe, which by no means express merely a reaction against overrefinement and a reversion to a misunderstood natural life, as cultural historians imagine . . .

> This is an illusion and the merely aesthetic illusion of the Robinsonades, great and small. On the contrary, it is the anticipation of "civil society" (capitalism), which began to evolve in the sixteenth century and made giant strides towards maturity in the eighteenth. In this society of free competition the individual seems detached from the natural ties, etc., which in earlier historical epochs make him an appurtenance of a particular, limited human conglomeration. The prophets of the eighteenth century, on whose shoulders Smith and Ricardo were still standing with their whole weight, envisaged this eighteenth-century individual—the product of the dissolution of feudal society on the one hand and of the new productive forces evolved since the sixteenth century on the other—as an ideal whose existence belonged to the past. Not as a historical result, but as history's point of departure. Not as arising historically but as posited by nature, because this individual was in conformity with nature, in keeping with their

idea of human nature. (Karl Marx, "Introduction to *A Contribution to the Critiques of the Political Economy*," *Grundrisse*.)

As we shall see often as we go along, far from repudiating, escaping or combatting capitalism and European civilization. Means has in fact adopted some of the insipid fantasies of the bourgeoisie and has capitulated to them. Further, the total backwardness of Means' adoption of this mythical "noble savage" stance leads to more than a bit of hypocrisy as he attempts to carry it through.

His assault against theory ("theory is an abstract, our knowledge is real") as a "European" development somehow hasn't prevented him from attempting to make his own "theoretical" contributions to the times in which we live. And while he complains early in his speech that "writing . . . is one of the white world's ways of destroying the cultures of non-European peoples, the imposing of an abstraction over the spoken relationship of a people," it was apparently within the scope of the "natural" philosophy of Russell Means to have someone write out, reproduce and distribute this speech so that people at the Survival Gathering could read it.

Considering Means' incessant chatter about Marxism being a "continuation of European intellectual tradition," he obviously feels it is best to have his own intellectual roots left underground. But Marxists have no need for such obfuscation. The philosophy of dialectical materialism did indeed develop out of the philosophies of the radical bourgeoisies of Europe, most immediately from the dialectics of Hegel and the materialism of Feuerbach. With the development of the modern proletariat, Marx and Engels were able to *leap* beyond the idealism of the former and the metaphysics of the latter to discover the true nature of material reality in historical society unhindered by the bourgeois viewpoint, which like that of all previous ruling classes, has the need to view its system as the culmination of all human development, eternal, unchanging, etc. As Bob Avakian pointed out in his book, *Mao Tsetung's Immortal Contributions*;

. . . this philosophy was not simply, or fundamentally,

the product of the brains of Marx and Engels. It was the result of the development of capitalism, of natural science and of the class struggle. And it was the product of a dialectical process of development of philosophy itself, reflecting these changes and upheavals in society and in man's comprehension and mastery of the natural world. Nor did dialectical and historical materialism represent Marx and Engels and a few others alone; it was, and is, the revolutionary philosophy of the proletariat, both objective and partisan, reflecting both the objective laws of natural and historical development and the interests and historic mission of the proletariat, which are fully in accord with these laws. For, unlike all other classes in human history which have previously risen to the ruling position and remolded society in their image, the proletariat aims not merely to seize power; its mission is not to establish an "eternal" unchanging system representing the "end point" of human development, but to abolish all class distinctions and enable mankind to continuously overcome barriers to development of human society and its transformation of nature. (page 139.)

We don't feel there's something shameful about the fact that Marxism has its roots in capitalism, that it developed out of the contradictions of bourgeois society. The proletariat itself is obviously a product of capitalism, and in fact everything develops out of the contradictions of what already exists. If Means finds it necessary to pretend that his ideas come from outside of the world of capitalism and imperialism, it is only because he has something to hide.

Shortly after the passage by Marx quoted above, he further notes, "The point need not have been mentioned at all, if this nonsense, which had rhyme and reason for the people of the eighteenth century, had not again been pulled back in all seriousness into modern political economy by Bastiat, Carey, Proudhon, etc." The same can be said about Russell Means. And the fact that he would go several centuries backward to fish up

aspects of bourgeois myth which has lost whatever feeble justification it may once have had, and which has by now become both
hackneyed and reactionary, and that he dredges it up in order to
attack revolutionary Marxism—well, all this should be a clue as
to what he has to hide and what he is actually up to.

And sure enough, we find that Means does after all draw a
certain *distinction* between capitalists and Marxists: "Capitalists,
at least can be relied upon to develop uranium as fuel at the rate at
which they can show a good profit. That's their ethic, and maybe
that will buy some time. Marxists on the other hand, can be relied
upon to develop uranium fuel as rapidly as possible simply
because it's the most 'efficient' production fuel available. That's
their ethic and I fail to see where its preferable." This thinly
disguised defense of bourgeois class rule is followed by a program
of total capitulation to imperialism in crisis. Now we are told:
". . . The European arrogance of acting as though they were
beyond the nature of all related things, can only result in a total
disharmony and a readjustment which cuts arrogant humans
down to size, gives them a taste of that reality beyond their grasp
or control and restores the harmony . . . Mother Earth will
retaliate, the whole environment will retaliate and the abusers
will be eliminated. . . . It's only a matter of time until what
Europeans call 'a major catastrophe of global proportions' will
occur. It is the role of American Indian peoples, the role of all
natural-beings to survive. A part of our survival is to resist. We
resist, not to overthrow the government or to take political
power, but because it is natural to resist extermination . . .
American Indians are still in touch with these realities. We
learned from the elders, from nature, from the powers. And when
the catastrophe is over, we indigenous peoples will still be here to
inhabit the hemisphere. I don't care if it's only a handful of Red
people living high in the Andes, indigenous people will survive
and harmony will be reestablished. *That's* revolution."

Sorry, Russell Means, but that's *capitulation*—to the hilt.
Here is program for withdrawal until some never-never time off
in the future *after* the "catastrophe," clearly referring to the
possibilities of nuclear weapons in the coming showdown
between the U.S. and the Soviet Union. As for any funny ideas
about trying to *prevent* inter-imperialist war through revolution,
any attempts to turn this around on the imperialists if they are

able to start it—forget it, just wait around passively for the new savior, this time Mother Earth instead of the old, discredited Jesus Christ to take care of it all for you. Means has adopted an old plan to let the real "powers" that today threaten the world's people with world war completely off the hook. Everything will work out, as long as some "survive"—even if it's somewhere in the Andes. And just in case anyone might not realize through all this that he is really quite comfortable with the way things are, Means let it all hang out at a later point in the Gathering when he said, "Part of the consumption society, the industrial society which they've laid on us, is impatience . . . we have to acknowledge that resistance is going to take generations, its' a process of education . . . I see no reason to stop it or hurry it up."

Anyone who has any sense of the dung heap that is this society, anyone who has come into political struggle against any of the atrocities of the capitalist system—from the wholesale slaughter and continuing degradation and oppression of the Native American people, to the massive threat of disease and death posed by the capitalist nuclear industry, and especially to the war feverishly being prepared by the U.S. imperialists and their Soviet rivals—anyone who wants to *do something* about all this shit should by now be going through a "process of education" themselves concerning the stand, the politics—and yes, the philosophy—of Russell Means!

*   *   *   *   *

Russell Means' speech is bogus. He has no more intention of leading a back-to-nature movement than the U.S. has of abandoning plans to mine uranium in the Black Hills. His ideological offensive against Marxism—and revolution in general—is serving an important function for the rulers of the U.S. at a crucial time in the history of this country. Just the same, while it is true that his speech, his "natural" path forward so to speak, has invoked hostility on the part of many activists, it is also true that the general ideology—on which his speech was based, one rooted in a basic idealist and metaphysical world outlook, is still widespread in the U.S. today including among those active in struggle against various aspects of imperialism, and that in particular, the spiritualism of the "revenger of Mother Earth" and the romanticized notion of an earlier, pre-industrial time is a widely held viewpoint among those active in the struggle against the oppression of Native Americans. In other words, many of both the particular and general ideas Means puts forward are shared by many who are friends and allies in the revolutionary fight. This is inevitable and will be true up to, during and after a revolution, for resistance, struggle, and even revolutions do not come to think just alike. People are drawn into struggle and revolution out of many different necessities and with many different ideas in their heads. But at the same time, revolutionary struggle will cease to go forward at some point and will ultimately *fail,* if the guiding ideology of the struggle does not consist of—and in the case of *this* historical epoch, this means *Marxism*—the most advanced and scientific ideas available and if this ideology doesn't increasingly become the property of the masses of people themselves.

Therefore, first, we recognize a clear and sharp difference between friends and enemies—between those who may have confused or backward ideas but fight against imperialism on the one hand, and those who are trying to use reactionary ideas to derail the fight and lead it in a counter-revolutionary direction, on the other. And second, we struggle against the incorrect ideas that confuse and mislead people.

Specifically, in this case we must talk about both a scientific world view in general and about a correct understanding of the history of American Indians in particular. The struggle for a scientific understanding of the historical development and present situation of Native Americans is an important task, but not because Indians are somehow innately superior to other people, as Means would have us believe. It is because such an understanding is an important prerequisite for the correct programme of the proletarian revolution in this country, and will also make great contributions to man's understanding of the overall development of society. Actually, one of the big problems involved in such an undertaking is that the vast majority of the studies done so far have been colored by the bourgeois prejudices and viewpoints of many anthropologists—ideas which in essence are little different from those of Russell Means. For example, the rampant idealism of Means' theories abounds in numerous studies of Indian cultural forms, separated off from and in fact raised above the development of the productive forces of the period being discussed.

This is also true of bourgeois anthropologists. (Incidentally, this state of affairs will itself be transformed one day. It is truly inspiring to consider the fact that once the proletariat has seized power and ended the bourgeoisies' monopoly over much of the knowledge of man's development, the class conscious proletariat will be able to unite with American Indians to discover the *actual* process of development. Such discoveries are *impossible* under the rule of the bourgeoisie, which aside from its overall metaphysical and idealist viewpoint also has the particular necessity of justifying its continuing national oppression of Native Americans.)

Still, there is much that has already been proven which is useful today. We know, for example, that at the time of the first lasting European contacts in the 1500s the Native American population of what is now the U.S. was made up of a wide diversity of tribes, some of which were mainly nomadic hunters and gatherers, while others were more agricultural and many relied on a combination of the two for their subsistence. Generally speaking, while there existed the beginnings of class divisions among some tribes, notably in the southeastern part of the U.S., overwhelmingly development had not gone beyond the upper stages of primitive communalist—that is, the initial stage of human society prior to the development of classes and private property. The low level of the productive forces meant that people lived at a subsistence level characterized by scarcity: there was no surplus to allow for the existence of a class that lived off the labor of others or for private ownership of the means of production. People were obliged to work together to avoid starvation or attack from animals and neighboring tribes.

Further, the level of society existing at that time was itself a product of development from earlier times. The first Native Americans were not really "native" at all, but came to this continent from Asia, most likely across a land bridge that formerly connected Alaska and Siberia. Archeological findings have shown that by about 10,000 B.C. at the end of the Pleistocene Period (also known as the ice age) man in this hemisphere was primarily a big game hunter, traveling in small bands and killing animals like the mammoth and bison antiques for his food. Perhaps the fact that these animals no longer exist explains

Means' reluctance to cite this particular pre-tribal period as part of the "traditional" ways he claims to want to return to; anyone who depended on the mammoth for food today would be in big trouble. In any case, early man's supposed "natural harmony with all related things" did not prevent him from unconsciously contributing to the disappearance of those animals with such inefficient slaughtering methods as the *jumpkill*—with this method a band of hunters armed only with spears would surround a herd of these much larger animals and drive them off a cliff to their death. (And here, where this society *was* able to create a—momentary—surplus value above subsistence needs, it couldn't be used and most of the meat had to be left to rot.)

Another way of life was developing as the big game hunting period was coming to a close—bands of hunters and gatherers moving around different regions, with somewhat different levels of subsistence based on the amount of small game and natural vegetation in the area. This was still marked by extreme scarcity. Perhaps Means would like to be transported back some 7,000 years to the days of the desert bands of the great basin of Nevada and western Utah to live in the ways of "the ancestors" of that period. Anthropolgists recently examined a cave in the area and the results of their findings were summed up in the *New York Times* on Tuesday, August 12: "In one of the middens (refuse heaps) the scientists found large deposits of coprolites, desicated human feces. Since it seemed strange that the ancient people would use a storage cave as a latrine, Dr. Thomas said, it is possible that the feces were stored there for what archeologists call the 'second harvest.' Other primitive people were known to have saved their feces so that, in time of famine, they could extract undigested seeds and other products for food. Analysis of the coprolites showed that the heads of cattails and other marsh plants were a substantial part of the lakeside people's diet."

And while we are on the subject of the supposed glories of earlier times, we wonder if Means would advocate a return to a part of the tribal traditions of the Chippewyans of Canada, who on occasion allowed their female infants to die—a practice viewed by some of the adult women as a kindness. Women were beaten frequently, and although it was a crime to kill a Chippewyan man, a husband was permitted to beat his wife to death with no punishment at all. The point here is not to lapse into some ridiculous argument that people now are better than people then, or that one area of the world produced better people than another—after all, most Europeans (themselves not indigenous) went through similar stages of development. (In the case of the question of treatment of women, the stage of development still exists to a great degree.) The point is to understand what is at the basis of the development of society and on what society itself is based.

As Marx put it in the course of a polemic against Proudhon (who has several points in common with Means) describing how the struggle of man against nature determines the overall course of human history: "what he has not understood is that these definite social relations are just as much produced by men as linen, flax, etc. Social relations are closely bound up with productive forces. In acquiring new productive forces men change their mode of production; and in changing their mode of production, in changing their way of earning their living, they change all their social relations in conformity with their material productivity, produce also principles, ideas and categories, in conformity with their social relations." (*The Poverty of Philosophy,* p. 109.)

Contrast this analysis of the development of society with Means' idealist childish attempts to demolish Marxist materialism by vulgarly terming it "gaining." Marxist materialism, says Means, is something "(seen by) American Indians . . . as still more of that same old European conflict between being and gaining . . . being is spiritual proposition. Gaining is a material act. Traditionally American Indians have always attempted to *be* the best people they could. Part of that spiritual process was and is to give away wealth, to discard wealth in order *not* to gain. Material gain is an indicator of false status among traditional people while it is 'proof the system works' to Europeans. Clearly, there are two completely opposing views at issue here, and Marxism is very far over to the other side of the American Indian view."

Where, even in the most primitive society that Means could invoke, is it not true that society's basis is the procurement ("gaining") of the means of subsistence? Certainly not in the previous example cited, whose "traditional way" somehow gets left out of the "being vs. gaining" fantasy. And beyond this, society is constantly in motion—nothing in Means' maternal

friend nature, including mankind, is unchangeable. The productive forces develop as a result of the struggle of man against
nature—and this is independent of anyone's subjective desires.
The Hopi tribe, whose "traditional ways" Means continually
upholds as an example of the type of society to which we all
should return, have themselves gone through this process of
development, attaining higher levels of production of the necessities of life with new developments in the productive forces. Their
ancestors hunted deer and mountain sheep by throwing wood
and later spears; they lived in caves and rock shelters. With the
invention of both the bow and arrow and certain agricultural
implements, their society advanced to a higher level. There was
now more certainty of meat and produce in their diet. The
formation of village communities developed where maize and
beans were cultivated. The later invention of the hoe led to
greater domestication of plant life, including cotton (which now
resulted in new apparel) and a much more complex, mainly
agricultural society. Clearly, there was a great deal of "gaining"
going on here.

Means' claim that Indians gave away wealth, "in order *not* to
gain," while true *within* many communal, that is classless tribes,
certainly doesn't apply to relations between tribes. He conve-
niently ignores the numerous nomadic tribes that went to war
with each other over the "richest" hunting areas, as well as those
that raided the agricultural settlements of others for their produce and implements. It is quite true that primitive communalism
was very egalitarian—and it is just such equality, of classlessness,
that communism of the future will reproduce, *but on a much
higher and qualitatively different level.* For in primitive society
this equality is quite restricted both in the sense that it applies
only within each tribe, and in the sense that it is based on a very
restricted level of material-productive development. And because of these facts, it also restricted human development. In
order to move beyond this level, it was necessary to negate
equality, to move through an epoch of class society, with all its
brutal oppression, in order to develop the productive forces of
humanity and make possible a far higher equality. As Engels
explains in *Anti-Duhring,* in a passage which is worth quoting at
some length:

The division of society into an exploiting and an exploited class, a ruling and an oppressed class, was the necessary outcome of the low development of production hitherto. So long as the sum of social labor yielded a product which only slightly exceeded what was necessary for the bare existence of all; so long, therefore, as all or almost all the time of the great majority of the members of society was absorbed in labor, so long was society necessarily divided into classes. Alongside of this great majority exclusively absorbed in labor there developed a class, freed from direct productive labor, which managed the general business of society; the direction of labor, affairs of state, justice, science, art, and so forth. It is therefore the law of the division of labor which lies at the root of the division into classes. But this does not mean that this division into classes was not established by violence and robbery, by deception and fraud, or that the ruling class, once in the saddle, has ever failed to strengthen its domination at the cost of the working class and to convert its social management into the exploitation of the masses.

But if, on these grounds, the division into classes has a certain historical justification, it has this only for a given period of time, for given social conditions. It was based on the insufficiency of production; it will be swept away by the full development of the modern productive forces. And in fact the abolition of social classes has as its presupposition a stage of historical development at which the existence not merely of some particular ruling class or other but of any ruling class at all, that is to say, of class difference itself, has become an anachronism, is out of date. It therefore presupposes that the development of production and of products, and with these, of political supremacy, the monopoly of education and intellectual leadership by a special class of society, has become not only superfluous but also economically, politically and intellectually a hindrance to development.

This point has now been reached. Their political and intellectual bankruptcy is hardly still a secret to the bourgeoisie themselves, and their economic bankruptcy recurs regularly every ten years. In each crisis society is smothered under the weight of its own productive forces and products of which it can make no use, and stands helpless in the face of the absurd contradiction that the producers have nothing to consume because there are no consumers. The expanding force of the means of production bursts asunder the bonds imposed upon them by the capitalist mode of production. Their release from these bonds is the sole condition necessary for an unbroken and constantly more rapidly progressing development of the productive forces, and therewith of a practically limitless growth of production itself. Nor is this all. The appropriation of society of the means of production puts an end not only to the artificial restraints on production which exist today, but also to the positive waste and destruction of productive forces and products which is now the inevitable accompaniment of production and reaches its zenith in crises. Further, it sets free for society as a whole a mass of means of production and products by putting an end to the senseless luxury and extravagance of the present ruling class and its political representatives. The possibility of securing for every member of society, through social production, an existence which is not only fully sufficient from a material standpoint and becoming richer from day to day, but also guarantees to them the completely unrestricted development and exercise of their physical and mental faculties—this possibility now exists for the first time, but it *does exist*.

Engels continues with a discussion of the future communist society:

The seizure of the means of production by society puts an end to commodity production, and therewith to the domination of the product over the producer. Anarchy in social production is replaced by conscious organization on a planned basis. The struggle for individual existence comes to an end. And at this point, in a certain sense, man finally cuts himself off from the animal world, leaves the condition of animal existence behind him and enters conditions which are really human. The conditions of existence forming man's environment, which up to now have dominated man, who now for the first time becomes the real conscious master of nature, because and in so far as he has become master of his own social organization. The laws of his own social activity, which have hitherto confronted him as external, dominated laws of nature, will then be applied by man with complete understanding, and hence will be dominated by man. Men's own social organization which has hitherto stood in opposition to them as if arbitrarily decreed by nature and history, will then become the voluntary act of men themselves. The objective, external forces which have hitherto dominated history, will then pass under the control of men themselves. It is only from this point that men, with full consciousness, will fashion their own history; it is only from this point that the social causes set in motion by men will have, predominantly and in constantly increasing measure, the effects willed by men. It is humanity's leap from the realm of necessity into the realm of freedom.

To carry through this world-emancipating act is the historical mission of the modern proletariat. And it is the task of scientific socialism, the theoretical expression of the proletarian movement, to establish the historical conditions and, with these, the nature of this act, and thus to bring to the consciousness of the now oppressed class the conditions and nature of the act which it is its destiny to accomplish.

At this point in history, when the leap of mankind into the realm of freedom is actually on the horizon, to preach instead the necessity for a "second harvest" of primitive life is an expression either of despair or of counter-revolution and reaction.

With Means, it comes down more to reaction. Here he is extolling primitiveness and telling how Indians like to give away their material goods—which fits in pretty well with the old capitalist tradition of stealing from the Indians all they have and forcing them to live in abject poverty.

Of course, Means might argue that his main beef is against machinery and industry, that machines pollute the water, that machines will destroy the world, etc. But really isn't this more than a little pragmatic, a "theory" based on the appearance of things and not their essence? Would Means argue, to take a notable example from the history of the capitalists' oppression of Indians, that instead of blaming the U.S. government for intentionally infesting blankets sold to the Indians with smallpox virus, that one should instead blame the *blankets* for the deaths caused by the disease?

There was, in the development of capitalism, a period in which the class struggle between workers and capitalists focused on the introduction of machinery. When new machines were introduced, vast numbers of people were thrown out of work, and as a means of gaining back their jobs, large crowds would destroy the machinery. The machines, on the other hand, were often consciously introduced by the capitalists as a means of repressing strikes. Marx, in recounting this historical period, remarks, "It took both time and experience before the workpeople learnt to distinguish between machinery and its employment by capital, and to direct their attacks, not against the material instruments of production, but against the mode in which they were used." (*Capital,* Vol. 1, page 429).

Here as elsewhere, we see a sentiment or idea which once had some historical justification, but which has long since been bypassed—and which Means now proposes to raise to a principle! What he cannot and will not understand is something Engels pointed out over 100 years ago (to quote again from *Anti-Duhring*):

The forces operating in society work exactly like the forces operating in nature—blindly, violently, destructively, so long as we do not understand them and fail to take them into account. But when once we have recognized them and understood how they work, their direc-

tion and their effects, the gradual subjection of them to
our will and the use of them for the attainment of our
aims depend entirely upon ourselves. And this is quite
especially true of the mighty productive forces of the
present day. So long as we obstinately refuse to understand their nature and their character—and the capitalist mode of production and its defenders set themselves
against any such attempt—so long do these forces
operate in spite of us, against us, and so long do they
control us, as we have shown in detail. But once their
nature is grasped, in the hands of the producers working in association they can be transformed from demon
like masters into willing servants. It is the difference
between the destructive force of electricity in the light-
ening of a thunderstorm and the tamed electricity of the
telegraph and the arc light; the difference between a
conflagration and fire in the service of man. This treatment of the productive forces of the present day, on the
basis of their real nature at last recognized by society,
opens the way to the replacement of the anarchy of
social production by the socially planned regulation of
production in accordance with the needs both of society
as a whole and of each individual. The capitalist mode
of appropriation, in which the product enslaves first the
producer and then also the appropriator, will thereby
be replaced by the mode of appropriation of the products based on the nature of the modern means of production themselves; on the one hand direct social
appropriation as a means to the maintenance and
extension of production, and on the other hand direct
individual appropriation as a means to life and
pleasure.

Russell Means bills himself as the exponent of nature and
the natural, but in fact he never strays outside the bounds of
capitalism and bourgeois ideology. As we saw above, the romantic longing for the supposed simpler and nobler life of primitive
man is a product and an expression of capitalist social relations,
as is the view that history will never advance beyond capitalism.
As Marx sums this up: "It is as ridiculous to yearn for a return to

that original fullness as it is to believe that with this complete emptiness history has come to a standstill. The bourgeois viewpoint has never advanced beyond this antithesis between itself and this romantic viewpoint, and therefore the latter will accompany it as legitimate antithesis up to its blessed end." (*Grundrisse,* p. 162.)

Well, if Russell Means wishes to return to the days of the "second harvest"—either economically or politically or both—he is free to do so; in fact, we are quite willing to help him in his quest. We ony plead that he not take everyone else along with him. His "being" is a head-long flight into fantasy over reality, spirit over nature, ideas over matter—all with the end result of keeping man perpetually helpless before forces he would obstinately have us refuse to understand or control. His idealism reminds us of an incident which took place in a college classroom in the early '70s. A professor, ideologically in the same camp as Means, theorized that even if one could not swim, but one *thought* one could swim, then one could swim. A rebellious Chicano student raised the point in the discussion: "Well, I had a friend who reasoned the same way. So one day he walked to the end of a pier and jumped in the ocean—even though he couldn't swim." The professor anxiously asked, "Yes, and *then* what happened?" Anticipating the professor's scholarly (and foolish) inquiry, the student moved in for the kill: "The damn fool drowned to death, what the hell do you think happened?"

In the interest of staying afloat, professor Means, we would hasten to inform you that even the religious ideas of the American Indians, which have themselves undergone a great deal of change and development with the corresponding changes in Indian material reality, have a material basis which can be explained by applying Marxism. Like the rest of the superstructure of any society, they correspond to that society's material development. In particular, since the Indian people were so much at the mercy of the forces of nature for their survival, it was thought that these forces commanded supernatural powers. However, the religious ceremonies and customs varied depending upon the manner in which they gained their subsistence. The Hopi, for example, being an agricultural tribe living in the semi-arid environs of the Southwest, held a religious belief that after people died, they turned into clouds which brought rain to irrigate the crops. The fishermen of the Northwest, on the other hand, put great stress on praying to Sea Spirits to bring them an abundance of fish, and the nomadic hunters developed ceremonies around gaining strength for the hunt or to do battle with other tribes. But more to the point of Means' particular argument, even the "revenge of Mother Earth" philosophy he promotes is a fairly recent development in the religion of many tribes in the U.S., having been adopted after the conquest and subsequent oppression by the forces of capitalism, as the Indians saw the world—as they had known it—being destroyed by the invaders. The use of the messiah who had come back to save those who were not lost after the apocalypse was, in many cases, borrowed from the Christianity of the Europeans.

Communists are opposed to the whole idea of *spirits* but not to the spirit, if this is understood to mean the advancing consciousness of mankind, based on the material world. In fact, we even write about it in our songs: ". . . To make the thief disgorge his booty, to free the spirit from its cell . . ." goes the famous line from the *Internationale*. But this is the opposite of what Means is talking about. We understand that it is only by correctly grasping the objective laws of nature and society, and thereby being able to change the material world, that man's "spirit" is truly unleashed—just think of the great difference if the would-be swimmer in the story told above had merely done a little investigation into how to avoid sinking to the bottom like a stone. But Means would condemn us all to a "being"—in fact a "drowning"—of backwardness, ignorance, and servility to the bourgeoisie and—despite protestations to the contrary—to productive relations characteristic of its rule. No thanks, Russell! We'll take communism and the elimination of classes altogether.)

As with religion, so with other aspects of the cultures of the American Indians—not only was it a historical creation, but many aspects which have come down as "traditional" were created out of the historical conflict between capitalist expansion and the primitive communal society of the Indians.

In fact, the tribes that were most successful in resisting and delaying their eventual defeat, like the Lakota tribe of which Means is a member, were those that adopted the more advanced technology of the invader. Actually, the entire Lakota way of life was conditioned by European contact. Originally, the tribe had been semi-sedentary farmers in what is now Minnesota. They were attacked by Canadian tribes like the Cree and Ojibwa who had gotten guns from French traders, forcing them westward into the Great Plains. There they first came into contact with horses which had been brought to the western hemisphere by the early Spanish colonists and subsequently slowly spread northward. (The indigenous horse had become extinct at the same time as the mammoth and big bison.) They quickly became known among all the tribes of the Great Plains as the finest buffalo hunters and warriors in the area. When they recognized that their bows and arrows were no match for the U.S. Cavalry's more advanced weaponry, they began to conduct raids to obtain the more modern weapons. They adopted the method of fighting involving a field commander giving tactical direction to the troops, as opposed to their "traditional" way of every man for himself that they had used in their previous fights with other tribes. In this way, they were able to inflict some of the most devastating defeats, if only temporary ones, on the westward expansion of the U.S. capitalists.

Generally speaking, all the tribes that existed adopted aspects of the invaders into their culture, or they were totally wiped out. The Navajos took not only horses and guns, but also developed their "traditional" sheepherding culture by raiding Spanish settlements for sheep. The Hopi expanded their agricultural complex many times over by adding domesticated plant strains from both the Spanish and the Americans.

Of course, not only was much of what is today considered "traditional" Indian culture a product of the clash of primitive communal society with capitalist expansion, but that culture was also then suppressed by the inexorable capitalist drive for total supremacy. In addition, genocide through disease and massacre reduced the Indian population from 10 million to 500,000 in the area north of Mexico within 300 years. As capitalism expanded westward, treaties were signed only to be broken a few years later, and Indians were repeatedly forced onto concentration camps called "reservations," only to be moved once again if valuable minerals were found, where the land was potentially productive for agriculture or where the railroad needed the right of way. As capitalism consolidated its victory over Native Americans, laws were passed mandating "forced assimilation" and Indian lands were broken up into smaller parcels to open them up for settlement. At one point, Indian lands were given to Christian missionaries to exercise trusteeship over them, while bringing "religion to the heathens." Of course, there was always fierce resistance to this repression and particularly to the attempts to make the Indian tribes disappear. In fact, the resistance was so fierce that by 1934 the imperialists amended their "forced assimilation" schemes. They passed the Indian Reorganization Act, setting up their own puppet tribal councils under the direction of the Bureau of Indian Affairs to facilitate the continued armed robbery of Indian land—a robbery that is intensifying today with tribal council sanctions, such as that offered by Navajo tribal chairman Peter McDonald. At the same time, political repression and outright murder is offered to all those who dare to resist.

A history of brutal oppression; a history of attempted genocide. In the face of this imperialist attempt to wipe Indians off the face of the earth there has been resistance, rebellion, and reaffirmation by Native Americans of their own culture against the onslaught of imperialism. As we've seen, Indian traditions are not capable of guiding the struggle on the path to real liberation, even though they have played a part in providing a "culture of resistance" in the Indian movement. But in Means' hands this culture of resistance turns into its opposite—into a theory of capitulation. From a fight against capitalism and imperialism, he tries to turn it into a fight against the future. He reiterates: "I do not believe that capitalism itself is really responsible for the situation in which we have been declared a national sacrifice. No, it is the European tradition; the European culture itself is responsible. Marxism is just the latest continuation of this tradition, not a solution to it. To ally with Marxism is to ally with the very same forces which declare us an acceptable 'cost'." But we think in the final analysis that you do understand the difference between capitalism and Marxism, between the revolutionary science of the working class and the reactionary theories of its enemy. The point is that you have adopted a reactionary theory yourself—the idealist and metaphysical theory of the bourgeoisie!

There is only one final charge made by Means in his speech to which we must respond. "Look beneath the surface of revolutionary Marxism and what do you find? . . . a commitment to guaranteeing the Lakota and other American Indian people real control over the land and resource they have left? No, not unless the industrial process is to be reversed as part of their doctrine. A commitment to our rights, as peoples, to maintaining our values and traditions? No, not as long as they need the uranium within our land to seize the industrial system of this society, the culture of which the Marxists *are still a part.*"

For the position of the proletariat on this matter—once it has seized power—we will let the draft of the *New Programme and New Constitution* of the Revolutionary Communist Party speak for itself:

> . . . (Native Americans) have been repeatedly forced off their land into concentration camps which are euphemistically called 'reservations.' In un-doing this longstanding atrocity the proletariat will, through consultation with the masses of the Indian peoples, establish large areas of land where they can live and work and will provide special assistance to the Indian peoples in developing these areas. Here autonomy will be the policy of the proletarian state—the various Indian peoples will have the right to self-government within the larger socialist state, under certain overall guiding principles. The overall guiding principles referred to are that practices and customs must tend to promote equality, not inequality, unity not division, between different peoples, and eliminate not foster, exploitation. The Indian peoples themselves will be mobilized and relied on to struggle through and enforce these principles. This will mean that policies related to local affairs as well as customs, culture and language will be under autonomous control, while at the same time the Indian peoples will be encouraged as well to take a full part in the overall affairs of society as a whole. Local customs and practices—such as medicine . . . will be studied for those aspects that have an underlying scientific content and these aspects will be promoted and applied generally by the proletariat . . .

This will not be done because the proletariat has the impossible and undesirable dream of going backward in time, but rather because it is a crucial part of moving forward to classless society.

> ...In particular, this will most definitely not be a new chapter in the history of oppression of the Indian peoples—forcing them onto reservations and treating them like special 'wards of the state' when they move off them. Instead the new proletarian state, while favoring and encouraging unity and integration, will ensure these formerly oppressed peoples' right to autonomy as part of a policy of promoting real equality between nations and peoples. (*New Draft Program and New Constitution*, Drafts for Disussion, pp. 62-63.)

This great historical advance can only come about through the overthrow of the existing social order and the establishment of the dictatorship of the proletariat—a period still marked by the existence of classes and class struggle, but with one important distinction from previous revolutions. The proletariat, the class whose ultimate goal is the elimination of all classes including itself, holds the reins of state power and exercises that power to consciously wage the struggle for the attainment of classless society. It is inevitable that this revolution will take place, and further that humanity will move beyond it to that new era where all mankind consciously grasps and applies the laws of nature to continuously transform it in the interest of mankind. But until that occurs, and the ultimate basis for the exploitation of man by man is eliminated, there will also inevitably be those—like Russell Means—who jump out to oppose the revolutionary forward march of history under the signboard of a retrograde retreat into the past—and whose "theories" are worth less than those specimens of the crop of the "second harvest" discovered in the Nevada desert.

3
The Same Old Song In Sad Refrain
Dora-Lee Larson and Ward Churchill

The official response of the Revolutionary Communist Party, USA to Russell Means' statement on Marxism at the Black Hills Survival Gathering induces a reaction of appalled consternation and sheer delight, in roughly equal proportions. The RCP position is distressing not only for its seemingly willful ignorance, but also for its obviously conscious distortion of known realities. On the other hand, it is perversely pleasurable to note that it could hardly have gone further in reinforcing virtually every point posited by Means, even if Russell had drafted the Party paper himself.

The authors first felt it most appropriate that a response be made directly by Means. Subsequent discussions, however, made it clear that he felt compelled to devote his time and energy to more pressing matters than the rhetorical posturing of the "caucasian left," that nothing in the RCP piece ultimately raised issues requiring (for his purposes) a theoretical position differing from those he'd already publicly assumed, and as a result he was more than willing to simply ignore "those idiots."

From a purely American Indian Movement members' perspective, Means' attitude seems incontestably correct in this instance. The authors, however, remained unconvinced of the propriety of this position beyond AIM. The RCP is—for better or worse—one of the more prominently vocal and visible left organizations in the contemporary United States. As such, it attracts certain attention to its formal elaborations, attention which necessarily transcends both its theoretical content and the absolute numbers having party membership. Marxists of other than Leninist/Maoist persuasion might argue that such attention is both practically and intellectually unwarranted. This is perhaps true, but does nothing to alter the fact that such attention is nonetheless paid; ignoring the RCP and similarly structured Marxist-Leninist groups accomplishes nothing in coming to grips with the content of their image or their ability to popularly project it, often through media facilities unavailable to more theoretically important left configurations.

Simply dismissing the RCP and kindred parties of the Leninist mold as being "tiny," "irrelevant" and "isolated" within the true flow of contemporary US Marxism is an evasion of considerations of their obvious longevity, continuity (in form, at least), organizational coherence and public visibility. Along with the bourgeois media, all these factors militate to identify sectarian dogma with the generic term "Marxism" in the popular mind. It seems inevitable, therefore, that these dogmas must be dealt with seriously; no real alternative appears for those who would claim the mantle of Marxism in terms other than those prescribed by Leninist doctrine.

Thus, we have set out to address the issues and distortions raised by the RCP in "Searching for the Second Harvest" in some depth and, in places, on a point-by-point basis. This is not done from a Marxist position, though it *is* done with the knowledge that the Marxist paradigm is hardly limited to the Leninist catechism. We also wish to make it clear that our writing does *not* constitute an official AIM response, but rather points offered by two people who share in the AIM perspective and who wish to offer a coherent analysis to those desiring to participate in a considered forum, who seek to further their understanding of the relationship of Marxian theory to Native Americans, and who wish to reach a realization as to why Marxism (the Leninist version in particular) tends to be dismissed rather harshly by the Indian population.

Before proceeding, however, we would like to observe that in certain very important ways, a point-by-point refutation of the RCP argument is insufficient in countering their technique. This is because the points they offer are, in the end, secondary to the real nature of their attack. First, this is purely ideological in the narrowest possible sense, i.e.: "Does the individual we are considering subscribe, and subscribe in every detail, to our ideological posture?" Such questions properly belong to grand inquisitors rather than debaters. Inquisition, however, is precisely the party's stock-in-trade, and from the party viewpoint, entirely warranted. The party is by its own description the sole agent of proletarian liberation and true revolution at large in this society today. Those who do not conform, intellectually or otherwise, to party strictures are by definition counter-revolutionary. That which is counter-revolutionary must be exposed and attacked. Hence, the substance of the RCP polemic is essentially an ideologically motivated personal attack on Russell Means himself rather than a reasoned argument against his position. With this in mind, we can turn to the material with which the RCP orchestrated its assault.

*   *   *   *   *

The first point of contention between the RCP's polemic and anyone aware of the circumstances leading up to Russell Means' address at the Black Hills Survival Gathering is the question of, as the party puts it, Means' "attempts to trade on his reputation as an American Indian *leader* (despite the obligatory false disclamers of "humility" to the contrary)." The facts of the matter are that several people other than Means had attempted, during the year prior to the event in question, to present essentially the same analysis (in both "scholarly" and "popular" formats), to a number of left publications.

RCP cadres were presented with such material at least as early as the Union of Marxist Social Scientists Conference held in October, 1979. Cadre response, however, was simply to refuse consideration of any position deviating from the various

"National Minorities" planks of the party's draft platform; RCP representatives flatly maintained through this posture that the party naturally possessed more inherent ability to deal with American Indian issues and perspectives than Indian people themselves. Clearly, the party demonstrated its unwillingness to grace the pages of either its "mass circulation" tabloid (*Revolutionary Worker*) or its "theoretical journal" (*Revolution*) with the views of Native American activists. Even during its later editorial campaign to "let 100 schools of thought contend," the content of debate in *RW* is restricted to an extremely narrow focus, entirely within the doctrinaire confines of standard Marxist-Leninist discussion.

In any event, the persons attempting to surface the analysis presented by Russell Means in July, 1980 shared a common attribute aside from being Native American activists and writers. None of them happened to have received any media acclaim as "Indian leaders." Thus they were quite universally ignored and frozen out of print. The difference in left response accorded Means, a figure hyped for nearly a decade by such various glamorizers as *Time, Newsweek*, and Andy Warhol, is stunning. The RCP article in question here is fully twice the length of the text of Russell's original speech.

In the event, it was calculated that only a person who had been established by the bourgeois media as a "leader" could hope to penetrate the monolithic elitism and caucasoid fantasyland prevailing in the contemporary Euro-American consciousness, Marxist or otherwise. As Means put it near the end of his speech, he is not a leader in the sense conveyed by the media, he is merely *used* by the media; a fact brought dramatically home by the RCP's snide commentary on his "obligatory" and "false" disclaimer, and compounded by the fact the the party itself refused categorically to consider the statements of any "lesser" personalities. Thus, the issue was forced from a matter of possible productive analytical dialogue into the propagandist arena of "the cult of the personality," an intrinsically Marxist proposition rather than an Indian one. The RCP itself was/is quite actively involved in creating the elitist context at issue.

*   *   *   *   *

With a sort of inevitable appropriateness, the RCP launches its analysis of "The Same Old Song" by utterly validating one of Means' primary theses. That is that "revolutionary Marxism" is hopelessly locked into the notion that production, and thereby industrialization, constitute *the* "advanced ideas" of humanity while those opposed to them are the "most backward." The RCP is confronted with the problem of proving that these "advanced ideas" are correct. This is precisely the situation which creates the necessity for the RCP writers to validate virtually every point within Means second thesis: that such a formula is inherently racist and a totally inaccurate view of the natural order.

By way of refuting the central thrust of Means' argument, the RCP once again arcs back to the snide, if meaningless, realm of assault on the personality of their opponent. Not only is Means a *leader* (horrors!), but he adapts the garb of the "noble savage" as well. This second descent into name-calling is grounded, intellectually, in the RCP assertion that Means' commentary on the natural order harkens back, not to his own Lakota heritage, but to Adam Smith and and the "Robinsonades." This is, on one level, merely distortion; Smith, along with Descartes, Locke, and a number of other thinkers of European origin are dealt with in Russell's talk, securely placed in the intellectual development of capitalism and therefore dismissed as *antithetical* to Native American interests. Nowhere in his defense of native cultures is there a suggestion of the ahistorical individualism for which the European theorists can be justly criticized.   .

On a second level, this attempt to link Means' thinking to a European school of idealist exponents of an invented "noble savage," *despite* his crushing critique of these same idealists, points to a much more serious problem. The RCP seems utterly incapable of placing Means' thought in any other context than their own. From their viewpoint, all ideas, no matter what the claims of their proponents, can be traced to European origins, and if not Marxist, they must be bourgeois; genuinely non-European ideas simply do not exist. It is as if to the Marxist-Leninist mind non-European thought itself is an impossibility; any tradition of thought alien to that of Europe therefore remains opaque to the polemicists of the RCP.

Given that the RCP views industrialization as constituting the indication of "advanced thought," it succeeds in linking thought itself (by way of its "inherent" technological deployment) to production of material attainment. A crude continuum is thus established: the more material attainment evidenced by a culture, the more advanced its thought; the less material attainment, the more backward the thought. But—this is extremely important—it also follows that the link between thought and production indicates that given levels of thought cannot be achieved *without* a corresponding level of material attainment. The implications of this should be immediately apparent. The Lakota, of which people Russell Means is a member, never evidenced a material culture similar to that prevailing in Europe at the time the "noble savage" idealists did their thinking. Thus, the Lakota could not have possessed a body of thought which equalled—much less surpassed—the thinking of these idealists; such would be *materially* impossible. The notion that the Lakota and other non-industrial peoples might have a completely autonomous heritage of thought on matters which intersect the thought of Europeans in certain superficial ways, but which follows the logic of their own cultural imperatives and perceptions to conclusions completely dissimilar to those reached in Europe, is an impossibility to the historical materialist mind.

The Leninist doctrine decrees that Lakota culture could not, in and of itself, have historically generated a body of thought at the level evidenced by the European idealists simply because the Lakota never exhibited a level of material attainment which would have provided the basis for thinking such thoughts. The Lakota in pre-contact times were, by purely materialist definition, a "stone age" or "primitive" culture, the thought of which *necessarily* would reflect such status. It was thus incumbent upon the RCP writers to assign Means a direct equivalent in European history, regardless of his conclusions, simply because of the internal structure of their own premanufactured theoretical assumptions. To acknowledge even the possibility that Means' thinking has its roots in Lakota rather than European culture would create a serious breach in the seamlessness of the production/industrialization paradigm.

Transparent distortions of Means' content were thus necessary to reconcile the RCP critique to the superstructure of

Leninist theory. But the matter does not rest with this single instance. Given production/industrialization as the measure by which all human advancement may be calculated, then *only* Europe can lay claim to ultimate leadership in terms of human progress and development. Given the productivist link between material attainment and conceptual ability, *only* Europe can lay claim to establishing the intellectual basis of planetary thought. All non-European cultures must be considered "underdeveloped" stages to be transcended. All non-European thought must be considered ' 'primitive" relative to that of Europe, consigned by "progress" to Trotsky's "dustbin of history." All non-European articulations not corresponding to the relative primitiveness prescribed by historical materialist assumptions must be pegged to one or another component of the European intellectual tradition; they are to be construed as "acculturative attributes." In essence, Europe must be the ideal against which all people and all things are measured, the source of all "valid" and "advanced" inspiration.

The mere fact that Means was, in most instances, simply applying the teachings of the Lakota tribal elders (who, it can be vouchsafed, have never heard of, much less read, the "Robinsonades") to the immediate context with which he was confronted,[1] is singularly lacking in interest to the party polemicists. Such facts do not fit the "party line." The nature of this willfully arrogant disregard for and diminishment of even the *possibility* of non-European cultural attainments and integrity seems sufficient to cause the Nazi theoreticians to turn gleefully in their graves; it is the penultimate in applied theoretical racism masquerading behind a liberatory facade. As Baudrillard has aptly observed, the analytical potential of Marxism is broken by the catechism, upon the "wheel of production."[2]

*   *   *   *   *

Attempts to tie Means' argument to a European tradition he clearly renounces, however, were hardly enough to carry the RCP polemic to a successful conclusion. In order to establish its counter-position, the party (logically enough) perceived the need to demonstrate the overall inadequacy of traditional Native cultures in relation to the "more advanced" European model. In order to accomplish this, a direct application of historical materialist cross-cultural analytical methodology was called for.

In what has, by now, become something of a pattern in party exposition, this argument leads off with a snide attempt to discredit the opposition; but this time the "opposition" is the whole complex of peoples and cultures referred to as Native American. As the party puts its, "The first Native Americans were not really native at all, rather they "came to this continent from Asia," and further this immigration probably occurred "across a land bridge which formerly connected Alaska and Siberia." The party then proceeds to cite "archeological" evidence as to the big game hunting habits of the North American population *circa* 10,000 BC. This sequence of introducing archeological evidence is rather important.

In the first place, the physical evidence used to support the bourgeois anthropological contention that American Indians crossed the Bering Strait land bridge from Asia to the Americas has been ambiguous at best. There is in fact considerable evidence which militates against the validity of any such notion. Geological evidence points firmly to the fact that the land bridge in question would have been passable approximately 12,000 years ago, essentially the same period that other data points to the existence of a population spread across virtually the whole of the North American continent—this is what RCP refers to as the big game hunting period. Worse, in terms of what the RCP is proposing, there is a vast surplus of evidence that the *South* American continent was even more thoroughly populated at the same time. Barring the existence of jet aircraft in the Americas twelve millenia ago, the RCP chronology is simply a physical impossibility. An impossibility which, incidentally, has been acknowledged in all but the most arcane anthropological circles (such as among the Mormons, who are still bound and determined to prove Native American origins among the Tribes of Israel) for well over a decade.[3]

In addition, more recent information tends to support precisely what "primitive" Native Americans have been saying all along: American Indians did *not* migrate to this hemisphere.[4] Indian accounts have been consistently chalked off as "legend and superstition" by more "knowledgeable and advanced" Europeans. Recently, however, a contemporary anthropologist, Jeffrey Goodman, finally got around to treating Hopi origin accounts as fact rather than fiction. When he initiated an archeological dig where the Hopis themselves state the tribe came from, he found precisely what they said he'd find: evidence of occupation old enough to validate the Hopi sequence of earth, fire and ice in literal geological rather that figurative mythological fashion.[5] In short, archeological/anthropological/geological data clearly tend to corroborate American Indian knowledge; as Means puts it, "our knowledge is real. . ."

It is interesting to note that the whole Bering Strait speculation originated with no less a personage than Thomas Jefferson in his musings entitled *Notes on Virginia,* published in 1781. Given Jefferson's particular outlook, the thesis may be viewed as something of a device to assuage the guilt experienced by a political theorist associated with the final phase of genocidal policy directed at the indigenous population of this continent. Although, as was noted earlier, nothing has ever emerged to validate the Jeffersonian proposition, it has generally been accepted by Euro scholars perhaps due to the need to justify the European invasion of America: not only was the indigenous population "primitive and savage," but it too "invaded" the hemisphere, held no *real* native title to the land, and thereby constituted just another usurping agent in the game of might makes right.

The RCP accepts this bourgeois abstraction (could anyone be more appropriately termed "bourgeois" than Thomas Jefferson?) fully and without reservation, thereby theoretically aligning itself with the most reactionary possible tradition of Euro-American culture in order to validate its own constructs. Thus it corroborates Means' assertion that beyond simply having its intellectual roots in the bourgeois tradition, Marxism continues this tradition full force. In this particular connection, it would seem "revolutionary" Marxism seeks to do so even when the bourgeoisie itself is quitting the myth in certain quarters.

*   *   *   *   *

Upon completing its abstract characterization of Native Americans as being non-native, the RCP turns to a more concrete agenda; historical materialist methodology does, after all, base itself in "the concrete and the real." In order to accommodate this necessity, the party turns to that "propaganda tool of the bourgeois," *The New York Times*, the contents of which are generally (and quite accurately) portrayed by them as a cesspool of capitalist distortion and fabrication. In its judgements on American Indians, however, the *Times* is suddenly sacrosanct in its objectivity.

The speculation of a single anthropologist (hardly a Marxist anthropologist, at that), concerning the practice by a certain "ancient people" in the Great Basin region of storing fecal matter in a given location, that perhaps the seed content of this fecal matter constituted a sort of reserve food supply, leads party polemicists to imply, in essence, that "all ancient American Indians ate shit." Russell Means' call for the preservation and enhancement of Native traditionalism is assumed to be analogous to searching through fecal matter for a few grains of nutritive value. The bourgeois anthropologist cited by the *New York Times* referred to this practice as a possible "second harvest" (reutilization of vegetable products). This newly appropriated term was then used by the party as the title of its polemic, and presumably as the crux of its argument.

Upon examination, one finds that even the *Times* was unwilling to stretch the quite tentative findings in a seemingly isolated location to cover all of Native America 7000 years ago. The RCP does so in one wild leap. The *Times*, in fact, nowhere demonstrates a readiness even to ascribe these tentative anthropological conclusions to the occupants of the site in question over any period of time; the RCP is perfectly prepared to advance this unproven speculation as an overarching historical reality. As Means succinctly observed: Marxism not only derives from identical sources as capitalism, it frequently *goes beyond capitalism* in its negative implications for Indian people.

Assuming that the "second harvest" thesis is correct in the sense that it was advanced in the *Times*, a possible interpretation of this would be that the group was undergoing a famine or other form of natural disaster requiring extraordinary survival measures. This scenario is at least as probable as the notion that these "ancient ones" consumed fecal matter due to the consistently "primitive" state of their economic practices.

Assuming, on the other hand, the RCP's utterly unsupported conclusion that such conditions were prevalent in a widespread and multi-generational sense, the party fails to mention exactly how this "backwardness" and "primitive" condition differs from the widespread famine prevailing in the USSR under Lenin's New Economic Program, during which it was not uncommon to find the rural populace separating undigested corn (seeds) from horse dung as well as their own excrement as a survival expedient. Nor does the RCP address the 9 million odd deaths attributable, mostly by starvation, to Stalin's forced labor reorganization of the Soviet economy which followed on the heels of the NEP. Were these victims of "advanced ideas" somehow exempt from eating the nutrient residue of their own stool during enforced and terminal starvation? Less so than the millions who were systematically starved to death in the Hitlerian organization of another "advanced" industrial context? These questions, much less the answers to them are nowhere noted by the party ideologues. Yet, spread across the face of both 20th century Europe and socialist Asia, one encounters precisely those conditions—and on a truly massive scale—which the RCP points to as indicative of the "backwardness" of Native traditionalism, which is somehow to be corrected by the "advanced" ideas of Marxist-Leninism.

To return directly to the RCP thesis that such conditions prevailed across the continent and over a substantial period of time in the "primitive" economies of Native America, the party is strangely silent in another connection: given the known death rates under similar starvation conditions under Stalin, Hitler, Mao, and Lenin, how is it that a Native population survived from a point 7000 years ago to the period of European invasion and genocide? Under such abject poverty, even cannibalism could not have prevented extinction in a much shorter time period.

A feeble attempt is made to reconcile this contradiction by stating elsewhere in the article that ". . . genocide through disease and massacre reduced the Indian population from 10 million to 500,000 in the area north of Mexico. . ." The oblique implication of this statement is that the precontact Native American population of North America was perpetually small enough in proportion to landbase to allow species continuation through the most "primitive" hunting and gathering economies coupled to a (newly discovered) "second harvest" economy. But once again the RCP relies upon a bourgeois dogma which was always unfounded, and has been fundamentally discredited, as a basis for its case.

The demographic methodology through which bourgeois anthropologists and historians have reduced (on paper) the precontact Native population of this hemisphere are no particular secret. The rationale for such statistical sleight of hand would not seem altogether different from that which caused (and causes) the persistence of the Bering Strait land bridge hypothesis: bad as the bourgeois figures show Euro genocide to have been, quantifiable guilt for that genocide is reduced if the precontact Native population can be "proven" to have been less than it actually was. Of course, the RCP has no particular vested interest in diminishing bourgeois guilt; no, it needs the bourgeois data not to minimize the implications of bourgeois genocide, but to "prove" its own theses on the implications of "primitive" economies. In actuality, the precontact population of the area north of Mexico probably exceeded 35 million, 3 1/2 times the number allowed in the bourgeois rearward projection fully accepted by the RCP.[6] Such a population stretches the economic structure imposed by the party on precontact Indian peoples well beyond the limit of any potential viability, and for good reason. The hunting and gathering economies which Euro scholars have always insisted categorized the Native "natural order" would also seem to be little more than a part of the myth of the "savage." There are substantial indications that agriculture played an important role in Native economies and that hunting and gathering was a form forced, in many instances, by massive dislocations induced in those economies by the European invasion itself.[7] In sum, the mound of dung the RCP has fixed on so obsessively may well have been a compost heap rather than an immediate food supply.

Thus, from start to finish, the central RCP thesis—the notion of the "second harvest"—is an absurdity. Its sources are spurious, its logic fallacious, its underriding metholology sheer self-serving propaganda. All credible evidence points directly *away* from the RCP conclusions; the party's insistence in the validity of its position regardless of data is not unlike the posture of Christian missionaries in relation to American Indian and reality in general—pure unadulturated faith.

*   *   *   *   *

Throughout its elaboration, the RCP maintains a theme of the ultimate sanctity of industrialization as *the* advanced form of human social organization. This is "supported" by a parade of quotations from a list of dieties: Marx, Engels, Lenin, Mao, etc., a strange automaton-like performance for "theoreticians" to engage in. Or perhaps *alchemical* is a more appropriate word. It is as if at bottom, the RCP believes that if the same incantations are recited, regurgitated, chanted in catechismic repetition often and long enough, then they will somehow *become* true, no matter how wrong they have been in the past.

Just as the party never manages to address the conditions of starvation prevailing under Lenin, Stalin, and Mao—which is understandable, coming from a party which tends to flank its speakers' platform with oversize portraits of Lenin, Stalin, and Mao—while lambasting other cultural economies for perchance leading to starvation conditions, so too does it evade the direct issues raised by Means in connection with the problems of industrial society as such.

Rather than confronting the questions posed, the party distorts Means' argument in order to label him as "reactionary" and "of service to capitalism." Means' statement that the planet would soon experience "a catstrophe of global proportions" is interpreted as referring only to nuclear war, whereas the point raised by "The Same Old Song" is that even in the absence of a nuclear holocaust, the imperatives of the European industrialization process are leading to an essentially similar result. And Marxism, rather than capitalism, now constitutes the theoretical (if not yet the practical) vanguard of this line of "development."

On this point the RCP is dumbfounded and consequently attempts to divert the issue in the manner noted above. Maximum production and industrial efficiency, as Means noted, is after all really their ethic, their theoretical pride and joy. The notion that it is ultimately the destructive element of humanity, as opposed to the liberatory element, is too heretical to be dealt with; the party polemicists are reduced to chanting "Not so. Not so." Yet not a single coherent counterargument is advanced. The closest they can muster is to make the wildly inaccurate analogy that Means is somehow equating industry to the smallpox contaminated blankets issued by US troops to the Mandans as an extermination device. Blame the troops who issued the blankets, not the blankets (which are in themselves benign) says the RCP, accurately enough. And industry is the same as blankets, subject to its employment by *people*, the party asserts with complete inaccuracy.

One difference between the blanket and industry, which should be rather obvious, is that the blanket (an industrial byproduct, in this case) consumes no energy; industry does. It seems more than slightly odd that staunchly Marxist-Leninist theorists, presumably steeped in that tradition's pretentions to status as a "science," might have missed something as elementary (to scientists) as the second law of thermodynamics. The second law states, among other things, that energy used for work can never be used completely efficiently, and that the waste energy is dissipated in a more disorderly form than the original source. The unusable energy is frequently in the form of heat but the same principle applies to the radioacive waste produced by nuclear reactors.

Industry—the European production process—is without doubt the most energy consumptive process ever conceived by the human mind, and produces the most waste energy as well as waste materials. Nuclear weapons are merely a by-product (like the germ-laden blankets) of that process; even without their use, the radioactive waste produced by the "peaceful" use of nuclear energy, along with the by-products of other energy-intensive industries, threatens to accelerate the termination of this planet's ability to sustain life. This thermodynamic disorder is a parallel to the social and political disorder being created on a global scale through the process of industrialization. Thus, Means' position not only opposes the deployment/employment of nuclear weaponry, it goes far beyond this surface concern to oppose the root problem, the European production fetish itself.

Clearly, such a position cannot derive from the likes of the Robinsonade idealists; their concern was with abstract social forms. Rather, Means' thesis is a physical proposition. It is based directly in the fundamental statement uttered by American

Indians ever since their first encounter with Europeans (and which, as Means noted, Europeans have resolutely refused to hear): "you *cannot* do this." Not "you shouldn't," not "please don't," but "you cannot." And why? "Because the planet will eat you alive if you do; because the universe will destroy you." There is no option here, it is a statement of fact, an assertion of knowledge. And it is a knowledge borne out directly by modern physics, the point being that Native Americans knew this centuries before European physicists arrived at the same conclusions. So much for the determinist correspondence between material attainment and conceptual abilities. So much for the "immutable iron laws of history."

At this point, the RCP falls back on precisely the faith noted by Means in "The Same Old Song." Not having a solution to the question of how to continue to actualize ever more and greater productivity and industrialization in an entropic universe, it simply *asserts* the validity of its doctrine without referring to the fundamental issue at all. "Trust us, we'll figure this out later; trust us, have faith, science will find a way." There is just no other way to assess the position the polemicists lay out; they are utterly religious in their exposition. At one point it was even asserted that the problem of traditional cultures was their "dependence on nature" as if somehow Marxism had, godlike, transcended nature and gone into another realm (which, of course, is one way to get around questions such as those raised by physical law.)

*   *   *   *   *

Finally, after all of the preceeding, a rationale is advanced to justify the trust in Marxist-Leninist intentions requested by the RPC from Native American people. Its nature? The contents of the party's *Draft Programme and New Constitution*, (to be actualized after the "proletarian revolution") which reads in part:

Here autonomy will be the policy of the proletarian state—the various Indian peoples will have the right to self-government *within* the larger socialist state, *under* certain overall guiding principles. . . the practices and principles must tend to promote equality, not inequality, unity, not division, between peoples, and

eliminate, not foster, exploitation . . . (and Indian
people) will be *encouraged* to take a full part in the
overall affairs of society as a whole . . . (emphasis
added).

This is hauntingly familiar rhetoric, virtually a paraphrase from
Stalin's writings concerning the "National Question" in the
USSR.[10] And small wonder; a primary intellect behind the prose
of the document in question, and the "Chairman" of the
Revolutionary Communist Party USA is one Bob Avakian,
unabashed career Stalinist, an individual who only lately reached
the dramatic conclusion that Josef Stalin "might have" made
several "relatively minor errors" in the course of his tenure of
leadership in the Soviet Union. Can there be question as to the
nature of the reality lurking behind the compelling early Stalinist
rhetoric concerning the "National Question"? Can there be real
questions as to the fate of the Soviet minorities so solidly assured
of "autonomy" within the "greater society" of the USSR?

The question of the pragmatic significance of a "guarantee"
of autonomy to American Indians by an intellectual/political
tradition which states, before the fact, "As we have seen, Indian
traditions are not capable of guiding the struggle on the path to
true liberation . . ." must be confronted. The question of why
Native Americans would be better off "within the larger socialist
state" than within geographically discrete territories (nations) of
their own as are other sovereign peoples, must be confronted.
The question of the advantage to the "larger socialist state" of
having those native groups within its corpus must be confronted.
The meaning of "socialist equality, unity," etc. within the
Marxist-Leninist tradition must be confronted in the light of
readily observable historical realities, as must the ultimate nature
of the "encouragement" referred to in the party document. The
time for such confrontation is now, while what the RCP calls "the
revolutionary ripples" which may become "mighty waves in the
not too distant future" are still ripples; *not* after a visionless and
theoretically bankrupt "cadre" has once again seized the power
necessary to continue "the same old song."

*   *   *   *   *

Russell Means' argument is anything but a call to reaction or a defense of capitalism; such a contention can be predicated only in the simplistically mindless view that the range of human option is prescribed within the limitations of the European cultural paradigm itself. Even then, it is vastly simplistic, an exercise in cynicism and manipulation. There are other options, other traditions, other heritages leading to observations, perceptions and conclusions external to the European cultural context; their validity cannot be dismissed *a priori.*

The anal retentive fantasies of the RCP are not an isolated phenomenon on the American left. They are merely presented in crystalline form by the party. Other schools of Marxism advance their thesis variants in more brilliantly sophisticated packages, calling upon more complex adjuncts to bolster the general theory, offering their positions in less obviously transparent jargon. But, in essence, they remain the same.

Terms such as "primitive," "precapitalist," "underdeveloped," etc. hold universal currency in Marxism, regardless of the sophistry within which they are buried. In the final analysis, they are racist and arrogant terms, unsupported by fact. No culture other than Europe has ever undergone the progression of material development experienced in Europe and indicated by such terminology; to presume that non-European cultures would inevitably have followed a trajectory from primitive to precapitalist to capitalist is sublimely speculative. To lock such speculation into a categorical and universal "law" is a cornerstone of all Marxist theory. To this extent at least, the RCP—for all its crudity and vulgarity—*is* representative of Marxian thinking.

The converse applies here. Europe, precisely because of the nature of its material developmental trajectory, has not undergone the experiences of non-European cultures. On that basis alone there is much knowledge to be gained and shared on a cross-cultural basis. Pretense at cultural hegemony in terms of knowledge, on whatever basis, is merely obfuscation, intellectual imperialism, a barrier to real understanding. It is faith, not science. Europe has exported the faith of its core ideology under the mantles of Christianity, capitalism, and Marxism *at the expense of knowledge* throughout its history. To this extent, the pretentions of European knowledge are and must remain a lie.

In the immediate sense, it seems obvious that the RCP knows little of Native Americans. Worse, it seems equally obvious the party seeks no more knowledge than it has already achieved. The willingness to distort, to fabricate, to twist reality beyond recognition in order to force theoretical conformity to its preconceptions is stunning. The pettiness of the polemics advanced as party theses, however, cannot be easily dismissed by either other Marxist schools or non-Marxists. The commonalities of assumption between Marxists are ultimately more compelling than the evident dissimilarities. The differences are tactical, the similarities strategic and theoretical.

In critiquing the inadequacy of the RCP position, non-Leninist Marxism must critique the ground it holds in common with the RCP. A reassessment of the Marxian core ideologies must occur. The alternative can only be that "Marxism no longer has anything to tell us," as Sartre so aptly put it. The redundancy conveyed by the phrase "revolutionary Marxism" can then only constitute a conflict in terms, rendering Russell Means' observations just that much more astute.

What is required at this historical juncture is an abandonment of faith in the fundamental role of production. In its present configuration, Marxism has nothing to say in the matter. Structurally, however, through its dialectical methodology, Marxism can hope to transcend its own intellectual/theoretical stalemate. Self-serving, mythologizing polemics such as the RCP illustrates so well can serve only to balk such a process; they are regressive in the extreme, they are truly "backward," truly "reactionary."

The absolute need to combine the knowledges of all the cultures of the world within a comprehensive world view has never been stronger than at this moment. Marxism can and should have an important role to play in such a dialectical endeavor. The imperative to accrue such knowledge must be established before, not after, some mystical "revolutionary" cataclysm. Presupposition must be ended and interaction begun. And the only valid point of departure for American Marxists is with the cultural knowledge of *Native* Americans.

PART TWO

At night, when the streets
of your cities and villages are
silent and deserted,
they will throng with the host
that once filled, and still
love this land.

The white man
          will never
                   be alone.

                -Chief Sealth Suquamish

4
Marx's General Cultural Theoretics
Elisabeth Lloyd

Can Marxist analysis be applied successfully to all of the diverse cultures on our planet? Critics often contend that Marxism possesses no theory of culture per se, and that its analysis tends to be advanced from such a narrowly European base that any conclusions drawn are strongly suspected of being inappropriate to Third World contexts. Such an approach to cultural diversity renders Marxism as potentially destructive to non-European cultures as capitalism/imperialism.

Various bits of evidence are offered to support this conclusion: these often constitute particular and useful criticism of contemporary Marxist practice. It might be argued, however, that it is precisely within the realm of practice that the defects occur, and that Marx's theories do contain material applicable within a multi-cultural arena; that Marxism does, in fact possess the essentials of a theory of culture in precisely the sense intended by critics. What follows is not intended as definitive, but as a brief summary of certain tendencies within Marx's general theories which go counter to the charges of mono-culturalism. Additional development of these points is appropriate, but must be left for another time.

A Question of Definition

We immediately confront a fundamental problem in terminology when we speak of "culture" in Marxian analysis. Critics are wont to point out that Marx customarily used this terminology in relation to *haute Kulture* and *volks Kulture,* that is, to define "high" and "low" realms in literature, music, dance, the plastic arts, etc. This usage supposedly "proves" that Marxism possesses only the most superficial conception of culture and has no sense of how culture provides the complete matrix from which artistic endeavors spring.

Given the broad anthropological definition employed by these critics, their argument is valid. Observation on arts and letters in no way begin to address questions of cultural differentiation between peoples. Aesthetic criticism *aux* Lukacs and Adorno is at best opaque and, more probably, is utterly irrelevant in terms of the revolutionary aspirations of an Afghani tribesman. If Marxism's conception of culture was limited to this aesthetic preoccupation, the critics would have their way. Marxism would be truly disfunctional as a tool in all non-European contexts.

The situation is not so simple. As has been observed elsewhere,[1] Marx frequently used concepts in varied and, at times, apparently contradictory ways. Purely semantic examination of his work can lead to erroneous observations regarding his theoretical conclusions. In the case at hand, the situation is even worse. The anthropological conception of culture was not current in Marx's time, but was actually popularized long after his death. Thus, to criticize Marx for not acknowledging the full cultural matrix *in those terms* is effectively to discredit him for not having foreseen and utilized a vernacular that only came into use decades after his last work. This is manifestly absurd. The point at issue is whether, terminology notwithstanding, the essential ingredients for a general theory of culture exist within Marxism.

Further exploration of this point demands some agreement regarding the term "culture." For purposes of this discussion, it may be posited (as it seems to be by the critics of Marxism's "defective" cultural theory) that culture involves characteristics which bind a particular group of people together socially. These would include language, basis of economy, kinship relations (marriage, blood linkages, matrilinear/patrilinear structure, etc.), spatial/temporal conceptualization, and religion, among other factors; in other words, the galaxy of base and primary superstructural characteristics which define a people as a people. This is a specifically anthropological view, but it has proven useful in cross-cultural considerations.

The Dialectial Method

Given the preceding working definition, a general theory of culture would not only have to explain how this array of traits and characteristics functions in a state of interaction (each element interacting with all others) to create a society, but should also provide cogent interpretation of the nature of that society, and its historical direction. Marxism seems eminently equipped to provide the necessary tools for such a constructive and dynamic cultural theory.

The fundamental methodology employed within Marxist analysis is dialectics, or more precisely, the "triadic dialectic." This conceptual formulation, borrowed by Marx from Hegel, consists of three primary properties or "laws": 1) the transformation of quantity into quality; 2) the unity of opposites; and 3) the negation of the negation.[2] These laws (particularly 2) indicate that all things, whether constituting the subject or object of examination, must be analytically treated as inherently relational to all other things. The same laws (particularly 1 and 3) necessitate the consideration of such relations in terms of dynamic process (i.e., transformation occurring through time).

Thus, Marxist methodology demands that an analysis of society occur in holistic fashion; any social element can only be fully understood in its relationship to all others. Epistemologically, dialectical thinking or methodology must imply a procedure which is constantly sensitive to the wholeness of the context from which the element of examination has been lifted; the consideration of any element alone, though often necessary and useful, is recognized as a potentially distorting abstraction.[3] Given this operational mode, Marxism possesses the conceptual tools requisite to an interactive examination of society in precisely the sense called for by cultural theory.

In practical application, the dialectical method is brought into play through a series of three generalities perhaps best articulated by Louis Althusser:

> In theoretical practice (q.v.), the process of the production of knowledge, Generalities I are the abstract raw material of science, Generalities III are the concrete, scientific generalities that are produced, while Generalities II are the theory of science at a given moment, the means of production of knowledge.[4]

Althusser goes on to state categorically that "knowledge" is "Generalities III." Given that dialectics per se constitute the essential framework for "the theory of science at a given moment," then Marxists must proceed from a given social element taken as raw data, process this known element in holistic or dialectical fashion, and finally return this element as a fully comprehended entity into its context. Through such full relational analysis, the context of elements itself is also comprehended.

Thus, on both the methodological level and in terms of an intellectual practice, Marxism is quite capable of accomodating the intrinsic complexity of culture, broadly understood.

If this is so, then why do critics claim that no adquate Marxist cultural analysis has appeared?

The problem lies in the practice and application of dialectics by Marxist theoreticians, most of whom have been unable to distinguish between their method and some of the more complex systems of purely causal relations such as co-causality, cumulative causation or simultaneous determination of a multi-variable structure where no variables have been identified as dependent or independent in advance.[5] In other words, there is a lack of clear differentiation between cause/effect (linearity) and dialectics (holistic relativity or circulinearity) within contemporary Marxist analysis. While Marxist theoreticians claim ontological allegiance to the tradition of dialectics, many of them seem confused as to what, exactly, dialectical methodology should look like. This confusion is often hidden through the mystification of language and values so prevalent in 20th Century Marxism, which serves as a rhetorical barrier obscuring the non-dialectical epistemology being practiced.

To return Marxist theoretical practice to its root holistic method, as opposed to ultimately abstract systems of causality, is simultaneously to perceive a Marxist methodological model capable of allowing an adequate (and unbiased) theory of culture. The question remains as to whether Marx himself acknowledged, or even intended, the potential of this model.

Semantic Considerations

Rather than sifting Marx for development of terminology not current to him, it seems more fruitful to examine his theories for material which approaches more pertinent subject matter, albeit with some interpretation necessary. For example, the substitution of Marx's term "society" for the term "culture" proves rewarding. As he stated in the unfinished *Introduction to the Critique of Political Economy*:

> In the study of economic categories, as in the case of every historical and social science, it must be borne in mind that as in reality so in our mind the subject . . . is given and that the categories are therefore but forms of expression, manifestations of existence, and frequently but one-sided aspects of this subject, this definite society.[6]

Clearly, Marx was referring to "society" in this instance in the same sense that "culture" is referred to within an anthropological definition. The categories referred to—in this case, economic—are understood as being "forms," "manifestation," and "aspects" of a larger whole, their context. This whole or context, which Marx calls "society," serves essentially the same function within his theory as does "culture" for the critics.

This interpretation is supported by another passage from the *Introduction* in which Marx states, "[the categories of bourgeois society] serve as the expression of its conditions and the comprehension of its own organization."[7] In this case the "categories" under consideration are not limited to the economic, but are more general, capable of encompassing the wide array of superstructural elements requisite to anthropological investigation of "culture."

Marx becomes more explicit when he asserts, also in the *Introduction,* that:

> The simplest economic category, say exchange value, implies the existence of population, population that is engaged in production with determined relations; it also implies the existence of certain types of family, class, or state, etc. It can have *no other existence except as an abstract one-sided relation of an already given concrete and living aggregate* (my emphasis).[8]

What is this "concrete and living aggregate", if not "culture"? We can draw certain conclusions from Marx's statements: that Marx understood each base and superstructural concept as a component of a whole, which he called "society"; that each component is linked, through its relation to the whole, to all other components; and, given the internal relations between these components, the whole can be said to be contained in each of its parts, each in its particular interconnections with the others providing us with a version of the whole. Insofar as this is true, the meaning of Marx's "whole" or "society" is clearly identifiable with "culture".

Thus Marx did, in fact, elaborate an entity which falls within the anthropological definition of "culture," terminological differences notwithstanding. The question still lies unanswered of whether Marx, having articulated a basis for such, actually *developed* something which looks like a "theory of culture." He can be understood to have done so, but within a context which he termed "social relations."

The Method Applied

"Relations" are the minimum irreducible units in Marx's concept of society. Put another way, his subject matter is society grasped in terms of relations. Family, religion, government, etc., are all conceived as superstructural relations containing in themselves, as integral to their identities, those parts with which they tend to be seen as externally tied. In Marx's view, these relations are conceived as holding properties internal one unto the other. Any alteration in one relation implies corresponding changes in all relations; the whole itself is altered. For instance, Marx declares it a tautology that "there can no longer be wage labor when there is no longer any capital."[9] Such a statement clearly indicates the interactive, interdependent qualities of "relations." Further, alterations of relations at the base level will not only incur changes in relations at that level but in the superstructural level as well. The inverse also holds true.

As Marx put it, "[society is] man himself in his social relations."[10] To paraphrase, it may be asserted that culture is man himself in his overall relations. Is this a misinterpretation of Marx's meaning? For Marx, all conjunction is organic, intrinsic to the social units he considers and inherent to each. Of the relations of production, distribution, consumption, and exchange, for instance, Marx specifies that ". . . mutual interaction takes place between various elements. Such is the case in every organic body."[11] Again, the "organic body" referred to can only be construed as the social whole, or culture.

In terms of theoretical application, consider Marx's clear statement regarding the connection between production and consumption, "Production is . . . at the same time consumption, and consumption, production."[12] The two are socially joined and integral to one another. In another passage, Marx emphasizes that "the economic conception (is incorrect in holding) that distribution exists side by side with production as a self-contained sphere."[13] In other words, the standard non-Marxist view that production and distribution are integral relations to each other is insufficient; consideration of these two factors as a system which is independent from the rest of the social system is incorrect. Marxism treats its entire subject matter as "different side of one unit"[14]; that is, of culture.

As yet, we have uncovered only an appropriate means to discuss an abstracted static model of a society or culture. Each unit or element defined as existing within a society may be fully examined (only) in its relations to all other elements so defined. However, once this significant task has been completed, we are left with only a dead and motionless model, and no real society is stationary. Thus, the model is of decidedly limited practical utility.

As Paul Lafargue has noted, however, Marx's "highly complicated world" is "in continual motion."[15] The processes of change and development constantly occur; structure is only a stage in this process. To introduce a temporal dimension into analysis merely implies viewing each social element as being related not only to all elements, but also (integrally) to its own past and future forms. Once this is accomplished, overall temporal context is established by relating the past and future forms of all other social elements as well. While the procedure is reasonably simple to conceive, the resulting analytical panorama is infinitely rich and complex.

This relational model offers the present as a point along a continuum stretching from the definable past into a knowable future. All social change is conceptualized as actualization of what already potentially is; it is simultaneously the unfolding of a pre-existing process and a spatial relation. The model in this final form can handle the vast array of changing human circumstances.[16]

The Relations of Production

The abstract components have now been established for the Marxist apprehension of culture in the broad sense. "Society," as Marx put it, is "the sum of the relations in which individuals stand to one another."[17] When Marx states, "society itself, that is man in his social relations,"[18] this assessment must be understood as extending throughout the realm of "the product(s) of man's reciprocal activites";[19] since people are related to one another not only directly, but also through the objects of their productive labor, a broad definition of "society" must include both people and their objects.

Marx's deployment of his theoretical cultural elements results in the specification and explication of these various social relations. We turn now to the particular products of Marx's analytical tools, that is, the actual descriptions of social relations which complete Marx's cultural theory.

It is people's need for other people and their assistance in the realization of human powers which holds society together in all periods and places. This "cultural cement" is considered by Marx to be a "natural necessity" (Naturnotwendigkeit) or "interest."[20] Marx stated in *Introduction to the Critique of Political*

Economy":

> Man is in the most literal sense of the word a *zoon politikon,* not only a social animal, but an animal which can develop into an individual outside society—something which might happen as an exception to a civilized man who by accident got into the wilderness and is already dynamically possessed within himself the forces of a society—is as great an absurdity as the idea of the development of a language without individuals living together and talking to one another.[21]

There are three points made in the preceding statement which should be emphasized. First, Marx once again asserts his view that people are inherently social/cultural beings. Second, he directly acknowledges language as an aspect of cultural cement. Third, he takes up the issue of production within this paragraph on the nature of the human individual. This last point is crucial. Marx holds that production is the area of life in which people's social characters emerge most clearly; for Marx, production is the primary example of human cooperation. An important implication of the above statement from the *Introduction* is that production cannot be separated from the social/cultural matrix of which it is an integral part, a *relation.*

Productive work is the core of "life activity" for Marx.[22] He states, "productive life is the life of the species. It is life engendering life."[23] Marx summarizes his understanding of the role of production in the shaping of human life as follows: "As individuals express their lives, so they are. What they are, therefore, coincides with their production, both with what they produce and with how they produce."[24] In this context, "what they (men) are" can be understood as man's entire way of being in the world, including his cultural existence. Through examination of the products and means of production, "the open book of man's essential powers" and "the exposure to the senses of human psychology" are revealed.[25]

For Marx, humans are inherently social beings through the necessity of being materially productive. Thus, consideration of people's relations to production are central to the apprehension of the nature of people's social/cultural character at any given historical moment and within any given geographical context.

Conclusion

The preceding formulation of society and the central role of production in an analysis of social relations completes the theory of culture implicit in Marxism. Reiteration of the main points of this argument should clarify the connections between a broad theory of culture and Marx's emphasis on production as a social relation.

The opening question was whether Marxist analysis could be applied to diverse cultures. Having established an anthropological definition of culture as appropriate, we asked whether the essential ingredients for a general theory of culture exist within Marxism, and found that Marxist methodology, i.e., dialectics, is equipped to explain how the different aspects of culture interact in order to create a society and culture. Through dialectical analysis, each factor in society is explored and explained in relation to all other factors; the result is a holistic analysis of the dynamic creation of society through time. Marxist methodology therefore fills the requirement as a tool for an interactive theory of culture.

Althusser's schema was used to explore the practical application of the dialectical method. Some problems arose at this point concerning actual practice by Marxist theoreticians; in order to arrive at a non-reductive cultural analysis, theorists must apply true dialectical analysis, rather than one of the various forms of causal analysis.

The obvious question then arose of whether Marx intended his analytic tools to be used in this way. Upon examination of his writings, it became clear that Marx's term "society" has the same essential meaning as the anthropological definition of "culture." With this bit of interpretation in mind, Marx's theory of social relations surfaces as the sought after "theory of culture."

Finally, we are in a position to summarize the key features of a Marxist theory of culture. All social relations are interactive and interdependent; when one changes, all others change, as does the whole itself. This whole is society, the sum of all social relations. At the core of Marx's theory of social relations is production. What people produce and how they do so serves as a *foundation* for all other relations, for culture.

Some comments are in order. Given the interactive and circular nature of dialectical analysis, production should not be understood as the one single determinate of all other social relations; "through its (production's) internal ties to everything else, each factor is everything else viewed from this particular angle."[26] A superstructural relation from any given cultural perspective cannot be properly understood in isolation from base structural relations, and *vice versa.*

This latter is missed all too often both by "practicing Marxists" and by non-Marxist critics. To a degree, this may be a result of certain misleading polemical tendencies on the part of Marx himself. Certain superstructural problems such as kinship and heredity at times threatened the coherence of the practical application of his general theories. This, as Engels explains, led to an ideological exaggeration of the determinant role of economic factors.[27] It has also been pointed out that Marx speaks of all history in terms of class struggle and often refers to formations within precapitalist societies as "classes."[28] This is indeed an example of Marx applying a concept where only a few of many requisite components are present (and the nature of these tends to vary with his immediate purpose) and is thus open to dispute in terms of accuracy. Such "lapses" hardly diminish the importance of Marx's general principles and it is also possible that ideological exercises along these lines were a tactical ploy designed to promote revolutionary consciousness among the European working class of his day.[29]

There seems to be nothing inherent to the dialectical principles employed by Marx and sketched in this essay which would limit their application to Europe alone. Any culture is necessarily composed of a number of definable social elements, each of which has an historical context, and all of which must function in direct interactional relationship to one another at all times. Regardless of superstructural dissimilarities, any given culture must—on pain of sheer survival—engage in basic (or "base") material production. With this as a common denominator or starting point for analysis, and in combination with an analysis of all other integral social factors which emerge, an accurate portrait of *any* culture can be drawn.

Marx's theoretical conception of society or culture appears quite sound today, and his general methodology for examination quite appropriate. Rather than presenting a dangerous or dysfunctional approach to cross-cultural *praxis,* these would seem to offer an immediate counter to the bourgeois anthropological device of lifting particular factors out of their social/cultural context for purposes of "critical examination", an approach considered by some to be a "Euro-specific" and all-encompassing methodology. Nor would it seem there is anything within Marx's work indicating that European norms be used as an evaluative standard against which a non-European culture should be measured. To the contrary, given valid application of Marxist dialectical methods, it seems obvious that examination of the integral components of the given culture itself is specifically mandated. This militates against a value-laden "comparative" methodology. To the extent that Marxists have been historically guilty of violating this procedure, there have been errors of practice; this is not, however, the same as a defective theory.

It should not be forgotten that entire cultures are themselves relational/inter-related entities. At the very least, European expansion and colonial practice has guaranteed this. Cultures, if they ever were, are no longer "pure," but are intertwined through economic relations, through kinship interaction, through religious interchange, language, and a host of other factors. Each component culture can then be treated as a facet or set or social relations in world-wide social context. Marx hinted at the necessity of a dialectical analysis on a world-wide scale in the *Economic and Philosophic Manuscripts of 1844:* "Man, much as he may ... be a particular individual [or culture: my note] .. is just as much the totality—the idea totality—the subjective existence of a thought and experienced society present for itself."[30]

Marxism provides the tools for an articulation of a theory of social relations (culture) which includes individual cultures as its relational units. There is no indication that this should be restricted to a European arena. Marx's theories are tailored not only to his unique vision of capitalism (the context of his own culture), but to his unusually broad conception of a truly universal social/cultural reality.

5
Culture and Personhood
Bob Sipe

The time is ripe for a dialogue between Marxists and Native Americans. America's European descendent Marxists can learn a great deal about their own culture and its effects upon everyday life through studying Native American culture. Native Americans can heighten their appreciation of their cultural traditions by examining the Americanized version of European culture.

To fail to engage in this dialogue will have serious consequences for both groups. For Native Americans, to fail to understand the absorbing tendencies of American Capitalist culture and its effect on psycho-social development threatens their ability to keep in touch with the traditions that sustain and revitalize their identity, community and spirituality. For Marxists, to fail to appreciate the cultural context in which they struggle is to fail to come to grips with critical variables which shape working class consciousness and praxis.

For Native and Marxist Americans alike, the meeting of cultures is critical for building a new integrated socialist culture to gladden the future. As Stanley Diamond observes:

> Our illness springs from the very center of civilization, not from too much knowledge, but from too little wisdom. What primitives possess . . . we have largely lost. If we have the means, the tools, the forms, the rational imagination to transform the face of the earth and the contemporary human condition, primitive society at its most positive exemplifies an essential humanity.[1]

II

Among the many approaches to explain the concept of "culture" is George Simmel's definition of culture as "human self-creation in the context of cultivating things, or self-cultivation in the process of endowing the things of nature with use and meaning."[2] Here we see an interactive dichotomy between subjective culture and objective culture. The interaction between these two cultural dimensions—persons and things—is essential for a critical theory of culture.

In this paper we will examine how the phenomenal growth of objective culture in American society has endangered subjective culture. The productive growth of things has produced a crisis in the psychic life of America's primarily white population. Through a dialectical methodology I hope to shed some light on how a one-dimensional culture maintains and expands the exploitive production relations of contemporary American capitalism. Yet, a deeper crisis, a crisis of being, of personhood exists in contemporary American culture. How shall we understand this crisis? How has culture changed from an integrative force which traditionally cultivated our sense of being human into a disintegrative force which fragments, specializes, stunts and reifies our humanness? These are critical questions.

The tension between the integrative and disintegrative function of culture in American society grows clearer if we view humankind as *homo faber* rather than *animal laborens*. Such was the view of Karl Marx, who understood the drive of our species-being to engage in creative and purposeful activity. To cultivate an integrative culture is the "everlasting nature imposed condition of human existence."[3] In shaping the world and themselves as a social totality men and women emerge as beings of praxis.

By praxis, Marx meant something radically different from the common meaning of "practice." Praxis is "conscious life activity" in which social life stands as an object of our will and our consciousness. In praxis, we unite the human facilities of reason, imagination, and communication to develop a critical consciousness. In this mode of awareness we are able to discover the structure of natural and social processes in which [we] take part . . . [and] . . . make extrapolations for the future, project goals, and look for the most adequate means to satisfy them."[4] Praxis is the creative activity of constructing and reconstructing our social totality in accordance with real, historically created human possibilities. Identifying our species as *homo faber* suggests criteria by which we can analyze and evaluate modern sociocultural relations. The charge of Western Marxism stems from the "emancipatory interests" of humanity in the convergence of reason, truth and freedom. Our quest is to transform the quality of social relations of men and women and their world. In the ideal state, a liberated, self-actualized humanity exists in synergism with the natural environment. This way of being existed in many cultures before it was swallowed by the wave of inevitable colonization, modernization, cultural devastation and rationalization churned up by developing Western Capitalism. Glimpses of this harmony can be caught in the past and present traditions of Native Americans. The quest for liberation is a quest for a lost unity to inspire our future.

III

Questions about the conflict of human and production relations were of prime importance to a group of German intellectuals known as the Frankfurt School. Its leading members—Max Horkheimer, Theodore Adorno, and Herbert Marcuse—drew heavily on the thought of Hegel, Marx, Freud and, of particular importance for this analysis, Georg Lukacs. These thinkers viewed culture and society critically, antithetically, as something permeated by a negativity demanding transcendance. They shared a vision of a radically different society founded on human happiness, the satisfaction of vital needs, and the end to domination. By this vision they criticized the established culture and planned future struggles.

The Frankfurt School of cultural analysis stands in perpetual opposition to those aspects of Western capitalism which serve the interests of domination—the social institutions, modes of consciousness and the culture industry. Yet the "criticism" of critical theory is of a specific dialectical nature. "By criticism," Horkheimer said, "we mean that intellectual, and eventually practical effort which is not satisfied to accept the prevailing ideas, actions, and social conditions unthinkingly and from mere habit; effort which aims to coordinate the individual sides of social life with each other and with the general ideas and aims of the epoch, to deduce them genetically, to distinguish the appearance from the essence, to examine the foundations of things, in short, to really know them."[5] Critical analysis attempts to reveal the world as it really is, devoid of rationalizations.

So the forms of socio-cultural life are neither accepted by custom nor practiced uncritically, but critically scrutinized in the interest of developing a foundation on which society can build for general happiness and emancipation. Critical theory would prevent us from losing ourselves among the common sense understandings of everyday life. It exposes the contradictions between what a society claims to be and what it in fact is. Critical theory thus attempts to explicate the "gulf between the ideas by which (persons) judge themselves and the world on one hand and the social reality which they reproduce through their actions on the other hand."[6]

Trent Schroyer further explains critical theory as an "immanent critique" which "restores missing parts to historical self-formation, true actuality to false appearance" so that we can "see through socially unnecessary authority and control systems."[7] In restoring the missing parts critical theory develops a socio-cultural analysis which is concrete in the Hegelian sense of being "many-sided, adequately related, complexly mediated."[8]

No single aspect of socio-cultural reality is complete in itself. All facets of reality are complexly mediated and have meaning in their totality. The positivists' independent and isolated "social facts" are replaced by the dynamic interaction between moment and totality, particular and universal.

Within the multidimensional universe, critical theory is not content to complacently register and systematize socio-cultural facts. From the potentialities of the immediate historical situation, critical theory employs constructive concepts which depict reality not only as it is, but also as it can be. According to Trent Schroyer, "critique reconstructs the constitutive genesis of the existing order to recognize the actual or the universal possibilities that are objectively present in the existing. The intent is to promote conscious emancipatory activity."[9] As missing parts are restored, new insights into the potentialities for social transformation emerge. Critical theory is a means of penetrating myths. It offers insights into the construction of less alienating societies.

The critical theory approach stands in sharp relief to "orthodox Marxism" which pays scant attention to how culture forms societies. The subject of orthodox Marxist analysis is the dynamic development between the forces and relations of production. The economic base is of paramount importance, while the cultural superstructure is secondary at best and "epiphenomenal" at worst.

Orthodox Marxists have studied the evolution of capitalism and its ensuing class struggles from guilds to modern factories. The evidence suggested, and rightly so, that the capitalist class was able to assume and subsequently insure its dominant position in the social hierarchy of production because it exerted increasing control over all aspects of production. By controlling the means of production and the organization of the workplace, the capitalist class was able to control the products of labor and the laboring class. As the social hierarchy of production was transmitted to other interlocking social institutions the domination increased. As family, church, social services and armed forces, all levels of government and education became increasingly bureaucratic, capitalism became life itself.

A unique cultural transformation which was virtually ignored by orthodox Marxists accompanied and perpetuated this socio-economic transformation. The power of the new cultural context emerges in the extent to which the values and worldview of the capitalist class are successfully internalized in the psyches of the workers. The interiorization of the capitalist hierarchy by those whom *it most* oppresses is an additional bulwark for corporate capitalism. In contemporary society, the slaves, so it seems, embrace their chains and find self-fulfillment in that embrace. We now turn to the manner in which capitalist socio-cultural relations shape our psyches.

IV

The extension of this all-embracing social, economic, political and cultural hegemony to all facets of life is the functional imperative to the survival of capitalism. Structural elements such as the growing role of the state in labor-capital relations, the ethnic and social divisions, and labor organizations help to maintain the capitalist social hierarchy. The capitalist social hierarchy further persists through one-dimensional socialization and acculturation. In the following pages, we will consider how the development of working class consciousness and praxis have been overwhelmed since World War II.

If alienation is almost complete, revolutionary class consciousness should, says Marx, develop first in the workers. However, the workers remain oppressed. Studs Terkel's oral histories of workers suggest that despite their anger toward their jobs and the conditions of their lives, workers have not recognized their right to control the labor process and the conditions that affect their lives.[10] Why have workers not achieved class consciousness?

Class consciousness does not demand that each worker understand the socio-historical laws of capitalist development or the totality of capitalist social relations. However, working class consciousness must reflect some awareness of the connections between everyday life experiences and the larger social order. Wilhelm Reich suggests the following dimensions of class consciousness:

* knowledge of one's own vital necessities in all spheres;
* knowledge of ways and possibilities of satisfying them;
* knowledge of the obstacles that a social system based on private property puts in the way of their satisfaction;
* knowledge of one's own inhibitions and fears that prevent one from clearly realizing one's needs and the obstacles of their satisfaction;
* knowledge that mass unity makes an invincible force against the power of the oppressors.[11]

Thus class consciousness stresses the essential unity between personal life and prevailing socio-cultural conditions. It demands that workers know the nature of their unmediated needs, the nature of their important interactions, the functioning of social institutions and the cultural context of capitalism. Most important is the psychic structure of the class. The conditions of socio-cultural life are anchored, reflected and reproduced in the psychic structure. Capitalist socialization reflects capitalist production and so integrates the conditions of domination into the psyche. Psychic reifications minimize the possibility of an emerging alternative consciousness and empowering social actions. The ultimate relationship between psychic reification and capitalism constitutes a key obstacle to the development of dynamic class consciousness.

In his early writings and in the more sophisticated "fetishism of commodities" section of *Capital,* Karl Marx explained how capitalist society transforms social relations into "the fantastic form of a relation between things."[12] Marx understood alienation as "the process by which the unity of the producing and the product is broken. The product now appears to the producer as an alien facticity and power standing in itself and over against him, no longer recognizable as a product."[13] His socio-economic explanation of alienation supports psychological reification "the moment in the process of alienation in which the charac-teristic of thinghood becomes the standard of objective reality."[14] Reification is a mode of alienation unique to capitalist society because only in such an environment can workers be so effectively reduced to commodities that they enter into exchange relationships in a money-form. The communal and humanistic norms, customs and habits of pre-capitalist societies are de-stroyed by the inevitable onslaught of capitalist market relations.

Max Weber also recognized this phenomena as part of the inevitable rationalization and de-magicization of industri-alization. For Weber capitalist development inevitably penetrated "all spheres of social life: the economy, culture (art, religion and science), technology, law and politics, and everyday life by a single logic of *formal rationality.* This logic is defined by the principle of orientation of human action to abstract quantifiable and calculable, and instrumentally utilizable formal rules and norms."[15]

Drawing on Marx and Weber, Georg Lukacs provides a fruitful insight into this tragedy of culture by re-examining the subjective and objective aspects of reification.[16] Many of his observations coincide with previous analyses that the dismemberment and fragmentation of the worker and the elimination of subjectivity, stem from the nature and organization of capitalist production.   But Lukacs extends his analysis to the inter-relationship of psychic reification and the phenomenon of commodity fetishism. Following Marx, he posits "the fetishism of commodities" as the central problem of modern capitalism. Its universality, according to Lukacs, "influences the total outer and inner life of society"[17] so profoundly that human consciousness is reduced to a reified "second nature" unable to grasp the real dynamics of capitalist production. Commodity fetishism produces reified socio-cultural relations which distort human subjectivity.

For Lukacs, commodity fetishism extends to all social relations. In the fully developed market economy, he says, human activity becomes estranged from itself and "turns into a commodity which, subject to the non-human objectivity of the natural laws of society, must go its own way independently of many just like any consumer article."[18] With the capitalist reduction of human society to the movements of commodities, men and women become parts in a mechanical system. Object relations replace subject relations. Quantitative relations replace qualitative relations. Human value is determined by the prevailing rate of exchange. Human needs are satisfied in terms of commodity exchange.

Commodity fetishism engenders a commodity consciousness among workers—a reified consciousness unable to penetrate the "mist enveloped regions" of the social relations of capitalist production and distribution. For Lukacs, the destruction of craft labor, the reduction of work to a set of repetitious, mechanical motions, the repressive organization of the factory system, and the extension of these processes into the larger socio-cultural institutions of society extends right into the worker's soul."[19] The psyche is likewise fragmented and the unified personality system into opposed strands.

Fragmentation in turn produces the passive subjectivity among workers necessary to the functioning of late capitalism. Says Lukacs, "the personality can do no more than look on helplessly while its own existence is reduced to an isolated partical and fed into an alien system."[20] Reified consciousness is also passive: a consciousness devoid of subjectivity, isolated from praxis.

The alienation of the worker is commodity fetishism extended throughout life. The power of the capitalist system is generated at the expense of the worker, who is transformed into a thing, a reified commodity. In the final analysis a major reason for the failure of the American working class to develop critical class consciousness is capitalism's penetration into the psyche.

V

Late capitalism has required the elimination of labor-capital friction and the containment of class antagonisms for its successful functioning. The complicated, hierarchically organized and technically specialized production requirements of late capitalism demand infinitely greater and more varied social and cultural control than ever before. This stems not only from the scientific, calculable and technological requirements of the production process, but also from the fact that the contradictions of contemporary capitalism are infinitely more manifest and difficult to contain. Accordingly, to obtain voluntary compliance with the irrationality of its relations of production, late capitalism must anchor the performance principle within the worker's mental and psychic structure. This anchoring occurs primarily through the one-dimensional socialization and acculturation process of late capitalism. Hence, fragmentation, atomization, and psychic reification assimilate the worker into an antagonistic social reality.

The essence of late capitalism is captured in what Herbert Marcuse calls "one-dimensionality." All forms of social and cultural existence are defined and operationalized within the parameters of the established society. A one-dimensional society effectively represses the emergence of a qualitative antithesis and the expression of various "moments of opposition" to the essential negativity of the established order. Marcuse describes late capitalism as a society which,

> militates against qualitative change. Thus emerges a
> pattern of one-dimensional thought and behavior in

which ideas, aspirations, and objectives that, by their content, transcend the established universe of discourse and action are either repressed or reduced to terms of this universe. They are redefined by the rationality of the given system and of its quantitative extension.[21]

In late capitalism we understand change as a quantitative relationship consisting of homogenous steps, incremental to the established economic base. The qualitative dimensions of socio-cultural life must be neutralized and redefined as quantitative components. Value must assume a homogenous interchangeable character best represented in the medium of money. In capitalist society, exchange relationships subsume social relationships. People and their needs become commodities to be bartered in the marketplace.

As the needs, personality, consciousness, and socio-cultural milieu of the workers conform to the needs of advanced corporate capitalism, the worker becomes one with society. The workers' needs belong to their positions in the occupational hierarchy. Identity becomes a function of activity. The traditional antithesis between proletariat and capitalist is transformed into a one-dimensional unity of opposites. The worker is integrated into the "performance principle" of late capitalism. That is our crisis of culture.

The performance principle is distinguished from other reality principles by the phenomenon of "surplus repression." Our instinctual, psychic and socio-cultural structures come to resemble the production exigencies of late capitalism. In order to reduce the tension bred by partnership with an antagonistic social reality, "substitute mechanisms" are introduced into our psychic and socio-cultural structures. Repression and manipulation of working class sexuality, destruction of the worker's autonomous ego, the imposition of a capitalist social character and a one-dimensional socio-cultural milieu are experiences of surplus repression. The crisis of the individual is matched by the crisis of culture. We are enveloped in a profound alienation— "neuroses, perversions, pathological changes in character, the antisocial phenomena of sexual life, and not least, disturbances in the capacity for work."[22]

One-dimensional society has integrated traditionally antagonistic social classes and cultural milieus into a single mass. Antagonism has been caused by the contradictions of capitalist production. The needs and interests of the working class were, when Marx wrote, in fundamental contradiction to those of the capitalist class. Today, this opposition has been assimilated into the ethos of bourgeois society. We have, Marcuse asserts, been flattened:

> If the worker and his boss enjoy the same television program and visit the same resort places, if the typist is as attractively made up as the daughter of her employer, if the Negro owns a Cadillac, if they all read the same newspaper, then this assimilation indicates not the disappearance of classes, but the extent to which the needs and satisfactions that serve the preservation of the Establishment are shared by the underlying population.[23]

The creation, manipulation, and exhaltation of false needs has co-opted the working class' revolutionary and emancipatory needs.

Workers identify with their factory, and find self-fulfillment there. Marcuse concludes:

> The same technological organization which makes for a mechanical community at work also generates a larger interdependence which integrates the worker with the plant. One notes an "eagerness" on the part of the workers "to share in the solution of production problems," a "desire to join actively in applying their own brains to technical and production problems which clearly fitted in with the technology.[24]

As the workers needs are reshaped to conform with advanced technological production, their personal needs are conditioned by the demands of the job. The worker becomes happily assimilated into the machine. Alienated labor becomes a source of self-fulfillment. The traditional antithesis between workers and bosses is truncated into a one-dimensional unity of opposites which reinforces the established order.

Integration extends to the culture. Traditionally, there has existed a higher or critical culture to oppose the prevailing social reality. Within art, for example, is the power of negation, the power to suggest images which transcend social reality. Here was suggested "the appearance of the realm of freedom: the refusal to behave."[25] Today this critical element has been incorporated into mass culture. Says Marcuse:

> Today's novel feature is the flattening out of the antagonism between culture and social reality through the obliteration of the oppositional, alien, and transcendent elements in the higher culture by virtue of which it constituted another dimension of reality. This liquidation of two-dimensional culture takes place not through the denial and rejection of the "cultural values," but through their wholesale incorporation into the established order, through their reproduction and display on a massive scale.[26]

Art, or critical culture, has become an instrument of social cohesion serving to unite and reinforce rather than refute and contradict the prevailing reality.

To translate and integrate the symbols and imagery of critical culture its subversive elements must be destroyed. Art then becomes less true. Our transcendent ideals become matter in the form of consumable commodities. "The music of the soul is also the music of salesmanship. Exchange value, not truth value counts," said Marcuse.[27]

The traditional alien and alienating works of critical culture become products themselves or reinforce the marketing of products. Invariably, one finds a print of Picasso's *Guernica* adorning a living room wall among America's liberal "hip" populace. Invariably too, one hears strains of Vivaldi in the halls of some modern shopping centers. The truth value of critical culture of these works has been effectively reduced. The market place has become the purveyor of "higher culture." American mass culture has become one-dimensional, homogeneous and sterile.

The crises of culture finds its mate in the crisis of the individual. Sigmund Freud postulated alienation and neuroses as an inevitable, functional imperative for civilized social life.

Despite the fact that all individuals suffer in varying degrees from instinctual renunciation and sublimation, the sacrifice maintains civilization by controlling the unruly instincts, the sexual instinct foremost. Sexual sublimation shapes the individual's future behavior. According to Freud: "the sexual behavior of a human being often *lays down the pattern* for all his other modes of reacting to life . . . but if, for all sorts of reasons, he refrains from satisfying his strong sexual instincts, his behavior will be conciliatory and resigned rather than vigorous in other spheres of life as well."[28] Thus, the manner in which a society's institutions, values and mores regulate the sexual behavior of its members will be a crucial determinant of all behavior patterns.

This observation is especially significant for our analysis of American workers. In light of the previous discussion, it is imperative to inquire how and to what end contemporary institutions and socio-cultural processes control the sexual behavior of American workers. Reimut Reiche believes that "the whole sphere of sexuality is today biased in favour of the system. Sex is reduced to a commodity, the human body is de-eroticized, and a false sexuality imposed on life in general and on people's relations to their products."[29] The social relations of capitalist commodity production have transformed human sexuality. Not only do sexuality and sexual relationships become object relations among things, but a general de-eroticization of the body also occurs. This has profound consequences for the successful functioning of late capitalism. Under the cover of false sexuality, instinctual urges and emancipatory impulses can be harnessed for the system.

The prevailing social structure is reproduced within our deepest psychic interiority. This anchoring has occurred through the repression of sexual instincts and through wholesale incorporation of the pleasure principle into the performance principle. The extent of this penetration determines the degree to which "voluntary" compliance between the worker and a repressive, irrational social reality is secured.

The preceding analysis suggests that in order to obtain the necessary integration and productivity from the laborer, contemporary capitalism requires an ever greater surplus repression of the pre-genital, erotogenic zones of the body. Superimposed upon our qualitative, objectless, autoerotic sexuality is a plastic, quantifiable sexuality more susceptible to manipulation and control. Reducing our potential for pleasure in being increases our potential for employment. Erotic and libidinal beings cannot be chained to the alienating, dull, repetitive jobs or to the repressive socio-cultural domination of late capitalism. Neutered, we have been harnessed to the market mechanism of corporate capitalism. "I am not exaggerating," Freud insisted fifty years ago,

> "I am describing a state of affairs of which equally bad instances can be observed over and over again. To the uninitiated it is hardly credible how seldom normal potency is to be found in a husband and how often a wife is frigid among married couples who live under the dominance of our civilized sexual morality."[30]

As Wilhelm Reich has observed, we become "orgastically impotent" when our ties to the world around us are mechanized.

So too the opposition which should prevail between the worker and an exploitative social reality is neutralized. Integration and assimilation are further achieved by socio-cultural institutions and processes which so fragment the personality that we cling helplessly to the forces which have shaped us. Finally the autonomous ego is destroyed.

According to Freud, we are shaped by our families. The child's ego develops through conflicts with the moralistic authority of the father. The ego becomes the dynamic aspect of the psyche, mediating between the id's pleasure-seeking impulses and the moralistic imperatives of the outside world, represented by the father. Hence, the conscious, autonomous ego plays a dominant role in determining the course of this struggle.

The *idealized* individual of bourgeois society develops a strong, autonomous ego capable of reconciling instinctual urges with moralistic demands. Such bourgeois character traits as orderliness, obstinancy and parsimony reinforce the power of the autonomous bourgeois ego not only to postpone the gratification of these unruly instinctual urges, but also to transform them into socially constructive achievements.

Freud's claim that this process of personality development is basically ahistorical and transcultural is not valid. The Oedipal ego is historicaly rooted in the particular time, place and cultural milieu of nineteenth and early twentieth century European society. It is a fact of socialization and acculturation reflecting the socio-economic dynamics of the emergent capitalism of the late nineteenth century.

So the Oedipal struggle may be rendered obsolete by contemporary corporate capitalism. The social relations of late capitalism have developed unique modes of socialization and acculturation.

Dying with the Oedipal situation are private and family enterprises. Since World War II, huge, multi-national, quasipublic, monopolistic corporations have replaced them. Eliminating the individual entrepreneur engendered a second effect. The father-dominated or patriarchal family declined as the primary source of acculturation. Says Marcuse,

the socially necessary repressions and the socially necessary behavior are no longer learned—and internalized—in the long struggle with the father—the ego ideal is rather brought to bear on the ego directly and 'from outside' before the ego is actually formed as the personal and (relatively) autonomous subject of mediation between himself and others.[31]

An external accumulation process occurs through the mass media, the entertainment industry, modern advertising, peer groups, the educational system—all enormous structures able to intrude the requisite mores, values and world view of contemporary capitalist society into the family.

The autonomous ego becomes a nascent ego apparently under the controlled social institutions. Manipulation occurs in what realities are presented or excluded and the very structure of the socializing institutions. Stanley Aronowitz suggests,

the real achievement of schools consisted in their ability to train children to accept the prevailing class structure and their fate as workers within the industrial system ... students learn the skills needed to accomodate to the first requirement of industrial labor; respect for authority, the self-discipline necessary to internalize the values of the labor process, and the place of the worker within the prevailing occupational hierarchies.[32]

Thus, the father-dominated family has been superceded by extrafamilial authorities in our hearts and minds. Throughout the preceding capitalist period the autonomous ego has been a source of "inner freedom." Hans Gerth and C. Wright Mills suggest that the autonomous ego constructs a sense of self by engaging in meaningful and critical social praxis with social reality. But the growing power and technological sophistication of late capitalism have progressively penetrated this inner freedom. Individual opposition to the status quo has given way to identification with the prevailing social relations of capitalist production.

Management of the nascent ego has produced vital changes in the psyche which have precluded the development of class consciousness through autonomous egos. Franz Alexander, noted ego psychologist, has observed "the ego becomes 'corporeal,' so to speak, and its reactions to the outside world and to the instinctual desires emerging from the id become increasingly 'automatic'."[33] The defense mechanisms by which the autonomous ego was previously able to regulate the instinctual urges of the id and behavior now come under the control of those who manipulate the external acculturations. In the words of Reimut Reiche,

> the ego loses most of its classic function of mediating between id and super ego and outside world and undergoes an involution to a state at which it simply acts as an agency for the internalization of external authority and compartmentalized influences from the super ego. With the collective decomposition of the function of the ego, a monopolization takes place in the mechanisms of domination. In psychological terms, the super ego and the ego become one; in political terms, institutionalized techniques of social and political oppression become one with the individual.[34]

Free space has become so narrowed that human reactions are almost Pavlovian. The ego's private space has become public space occupied by the social order. When ego merges into the super ego, rich and many dimensional interactions give way to static, one-dimensional identification with the administered reality principle of contemporary capitalism.

The result of one-dimensional acculturation is alienated individuals unable to recognize themselves as conscious subjects. According to Ronald Laing, we live in our new "ontological insecurity" like zombies.[35] The inheritance of our time is engulfment, implosion, petrification and depersonalization. We do not develop a secure sense of self in relation with other selves. The most important consequence of this lack of identity, this inability to experience the "I," is that "it prevents integration of the total personality; hence it leaves the person disunited."[36] The reification and automation of the ego produces an ontologically insecure working class unable to develop meaningful social praxis. Destruction of the private space of the ego prevents workers from developing the requisite subjective autonomy to revolt against exploitation. We become reified objects of administration that are acted upon. We become commodity fetishes.

VI

We have suggested that the interlocking crisis of culture and the crisis of the individual in contemporary American society be understood as results of the functional needs of the capitalist production-consumption process. A one dimensional culture finds its prototype in a one dimensional person. Reification engenders subjectless subjects married to an antagonistic society.

However, a further manipulation of the workers' subjectivity causes the smooth and efficient functioning of the established social relations of corporate capitalism. The transformation of the individual ego ideal into the social character of corporate capitalism completes the dialectical triad of domination within the psychic apparatus. For Erich Fromm social character is embodied in

> the organization man, a man without conscience or conviction, but one who is proud of being a cog, even if it is only a small one, in a big and imposing organization. He is not to ask questions, not to think

critically, not to have any passionate interests, for this would impede the smooth functioning of the organization.[37]

With the advent of modern technology, mass communication, behavior modification, and the production-consumption requirements of late capitalism. Our critical mental faculties, our sense of personal conscience, responsibility and autonomy have declined in proportion to the decline of the autonomous ego and the individual ego ideal.

The established order has massified our privacy and permeated our private space. As Marcuse has observed, "the member of society apprehends and evaluates all this, not by himself, in terms of his ego and his own ego ideal .. but through all others and in terms of their common, externalized ego ideal."[38] This external ego ideal is not imposed by force; there is no harsh conflict with the father. Rather it is comfortably acculturated into the worker's psyche in the normal course of everyday life. The mass media, peer groups, school, recreational activities, jobs, are the exclusive forces of psycho-social and cultural development from infancy until death.

Thus we see that the redirection of the id, ego, and ego ideal of the workers' psyches toward the performance principle of late capitalism has created social character among workers which channels their energy and behavior into system-supporting outlets. The increasing proletarianization of the work force has extended this social character to ever greater numbers of workers. This expanding social character has prevented self-realization from theatening the social dynamics of the established order. It also serves as an important mechanism for adapting workers to the increasingly dull, mechanical work relations of capitalist society. The "social character" has minimized the workers' freedom to oppose the established social order. Workers are increasingly unable to develop critical consciousness and praxis as a revolutionary class. Thus the development of a pervasive social character completes the transformation of the workers from conscious subjects to reified beings reflecting the commodity fetishism of the era.

Conclusion

We have explored how the production/consumption processes of contemporary capitalism have shaped the psychological aspects of human social life. And we have offered an integrative framework for understanding the crisis of culture and crisis of the individual which so powerfully engulf contemporary American society.

The traditional Marxist understanding of socialist revolution as the inevitable resolution of the socio-economic contradictions—the objective conditions—of the capitalist system is no longer sufficient. Psycho-cultural contradictions—the subjective conditions—have urgent importance for effective revolutionary strategy. The social contradictions of capitalism are interiorized in the psychic apparatus of workers, there producing ever increasing levels of neurosis and mental pathology. The progressive resolution of the objective crises has been transformed into a regressive neutralization of the crises within the subjective conditions—the psychic life of workers. The enormity of the psychic and physical illness accompanying the reification of contemporary life can only be guessed at. But its effect is obvious. While the crisis deepens, no radical working class consciousness or praxis is born. New strategies and theories must be developed to penetrate this psychic and cultural reification. These strategies must restimulate our vision of a radically different society based upon human happiness, an end to domination and the realization of our species-being.

To resolve the twin crises of the individual and of culture we must develop an integrated culture which recaptures the holistic and liberatory aspects of primitive and non-Western cultures. We must develop a new culture congruent with the non-exploitive socio-economics we read of in the past and present socialist theory. To reconceptualize the relationship between individuals, culture and institutions, Marxists must engage in a dialogue with Native Americans and other non-Western people. We must try to discern those non-European elements, traditions and relations which prefigure our integrated and synergistic vision for Americans in a post-capitalist society. The contrast between the quality of life among integrated cultures of the past and modern American capitalism is immense. Stanley Diamond explains that

The average primitive, relative to his social environment, and the level of science and technology achieved, is more accomplished, in the literal sense of that term, than are most civilized individuals. He participates more fully and directly in the culture possibilities open to him, not as a consumer, and not vicariously, but as an actively engaged, complete man.

A major reason for this functional integrity is in his control of the processes of production; that is, the primitive, in creating a tool, creates it from beginning to end, uses it with skill, and controls it. He has no schizoid sense of it controlling him, and he has direct access to the fruits of his labor, subject to the reciprocal claims of his kinsmen. He stands, in the face of nature, much less elaborately equipped than ourselves, with his whole being and all of his faculties and activities geared for the survival and perpetuation of his family, clan, village, or tribe.[39]

How can the values, the imagery, the way of life of the original affluent societies show the way to a new American culture? Better yet, how can those elements be preserved within indigenous Native American cultures threatened with the intrusions of the U.S. Government and its corporate allies?

This analysis is written to Native Americans as an explanation of the debilitating effects of the capitalist system. Capitalism is more than a system of economic exploitation; inherent in its development and operation is the ability to destroy non-capitalist cultures, to reshape their disbursed people in its own image, and to engender profound alienation and unhappiness for individuals under its yoke. Psychological and cultural colonization is an inevitable companion to economic colonization. No primitive or Native American culture has opted freely for the American way of life. Some have chosen death and extinction rather than succumb. As Native Americans you must develop strategies for preserving your integrated past and for resisting the hegemonic encroachment of the capitalist way of life. Times are increasingly perilous. Critical analysis and action is imperative.

And how can the working people of corporate America resolve their psycho-cultural crises and realize the awesome potentialities for happiness and emancipation which lie beneath the surface of capitalism? I believe this is a threefold process. First, we must penetrate the psychic and cultural reification of our time. We must demystify the glossings and ideological trappings of corporate capitalism and understand it as it is. Emancipatory Marxism, critical theory, is our best tool. What you have read is a contribution in this effort. New research will point new ways. Dialogue with Native Americans and other non-European people offers new insights to penetrate our psycho-cultural amnesia. The perilous nature of the times makes dialogue crucial.

Second, we must develop our sense of the objective and subjective potentialities for our American future. Ideally, through research and dialogue, we must develop sense, vision, intuition, fantasy of what can and ought to be. This is the vision of an integrated culture, once enjoyed by certain Native American and primitive cultures which can rise again. The new integrated culture must be through non-exploitive emancipatory socialism. The visions of the past must be revitalized to accomodate the new technological potentialities of the current age.

Third, and most important, we must put our analysis and vision into practice. We must begin a long march through the institutions of corporate capitalism. We must dismantle, disspell and root out the internalized psychic reification, the hegemonic influences of cultural one-dimensionality, and the socio-economic oppression stemming from the institutions and processes of contemporary capitalism. We shall have to find strategies for developing authentic everyday lives. We will have to struggle for free space in which to explore our needs and redefine our potentialities. In new families, new networks, and intimate small groups, together we shall have to cast off our chains and begin to live our vision.

6
Circling the Same Old Rock
Vine Deloria Jr.

Several years ago, after delivering a speech on Indian philosophies, I was astounded when the questions raised by the audience almost all centered on the relationship of Indian customs to Marxism. I passed off most of the questions with the cryptic comment that as I did not distinguish between the brothers, and preferred Harpo, I saw no reason to go into the subject. Yet the questions persisted and today I suspect that hardly an Indian can address an audience unless he is prepared to deal with questions regarding the relevance of Marxist thinking to Indian conditions, customs, and existing view of the world. This past year I have devoted a considerable amount of time to reading a variety of materials which would give me some insight into the nature of Marxism and enable me to give more intelligent answers to these questions. I think I am now able to see why non-Indians feel that Indians and Marxists are saying basically the same things. I think, however, that a considerable gulf separates the two traditions and that this gulf cannot easily be bridged.

Marxism, Indian traditions and Christianity all share a common fate, in that they represent not clear channels of thought but broad deltas of emotion and insight so that attempting to articulate one in order to compare it with another involves considerable hazard. Whichever tributary of thought one might choose for comparative analysis is almost immediately disclaimed by adherents of the respective faiths in favor of the interpretation that appears most similar to the positive interpretation which they wish to give, with the result that virtually no comparison takes place. An articulation of the Indian idea of the physical world, for example, will immediately invoke Christian claims that St. Francis, not St. Thomas represents the Christian mainstream or will produce a Marxist arguing vehemently that nature includes man and society and precludes human institutions which alienate and enslave. No one is ever convinced of the arguments, but somehow the audience feels that it has preserved some kind of tenuous unity which we should enjoy as human beings, given that the insights it admires speak to all of us as human beings.

In this paper I do not wish to debate the effects of industrialization. It seems to me that Marxist analysis is superior at this point to the hopeless defense which Christianity seems to offer in behalf of various forms of capitalism and to the Indian refusal to take seriously the presence of industrial society on the planet. The best arena for intelligent comparison, it would seem to me, would be the discussion fo human personality as each of the three traditions views it. Clearly in this area we speak of articulated goals and not products of the process. Indians would clearly emerge as superior if we restricted discussion to the results of beliefs on human personality. After all, we do not have countless coffeetable albums of photographs of old Marxists or old Christians—they really don't have interesting faces. In most respects, Marxists and Christians simply grow old; they do not appear to grow wiser while doing so.

Prior to a discussion of human personality, and certainly prerequisite to any meaningful comparison, I believe, is the subject of alienation and it is here that we can make clear points and enhance the communication of ideas. In a nutshell, Christians and Marxists spend a great deal of time looking for the roots of alienation and seeking techniques and institutions through which this problem can be addressed. Alienation is clearly a critical building block for both systems. Indians, on the other hand, are notably devoid of concern for alienation as a cosmic ingredient of human life, a question to be answered or a problem to be confronted. This is not to say that Indians do not *feel* some degree of alienation. Rather they do not make it a central concern of their ceremonial life, they do not feature it prominently in their cosmic mythology, and they do not see it as an essential part of institutional existence which colors their approach to other aspects of life. Alienation, therefore, is an essential element of Western cosmology, either in the metaphysical sense or in the epistemological dimension; it is a minor phenomenon of short duration in the larger context of cosmic balance for American Indians.

Alienation is not a wholly Western idea since Buddhism and other Eastern systems posit human relationships to the physical world and/or reality as one system in which alienation appears almost *sui generis*. The peculiarity of Western alienation, however, is that while it appears at the earliest stages of that tradition, the wrong questions are asked regarding its historical genesis. Christianity, building upon Near Eastern religious models, saw alienation in the first act of disobedience of Man towards the Creator. It thereafter posited a Saviour or Messiah whose task was to restore the cosmic balance by offering himself as a cosmic sacrifice thereby atoning for the primordial sin. The problem with this cosmic drama is that it fails completely to become concrete. It is one thing to understand the ancient drama of blood sacrifice; it is another to feel cosmically cleansed by it some two thousand years later.

In identifying alienation as a peculiarly human emotion, Christianity is clearly prior to Marxism, but its failure to provide a satisfactory emotional/intelligible solution to the problem only made actual alienation, observable in the industrial society of the nineteenth century European nations, of such clear importance as to attract Karl Marx and Frederick Engels to the quest for its solution. Marxism, in describing the process of objectification whereby the product of human hands becomes the agent of human alienation, seems to me a powerful model for explaining a great deal of contemporary unrest and acts as a beacon for suggesting alternative paths that might be walked. But a form of alienation, discovered only two centuries ago, and clearly related to certain institutional structures which speak primarily to the economic aspect of modern societies, does not deal with the metaphysical presence of alienation which must certainly lurk in the background of the western European pscyhe. That is to say, the Marxist description of alienation serves more to condemn existing and discernible institutions, thereby making some aspects of alienation concrete (a task at which Christianity was spectacularly inept) than it does to deal with this problem in a comprehensive and comprehensible manner. Adam Schaff admits as much: "Together with private property, socialism abolishes alienation in the form in which it was known in capitalism. *But this eradication is by no means complete*: in a modified form all the elements of this alienation as specified by Marx remain, at least in socialism."[1]

Socialism speaks specifically to alienation which originates in, is generated by, or is intensified by capitalist industrialism. Insofar as socialism removes the specific manner in which capitalism aggravates or makes concrete existing Western alienation, it contains the potential for reform and healing needed by Western civilization and those societies affected particularly by contact with it. It is, perhaps, the light side of an otherwise dark step in human experience which can be seen in a broader perspective of systematic alienation through the establishment of an abstract dimension separating the worker from his product. Yet involved in even this analysis are salient points which differentiate Western civilization from other traditions and from its basic view of life and the place of human beings in the historical process.

A critique of socialism of the Marxist variety would then necessarily involve an examination of the presuppositions of Western civilization which go to form its basic perception of the world. Although these elements exist primarily within the Western milieu, they are believed by Western peoples to be of universal significance. Thus statements about the nature of, historical experience of, or ultimate destiny of human beings within the socialist context are not necessarily applicable to non-Western peoples in a philosophical or theological sense. Offering a critique of Western thinking from outside its cultural boundaries means that one must inevitably choose those elements most closely related to alternatives found in societies and traditions other than the Western mode of expression. Such an arrangement necessariy precludes logical linkages that are familiar and anticipated by Western thinkers. My arrangement of ideas may seem wholly arbitrary to the schooled Marxist thinker but it does indicate for the astute reader the probable hierarchy of values existing in one non-Western tradition and suggests the possible rearrangement which would be necessary if Marxist thinking were to attempt serious discussion with people of the American Indian tradition.

A common assumption underlying Western thought is that things must have had a beginning. From Christian theological speculations through Rousseau's noble savage, into modern scientific fictions concerning evolution, and in the Marxist analysis, beginnings or origins are critically important. While American Indian tribes all have creation stories, these are regarded simply as the accumulated knowledge that has been passed down from generation to generation. No effort is made to ground contemporary philosophies, institutions, or systems of belief in the reality of events long ago. Other customs may buttress these stories of creation and ceremonies may be regarded as deriving from creation events or subsequent revelations which organically relate to such events but the truth or falsity of the stories themselves is not a terribly important matter. A narrator of a creation story will simply recount what has been told to him or her by elders, shrug, and indicate merely that the story has been repeated in as literal an account as when it was first heard by people of this generation.

The Western propensity to absolutize primordial events or to suggest that certain conditions *must* have existed at the beginning—either by a projection backwards of present conditions or by assuming the relevance of certain conditions—seems to me to create unnecessary difficulties in understanding for Westerners. In describing the nature of consciousness prior to explaining the Marxist awakening which insight into the workings of capitalism invokes, Herbert Marcuse states:

> The first form consciousness assumes in history is not that of an individual but of a universal consciousness, perhaps best represented as the consciousness of a primitive group with all individuality submerged in the community. *Feelings, sensations, and concepts are not properly the individual's but are shared among all, so*

that the common and not the particular determines the consciousness. (Emphasis added).[2]

This hypothetical scenario suggests that individual pain, love, weariness, and so forth could not be individual expressions at all but must be simultaneously experienced by the group and that individual consciousness is actually a very big step in the formation of human history. This mythical (in the worst pejorative sense conceivable) state of existence is, of course, absurd, yet it is seriously cited as the precondition from which human beings emerge through a variety of experiences not the least of which is labor in the anthropological-philosophical sense which Marx felt was his unique discovery.

I would like to suggest that this primordial state of emotional being is a projection backwards from a contemporary state, perhaps intuited, in which we can observe certain functions of a group consciousness, with this word given a very precise objective referent. For example, Marcuse suggests that "the consciousness of men will continue to be determined by the material processes that reproduce their society, even when men have come to regulate their social relations in such a way that these contribute best to the free development of all. But when these material processes have been made rational and have become the conscious work of men, *the blind dependence of consciousness on social conditions will cease to exist.*"[3] (Emphasis added). Here I believe that we have a contemporary observation of seemingly mindless group behavior which provides the model for visualizing primitive conditions. Proper perception of the present state of confusion would then lead not simply to Marxism but to original purity. Deprived of the assumption concerning the original state of consciousness as a group phenomenon, means other than Marxian analysis would be required to really break through present herd-insensitivity.

Regardless of the disposition of consciousness, one of the avenues out of the primordial communal-tribal-herd mist into individuality seems to be the creation/invention of language, although, according to Marcuse, it performs a dualistic function:

> Language is the medium in which the first integration
> between subject and object takes place. It is also the first

actual community (Allgemeinheit), in the sense that it is objective and shared by all individuals. *On the other hand, language is the first medium of individuation, for through it the individual obtains mastery over the objects he knows and names.* (Emphasis added)[4]

The difficulty of starting at a hypothetical beginning and attempting to explain both human history and the philosophical meaning of human individual and social life should be apparent. Marcuse sees no inconsistency in suggesting that language is the first effort to transcend the subject-object gulf while maintaining that language is the first medium of individuation—which creates the subject-object polarization of the world. Perhaps more disappointing is his reliance on the Biblical interpretation of naming as the critical element in human beings gaining mastery over other life forms.

Whether we take the individual in his/her realistic context or as the pattern for explaining readily observable facts of daily existence for numbers of people, neither the Marxist nor the Christian concept of the individual is sophisticated enough to carry the burden imposed on it. Christians, of course, basing their concept on the relationship of the solitary individual before his/her maker, forego any realistic analysis of what we mean by the individual in favor of omnipotent absolutism vested in the person of the deity. Marxists seem to transcend this crude conception. Adam Schaff writes:

> The human individual as part of nature; as an object; the individual as part of society—whose attitudes, opinions, and evaluations are explained as a function of social relations; finally, the individual as a product of self-creation, of the practical activity of men as makers of history—these are the foundations of the Marxian concept of the individual.[5]

This complex of ideas tells us how Marxist thought takes diverse strands of interpretation and merges them into a complex around which additional insights can be clustered, but it does not tell us how individuality originates or why this is considered important. Traditional Marxian rejection of religious interpretations may help to account for Marxist concern with the individual, but it essentially restricts the data from which the concept of "individual" can draw meaning. It fails to suggest an interpretation capable of resolving under its umbrella all conceivable commonplace experiences of the individual, thereby making it useful beyond the borders of Western thought. "The interpretation of the individual both as part of nature and as a function of social relations fits into the man-centered autonomous conception that takes the human world for its point of departure, remains within it, and dissociates itself from all theories that hold that man's destiny is governed by the influence of any extrahuman factors."[6] Adam Schaff suggests.

Obviously the concern that extra-sensory entities not intrude upon the analysis or the awareness of the problem lies behind Schaff's insistence that the idea of the individual be generated within the human world and remain within it. Yet it is at precisely this point that American Indian peoples would have great difficulty with the Marxist position. Rejecting the idea that there is a human world distinct from the rest of existence, American Indians would include experiences of wholly religious content within their scope of inquiry, thereby rejecting that portion of Marxian thought and presenting a dilemma for the Marxist who wished to convince them otherwise. Quite properly the American Indian would insist that everything falls within human perception, and that we have nothing of extra-human origins except those ideas which we revere above our own experiences. Even should an experience testify to the ultra-sensory nature of reality, nevertheless it happened to a human being, was communicated by him/her to others, and came to form a part of the collective social consciousness/history while still remaining as a natural part of life. Marxist exclusion of some kinds of experiences, particularly those which seem to motivate human beings, appears wholly unnecessary and weakens the explanation that Marxists would expect us to accept.

Schaff provides us with a better philosophical statement of Marxist ideas about the individual when he writes:

The individual's ontological status is clearly defined within the framework of the Marxist doctrine: the individual is part of nature and society, and this determines his ontological status. He is that part of nature which thinks and consciously transforms the world, and as such he is part of society. As a natural-social entity he can be apprehended with no additional factors, apart from objective reality.[7]

Putting aside the continuing objection that we cannot establish arbitrary and artificial limits concerning objectivity, this definition approaches what the American Indian might accept regarding the individual, were it not for the idea that the individual, while nature's thinking part, necessarily must be involved in the transformation of nature and thereby gain entrance into society. Transformation is a wholly Western idea, linked to the notion of Man's initial dominance over the other life forms, and suspect in that no direction for the transformation is given (even within the evolutionary process, were that to be regarded as valid). The human role respecting the world is thus left open to prophetic interpretations which can be seized with intense fanaticism. Transformation, in fact, is one of the innovations suggested by Hebrew prophets to describe the events of the last days and in effect degrades and destroys any value inherent within nature as we presently find it.

In the Marxist analysis we are actually unable to move from beginnings to present realities because of the insistence on the independent reality of primordial conditions from which beginnings would be made. In this respect Marxism gives us little more than Christianity or other world religions, which suggest a negative world in need of redemption, and then suggest that redemption is the natural outcome of the present state of the world—in effect negating the existence of the creator (or suggesting that He was really not very bright after all). Compare these two statements which attempt to move us beyond our starting point.

Herbert Marcuse writes:

Through his labor, man overcomes the estrangement between the objective world and the subjective world; he transforms nature into an appropriate medium for his self-development. When objects are taken and shaped by labor, they become part of the subject who is able to recognize his needs and desires in them.[8]

Erich Fromm writes:

> For Marx the process of alienation is expressed in work
> and in the division of labor. Work is for him the active
> relatedness of man to nature, the creation of a new
> world, including the creation of man himself.[9]

Neither thinker really departs from the curse of Genesis regarding the need for work, although Fromm appears to distinguish between work and the division of labor. Nevertheless, both find inherent in the situation either estrangement or alienation, and if we regard these words as similar in content if not wholly equivalent, we still have alienation as a given condition of human existence and not as something produced by the historical process Further, we have accepted the unarticulated premise that people must be working on and transforming nature to be natural—at least a contradiction in conceptions if not in terms.

Of much more relevance is Schaff's analysis of the type of human activity that seems to produce alienation:

> It is only in certain conditions that the objectification
> and reification of human activity lead to alienation:
> namely when man's products acquire an existence that
> is independent of him and autonomous, and when man
> is unable to resist, in a conscious way, the spontaneous
> functioning of his own products, which subordinates
> him to their laws and can even threaten his life.[10]

Schaff here describes a process whereby human beings delude themselves into thinking that their products somehow transcend in value the perceived reality which they experience. Alfred North Whitehead described this delusion as the fallacy of misplaced concreteness and Christian theologians label it idolatry. Of fundamental importance in this discussion is why western peoples would be peculiarly subject to this delusion and why they would not recognize it for what it is and reject it. At any rate, it was certainly a historical/sociological propensity long before Marx examined Western industrialism.

Identification of this process of alienation inspires me to side with Marxist analysis regarding the place of religion in Western civilization. In the words of Adam Schaff: "God, a supernatural being, is a creature of man, an externalization and objectification of his own characteristics and attributes. This impoverishes man, because it robs him of his own features and content in favor of a projection, a product of his own mind, which acquires the guise of a social belief—and so, by making its existence independent of its maker, becomes an alien and often hostile force, *gradually coming to rule over man.*"[11] No question that this summarized the role of Western religions and their institutions. With the creation and promulgation of creeds, doctrines, dogmas and catechisms, Western religion became the highest expression of graven images because it made intellectual formulas a substitute for human experiences. Discussions of the status of the Son, nature of the Trinity, status of the saved, freedom of the will, and necessity to preach the Gospel all produced a dreadful sense of alienation in Western people and induced in them the belief that differences in practice of religion were the ultimate criteria for discrimination and violence.

Western historical experiences are not, however, the standard by which human experiences should be gauged. For every religious fanatic who saw in God the Father a justification for putting pagans to the sword, there were other peoples, particularly American Indians, who exerienced God as Grandfather, who could not conceive of commiting violence because of religious differences. If we have ample evidence that other peoples experienced God in terms of human images and characteristics and did not find it an occassion for murder, I would suggest that the difference can be explained using Marxist logical categories. Christians were taught that God was their father but rarely experienced the deity as such; American Indians experienced God as a grandfather but refused to speculate further on the subject, thereby precluding the alienation which is produced by our own thoughts when they become independent of our experience.

The history and present configuration of Western civilization can be explained quite easily when we reformulate it in terms of misplaced concreteness (or original sin, or independent objectification of work product) and we need not rely upon the Marxian analysis as the definitive account of this process. Nevertheless, Marx does give us the formula by which we can make further observations on the illness which infects Western civilization. In describing the inevitable economic logic of capitalism in *Economic and Philosophical Manuscripts,* Marx observes:

> . . . the more the worker produces the less he has to consume; the more value he creates the more worthless he becomes; the more refined his product the more crude and misshapen the worker; the more civilized the product the more barbarous the worker; the more work manifests intelligence the more the worker declines in intelligence and becomes a slave of nature.[12]

The process inevitably produces, as Christopher Lasch describes it, the culture of narcissism. Alfred North Whitehead commented in a similar vein when he said that while it takes a stroke of genius to devise a system it took only routine reflexes to operate it. Again the question bounces back to an examination of the origins of Western civilization, the intuited or apprehended existence of alienation and estrangement at its earliest period of awareness, and its subsequent failure to resolve this problem either religiously, economically, or politically.

Marxism appears to provide a different answer than Christianity in the sense that it seeks to combine nature and history within a process that can best be described as evolving social sophistication—that is, a greater qualitative social response to experience than mere increase in the quantity of goods or the conquest of nature. Marx wrote that the "*human* significance of nature only exists for *social* man, because only in this case is nature a bond with other men, the basis of his existence for others and of their existence for him." And, he argued, "the natural existence of man has here become his human existence and nature itself has become human for him. Thus *society* is the accomplished union of man with nature, the veritable resurrection of nature, the realized naturalism of man and the realized humanism of nature."[13] While one might argue that such a format produces basically the same result as Christianity, in fact it escapes the other-worldly, judgment day eschatology that characterizes the Christian faith in favor of a progressive and seemingly inevitable goal which nature finds in the historical process. This projected conclusion to the historical process whereby nature and our species are reconciled assumes without further questioning that nature and our species are initially at odds and that the transformation of nature through the fulfillment of human personality provides the final linkage which restores the separation. This scenario, while comprehensible to Western minds, fails to confront the American Indian apprehension that nature and our species are not opponents. Not only would American Indians seriously question the gulf between our species and nature, but of equal seriousness would be the critique leveled by Indians against the Marxian view of social institutions.

Marcuse writes that "the institutions man founds and the culture he creates develop laws of their own, and man's freedom has to comply with them. He is overpowered by the expanding wealth of his economic, social, and political surroundings and comes to forget that he himself, his free development, is the final goal of all these works; instead he surrenders to their sway."[14] Here we seem to move one step beyond the idea of misplaced concreteness or alienation and deal with the reality of group identity which forges new emotions and energies unpredictable by a simple statistical analysis of individual wants, goals or dreams. Yet Schaff seems to imply that these social institutions are so much predetermined as to constitute a barrier to human fulfillment because of their inevitable domination by economic considerations. "Man is born into a definite society under definite social conditions and human relations," Schaff reminds us, "he does not choose them: rather, they exist as a result of the activity of earlier generations. And it is the foundation of these and no other social conditions—which are based on relations of production—that the entire involved structure of views, systems of values, and their concommitant institutions is erected."[15] Granted that social relations are a cumulative factor in human existence, Indians would argue that customs, sparking spontaneous behavior on the part of individuals who are oriented toward tribal life, moderate the effects of the economic factors and keep them in line.

Both these views agitate against continued reliance of societies upon the fictional social contract which underlies Western capitalism. Indians would see the social contract as a phenomenon having primarily verbal reality which in turn creates the gulf between promise and performance now sadly recognized by Western libertarians. Marcuse attacks the question of social contract directly by noting that the common interest can never be derived from the separate wills of isolated and competing individuals. Marcuse further suggests that the social contract anthropology is faulty in the extreme: "as he appears in the natural-law doctrine, man is an abstract being who is later equipped with an arbitrary set of attributes. The selection of these attributes changes according to the changing apologetic interest of the particular doctrine."[16] There should be no question that the Lockean or Montesquieu version of man in the social contract appears without gender, age, language, education, or emotional commitment. But so does the Marxian socialist, and the socialist is further hampered because while he lacks the positive attributes of reason and self-interest which dominate English and French rationalist theories of the social contract, he carries the burden of economic deprivation which is assumed (although quite wrongly) not to exist in the Lockean model. An exceedingly strange version of the social contract is presently articulated by John Rawls and represents the ultimate abstraction produced by this line of thought.

Ultimately the social contract represents a generalized version of the Christian doctrine of the personal relationship between deity and the individual. Marcuse notes that "the social-contract hypothesis cannot serve, for no contract between individuals transcends the sphere of private law. The contractual basis that is presumed for the state and society would make the whole subject to the same arbitrariness that governs private interest."[17] It is this very flaw that continually undermines Christian efforts to derive a doctrine of the church from a theology that grounds itself in group-shattering demands of individual conversion. In the same sense that individual contracts must always remain as private law, so individual conversions really cannot and do not issue in the creation or sustenance of a corporate body of believers. Reduction of the human being to an interchangeable unit within a larger political, social or economic theory or theology simply restricts analysis to that concept. It prevents the practical realization of the intended goal because of its failure to take with any degree of seriousness the real differences existing within the spectrum of human personality.

Marxist thought, while recognizing the existence of classes and trying to account for their ultimate positive contribution to society as a whole, fails as miserably as does Christianity. Schaff writes that socialism is by definition a system in which every individual is guaranteed full development. But in practice, he sadly notes, "it did not check the spreading of anti-individualistic tendencies—not only in the sense of combating the psychological legacy of capitalism, but also in the wrong sense of denying the right to individuality."[18] Schaff admits that "in all the socialist societies that have so far existed, various forms of alienation have appeared. In other words, there is no automatic process whereby abolition of private ownership of the means of production eliminates alienation—if only because of the continued existence of the state as a coercive machinery."[19] Finally Schaff confesses that "within the framework of a class society there are groups, for example, occupational, social, and other groups that lead to a certain division of society along lines of prestige, position in a social hierarchy and the like. Similar divisions cannot be ruled out in a society that has abolished privated property and classes, on the contrary, previous experience indicates that their existence needs to be taken for granted."[20] One need not recount the sense of helplessness within existing socialist countries, the periodic purges, and the dreadful shifts in power marked by dictatorial excesses and secret police to understand the failure of the Marxist analysis to produce the classless society which fulfills human personality.

The parallels between Marxist thought and Western religious thinking, in particular the Christian religion, would seem to indicate that they differ only in the degree of realism which they are willing to acknowledge in selecting their supporting data. Christian thinkers always seem to be content to see sin in universal generalities, carefully preparing loopholes for their flock, who are devoutly convinced that the proper external behavior coupled with proper recitation of creeds and slogans is sufficient to ensure their ultimate cosmic salvation. Marxists reject after death salvation and the judgment day and rely upon the inevitability of the workings of historical, economic processes to produce basically the same result. In both instances the systems of thought are based upon the individual as the fundamental concept used in analysis, both systems project the fulfillment of human personality as the end product of their historical process. It is not strange, then, to discover that both systems see in education the final tool for socialization of individuals into the grand movement which they purport to describe.

Education was initially an ecclesiastical function. Designed to produce a continuing horde of true believers; the churches devoted considerable time and energy in educational pursuits. The United States, and particularly the midwest, still evidences many institutions founded by church bodies which were supposed to ensure the continued survival of the devout. While paying lip service to brotherhood, church colleges nevertheless provid'ed education to the elect. Marxist thinkers seem to place as much credence in education as did the American church fathers. But they seem to base it as much on historical conditions as on anything inherent in socialist ideology. Schaff represents the basic Marxist stance toward education:

> The historical genesis and traditional structure of modern societies still prevents all cultural goods—especially those whose assimilation requires special preparation and knowledge—from becoming generally accessible. There is only one conclusion to be drawn from this, particularly from the point of view of the educative tasks of socialist society: *everything must be done to fill this gap in the education of the masses as quickly as possible and raise them to a higher level, that is, make them into a cultural elite.* (Emphasis added.)[21]

The desired goal of this program, and the content which will illuminate the new cultural elite, according to Schaff, "is to disseminate through practical example the ideal persuasion an attitude of judicious egalitarianism that precludes the pursuit of wealth and the enlargement of individual property for the purposes of social elevation."[22]

One cannot examine the idealistic goals of socialist education without seeing the similarity between it and traditional Western theories of education. Although the Christian church has long since abandoned its role as educator in favor of the state, the underlying assumptions by which the Western state now engages in universal education at the primary and secondary levels is identical to both ancient ecclesiastical goals and more modern desires to create a responsible citizenship. Ideally, within the Western tradition, such an education, regardless of its civic goals, must consider knowledge in the rational format in which clear ideas and concise logic (the scientific methodology) inform, present, and formulate concepts and theories. Reason underlies Western theological education, secular Western education, and Marxist socialist education. Without reason the West would be unable to classify and pass along its version of human knowledge.

This passion of the West is not without its flaws and few Western thinkers are capable of understanding how much conflict such an education produces in the body politic. "Social and political reality cannot, for any length of time, conform to the demands of reason," Herbert Marcuse notes, "for the state seeks to maintain the interest of that which is, and thus to fetter the forces that tend to a higher historical form. Sooner or later, the free rationality of thought must come into conflict with the rationality of the given order of life."[23] Both responsible social contract citizens and committed socialists depend upon the ultimate rationality of their beliefs to guarantee the proper functioning of their respective political/economic orders. Education, while advanced as the solution to existing problems, becomes the ultimate nemesis of the system.

American Indians have continually rejected the Western educational format all the while insisting that their children receive an education which enables them to understand whites and compete successfully with them in the social, political and economic realms. The inconsistency in this position is not as profound or hopeless as it would seem. The reference point is never the transformation of tribal cultures but the opening of the inner workings of white society to the understanding of tribal members. Unfortunately, but predictably, American society has responded to Indian educational demands by attempting to change Indian social and cultural patterns—revealing that American education is a socializing process, not one that imparts insights and information about the world. In short, Indians want to learn and are offered indoctrination. In the same manner, socialist countries will eventually produce internal strife by confusing education and indoctrination, but this propensity to confuse one with the other seems a trait as old as Western civilization itself and must certainly derive from its religious origins and foundations.

Western knowledge, and its component parts, including education, produces alienation because it refuses to focus on the real knowledge that can be gained from particulars, in favor of universal categories of classification which purport to give a transcendent knowledge able to provide instant orientation to things known and unknown alike. Marcuse puts it best when he writes:

> Common sense and traditional scientific thought take the world as a totality of things, more or less existing *per se,* and seek the truth in objects that are taken to be independent of the knowing subject. This is more than an epistemological attitude; it is as pervasive as the practice of man and leads them to accept the feeling that they are secure only in knowing and handling objective facts. *The more remote an idea is from the impulses, interests, and wants to the living subject, the more true it becomes.* (Emphasis added.)[24]

This insight is equally applicable to democratic and socialist attitudes about knowledge and it certainly describes the fundamental appeal of Western theology. Unfortunately it also gives eloquent testimony regarding the sense of alienation experienced by the West—including Marxist thinking.

Erich Fromm, in introducing Marx's *Economic and Philosophical Manuscripts* to American readers in 1961, paid particular attention to the place of Karl Marx in Western intellectual and religious history. "The mainstream of Messianic thinking after the Reformation, however, was expressed no longer in religious thought," Fromm suggested, "but in philosophical, historical and social thought." And, he concluded, "it found its latest and most complete expression in Marx's concept of socialism."[25] Further, Fromm maintained, "Marx's philosophy was, in secular, nontheistic language, a new and radical step forward in the tradition of prophetic Messianism; it was aimed at the full realization of individualism, the very aim which has guided Western thinking from the Renaissance and the Reformation far into the nineteenth century."[26] Marx himself issued a philosophical clarion call to redemption:

> *Communism* is the *positive* abolition of *private property,* of *human self-alienation,* and thus the real *appropriation* of *human* nature through and for man. It is, therefore, the return of man himself as a *social,* i.e. really human being, a complete and conscious return which assimilates all the wealth of previous development. Communism as a fully-developed naturalism is humanism and as a fully-developed humanism is naturalism. It is the *definitive* resolution of the antagonism between man and nature, and between man and man.[27]

If not as poetic as Isaiah, we certainly have here the promise of salvation and the announcement of the day of the Lord, albeit in secular clothes.

The implications of Marxist thinking may be revolutionary for Western peoples but they raise a strange response in American Indians. Why is it that Western peoples feel themselves alienated from nature? And why is it that they seek some kind of messianic, ultra-historical solution once they have identified this estrangement? To consider communism, even in its purest form, the *definitive* resolution between humanity and nature is basically to announce that the alienation of humanity and nature is the fundamental problem around which all others revolve. Since this problem is so continuously on the minds of Western peoples, and since, after all the economic analyses are concluded, Marx returns to this theme, a better use of one's time than advocacy of capitalism or communism might be an examination of how Western peoples decided or when they first experienced this alienation—since it does not occur within the American Indian context as a problem of this magnitude. Marxism would therefore appear to be simply another Christian denomination, albeit a highly secularized version, seeking to discover the Messiah and opposing the "Kingdom of this world". If one needed further confirmation of this identification, it is readily apparent in the Marxist concern for international struggle. According to Adam Schaff, "internationalism . . . in the Marxist system is not simply a councel of battle dictated by the need to unite forces of one class against another on a supranational scale, but it is also a principle of equality that makes the notion of brotherhood realistic."[28] Could Christianity have made a better case for itself? Schaff emphasizes this argument quite eloquently when he writes:

. . . it is beyond dispute that *internationalism* is an inseparable part of the attitude of communists and that both the founders of Marxism and all their disciples and followers regarded it as one of the characteristic features of the personality of the communist man.[29]

Go ye therefore into all the world, preaching my Gospel. "It is also unchallenged," Schaff concludes, "that *internationalist* attitudes should be fostered consciously, that they do not arise spontaneously, least of all in periods laden with nationalist moods, but can only be formed in a struggle against nationalism and racism of all varieties and shades."[30] The Marxist message, therefore transcends local, tribal, and national boundaries and is and must be aggressively missionary-minded not simply to succeed but to realize itself in all its essentials.

Marx truly stands within the Western tradition and his message is hardly new or innovative. F.S.C. Northrup, in his book *The Taming of the Nations,* described Western universalism as follows:

The great achievement of the West as compared with Asia is its capacity to achieve political unity over social groups and geographical areas extending far beyond the Hebrew or Asian joint families or tribes, a political union, moreover, the moral communal roots of which have nothing to do with family, tribe, status, or inductively given station. The concept of such a society was first envisaged by the Stoic philosophers who created Western law. This new, more universal concept of law and political organization the Roman Stoics derived from Greek natural science and philosophy.[31]

Of particular interest in understanding this political unity is the type of morality which acts as its glue, providing the internal consistency, apart from force, to make it acceptable to individuals.

To be a moral man means to be a citizen not of one's family or one's tribe or of any particular geographical area, but *to be a citizen of a community of theoretically constructed, technically conceptualized relations.* Thus large numbers of men living too far apart for intuitively felt contact can achieve a common bond of unity by free individual acceptance of a common constitutional contract which has nothing to do with inductively observed family, caste, or tribal status. (Emphasis added.)[32]

Northrup was, I think, wrong in tracing this belief backwards only to the Roman Stoics or even to Greek natural philosophy and science. But if it can be traced back that far with a fair degree of consistency, then we can at least make one incisive comment which should distinguish American Indian from Western thought. Western mathematicians conceive zero as indicative of nothingness and the concern of Greek philosophy, Socrates, Plato and Parmenides particularly, revolves about the interplay of being and non-being. American Indians, particularly the more advanced groups in Mexico, Central and South America, conceived the zero to represent fullness, not nothingness, and thus the ultimate value in abstractions takes fundamentally and diametrically opposed viewpoints as between the two groups.

Even more significant, however, is the observation made by Robert Bellah in his essay on religious evolution. Bellah finds considerable significance in the fact of the "emergence in the first millennium B.C. all across the Old World, at least in centers of high culture, of the phenomenon of religious rejection of the world characterized by an extremely negative evaluation of man and society and the exaltation of another realm of reality as alone true and infinitely valuable."[33] Bellah further observes that "world rejection marks the beginning of a clear objectification of the social order and sharp criticism of it. In the earlier world-acceptance phases religious conceptions and social order were so fused that it was almost impossible to criticize the latter from the point of view of the former. In the later phases the possibility of remaking the world to conform to value demands has served in a very different way to mute the extremes of world rejection."[34] Unless we can accept the idea that whole societies could suddenly and convincingly accept a complete reversal of their understanding of life—*without any external event motivating the change*—I suggest that Marxism, Christianity, and Western civilization would do themselves well to pursue their historical investigations into their own past and discover *what happened*. What even triggered a complete and apparently humiliating acceptance of the belief that this world, nature included, no longer had any value?

Marxism looks forward to the production of "universal man" who has the emotional, intellectual, political, and social resources to transcend his (sic) own alienation and fulfill his personality. Marxism makes the claim that it can succeed where other interpretations of human destiny have failed by concentrating on conditions and historical forces to the exclusion of extra-human concepts. Yet it must, like all other Western institutions, confront the reality of its cultural past and deal forthrightly with the heritage of the West which suggests that an event long shrouded in the past provided the significant trigger for radical change—a change that has yet to be controlled or understood. Of particular importance in beginning to confront this event is the recognition that American Indians and other tribal peoples, indeed those societies which lacked sophistication and complexity, did not suffer the emotional trauma of the first millennium and consequently did not find it necessary to look beyond nature and outside of themselves for meaning.

Today Western thinkers are greatly agitated with the insights of Marxism and with good reason. If applied primarily to an analysis of the effects of industrialism, the segregation of wealth and power by a miniscule group of our species and their subsequent inhuman treatment of the rest of us, Marxism gives us significant insights into our condition. It helps to explain the crude functioning of the capitalist system and its oppressive machinery which exploits the mass of people on the planet. But capitalism, as Marx well knew, is based upon a rigid moral principle: the renunciation of life itself:

> The less you eat, drink, buy books, go to the theatre or to balls, or to the public house, and the less you think, love, theorize, sing, paint, fence, etc. the more you will be able to save and the *greater* will become your treasure which neither moth nor rust will corrupt—your *capital.* The less you *are,* the less you express your life, the more you *have,* the greater is your *alienated* life and the greater is the saving of your alienated being. Everything which the economist takes from you in the way of life and humanity, he restores to you in the form of *money* and *wealth.*[35]

The applause which Northrup reserves for Western genius is therefore sadly misplaced if we are discussing human beings and the new morality which Western thought produces. Marxist abolition of this form of personal expression, while it may resolve some historical inequities, hardly provides any ultimate solutions to the human problem.

From the perspective of American Indians, I would argue, Marxism offers yet another group of cowboys riding around the same old rock. It is Western religion dressed in economistic clothing, and shabby clothing it is. It accepts uncritically and ahistorically the worldview generated by some ancient Western trauma that our species is alienated from nature and then offers but another version of Messianism as a solution to this artificial problem. Its universalism, disguised in the costume of international concern and application, poses as much threat as ever did the Christian missionaries. In educational theory it provides outmoded and inapplicable socialization with abstract and useless, if not invalid, knowledge; at least generalizations which have little relevance to the tribal situation.

American Indians and other tribal peoples stand today as the sole example of true humanism because they willingly recognize the attributes that serve to compose and define the human being. They revere age and recognize the growing process. They establish with some degree of clarity the difference which gender creates in human perspectives. They admit that family considerations play a critical role in the distribution of goods and the application of justice. they recognize law but they also see the fullness of the moment and ask legal and political solutions to be just as well as lawful. They reject a universal concept of brotherhood in favor of respectful treatment of human beings with whom they have contact. It is not necessary, they argue, that crows should be eagles. Both Marxists and Christians should heed that insight since in attmepting to transform the world into eagles they have merely produced vultures.

7

Observations on Marxism and Lakota Tradition
Frank Black Elk

I have been asked to make some observations concerning the relationship between Marxism and the spiritual traditions of the Native Peoples of this hemisphere. First, allow me to say that I am no Marxist scholar. I suppose my understanding of the subject is the result of what has been popularly projected to me, often enough by people calling themselves Marxists or Marxist-Leninists. I assume that what they've passed along to me is an accurate enough summary of the main points of their tradition. Second, allow me to say that no individual can hope to accurately address the range of spiritual tradition indigenous to the Americas. There are a great number of cultures among Native People, each with its own infinitely complex spirituality. To do justice to the subject, representatives of each tradition would be necessary.

Of course, this is impossible in the context of a book such as that which has been proposed to me. Coverage of just the question of spirituality would require volumes, if done in full, and then the balance of the subjects to be covered would remain, requiring additional volumes. Obviously, few people would possess the time and energy to read such a lengthy work and so it is impractical.

Of necessity, then, I will restrict the bulk of my observations to the traditions of my own people, the Lakota people. I am not a spiritual leader or an "expert", even in this. Spiritual leadership is the role of the tribal elders, for the most part, and I am young. I have nonetheless, been fortunate enough to have benefited from the wisdom and knowledge of my uncle, Wallace Black Elk, my aunt, Grace Black Elk and various other elders. I know enough to speak in generalities, which is what is needed here.

Finally, my limited focus upon the Lakota traditions is not as potentially misleading as it may appear at first glance. I believe that, despite their great differences in some very important ways, most spiritual traditions of the Americas share certain central values and understandings. This is, in a way, the same as that the various factions of the Christian Church hold certain core features in common, despite other dissimilarities. This is not to say that I believe that all native spirituality sprang from a single source as the Christian religion is reputed to have, nor even that I believe Christianity is the product of a given source.

Along with Vine Deloria, Jr., in his book *God Is Red,* I feel that spiritual traditions were probably born of and continued by such things as the geography from which they sprang; they are *truly* indigenous to certain areas and are the only forms of spirituality appropriate to those areas. In any event, an understanding of the Lakota tradition in its possible relationship to the Marxist tradition should prove helpful to those seeking to understand similar relationships between Marxism and other natural spiritual traditions.

II.

My first impressions of Marxism came through hearing statements such as "religion is the opiate of the people." Since Europeans often have considered Native spirituality as being "religion", such statements were confusing to me. I asked several people for an explanation of this and, in each case, I received essentially the same answer. Yes, by religion, spirituality was being referred to; spirituality or religion is one of the ways the "ruling class" subverts the revolutionary energies of the people. By promising a glorious "afterlife" or "heaven" to those who stay in line during their lives on earth, and by threatening a horrible and eternal afterlife called "hell" to those who do not stay in line, the ruling class is able to maintain its position of social power by frightening the people away from revolting and taking power for themselves. The church is obviously associated with the ruling class and helps to define what staying in line means.

This description of religion obviously served to describe the Christian Church, an institution which has nothing at all to do with the traditional spirituality of the Lakota people. I pointed this out to each of the individuals who were explaining the various negative social effects of religion to me, in hopes that this would cause them to consider that my people's "religion" was not addressed by their analysis. But it did not. In each case, it was asserted (with various twists, according to the speaker) that, while religious forms tend to vary from culture to culture, or even within a given culture, the net social result of all religions is essentially the same: the people are "drugged" by religious "superstition" to the point of not reaching their full potential as human beings.

But, I asked, have you really examined all the spiritual traditions of all the different cultures on earth in order to reach this conclusion? Well, no, was the general reply, that would be much too lengthy and complicated an understanding. Besides, there's really no need, it has been dialectically determined that this is the social result of religion. Instead of wasting large amounts of time and energy analyzing what it already understands to be a socially negative condition, Marxism wisely devotes its resources to the understanding of a positive social vision which can overcome religion and ruling classes in general.

Usually, I tried one last time. But traditional Lakota spirituality could not serve the social purposes you describe, I insisted, again and again. The Lakota have never had a ruling class; leaders serve by consensus of the people. The Lakota have never been concerned with heaven and hell. The Lakota have never even had need for a church, at least not in the sense that Christianity has a church. Wouldn't it be wise for Marxists to take a look at traditional Lakota spirituality, in its own right, and see if it weren't something other than the religious "opiate" condemned by Marxism.

But my informants would have none of this. They were sorry, of course, perhaps even a bit embarrassed, to have to explain to me that what I was saying, while perhaps true as far as it went, didn't really matter. The problem, as they saw it, was that religion possessed socially useful attributes at certain, rather primitive levels of social organization. History shows that, as societies develop, religion assumes less and less useful social characteristics, becomes more and more socially repressive as a means to continue its existence (once the real need for it has passed) until finally it assumes a role as one of the most reactionary social forces. So, even if Lakota spirituality seems to retain certain superficially appealing characteristics now, as Lakota culture goes through its inevitable evolution "into the twentieth century," this same spirituality will just become like a dead weight around the neck of the people, a weight always attempting to pull them down into the mire of primitive superstition.

Finally, one individual (gently) explained to me that, while he was thrilled to see me standing up for the sovereignty and self-determination of my people—as a Third Worlder—I had to be constantly alert to the dangers of "glamorizing" my heritage and traditions. After all, he cautioned, it is absolutely essential to a "correct" understanding of the situation that one bear in mind that traditional Lakota and other indigenous spiritual forms of this hemisphere are aspects of *stone age culture,* and, of course, no sane human being would consciously advocate a return to life in the stone age. One must be realistic, one must carefully separate "advanced" ideas from "backward" ideas; a "new age" is dawning. What was done to the Indians was genocide, was horrible, but it's past; the duty of all Indians now is to leave the past behind and move on into the future, a new social order is emerging and Indians should take an equal place in that order.

That tore it. The guy sounded just like the headmaster at the old boarding school I was sent to after being kidnapped from my parents by the Bureau of Indian Affairs. Although you can be assured my old headmaster was hardly trying to convert me to a belief in Marxism, both he and the Marxist were equally sure that they possessed the "keys" to solving the problems of Native People. They were also, despite their prepackaged "solutions," equally and completely ignorant of the people they figured to "help". And they were equally disinterested in doing anything at all to overcome that little matter of abject ignorance.

"Listen, my friend," I said, "the *only* social order *I* have the least bit of interest in joining is an independent Lakota Nation, the same independent Lakota Nation *you* folks guaranteed us you wouldn't mess around with before *you* started coming up with better ideas of how *we* should live our lives."

"Frank," he replied (laughing, of course), "you're a hopeless romantic."

"Romantic," I retorted (getting really hot at his too smug amusement), "refers to Rome. I, in case it hasn't dawned on you, am an Oglala Lakota. You will kindly keep your racist bullshit in your mouth."

"Let's cut this Indian crap. . . "

But, I was already walking away rapidly. He was lucky I didn't put serious pressure on his jaw with my fist. Maybe if, as always, he hadn't been forty pounds and four inches bigger than me, I would have. And so it goes. . . .

Anyway, at that point, Marxism and I experienced a decided parting of the ways. Officially. Unofficially I remained intrigued by the "liberation" rhetoric of Marxism and the obvious willingness of at least some Marxists to put their all on the line in efforts to resist oppression and to overturn the status quo. Anyone possessing any familiarity at all with the contemporary colonial conditions imposed on Native Peoples throughout the Americas by the status quo, should be able to readily understand the appeal for me that comes with the idea of overturning it. I kept my eyes open, but I was (and remain) wary.

III.

I can't say that I've exactly been obsessed with thinking about Marxism since I first investigated it. But, as I said, certain aspects of it retained a sort of natural appeal. So, I considered the problems which had turned up in my discussions with Marxists, at least from time to time. Basically, I came up with what I think are a couple of major points.

First, it seems Marxists are hung up on exactly the same ideas of "progress" and "development" that are the guiding motives of those they seek to overthrow. They have this idea that Lakotas are (or, at least, were) a primitive people in relation to Europe. Any rational person would have to ask what's so "primitive" about a people which managed to maintain a perpetually democratic way of life, which shared all social power equitably between both sexes and various age groups, which considered war essentially a sport rather than an excuse to indulge in the wanton slaughter of masses of people, which killed game only for food rather than as a "sport," which managed to occupy its environment for thousands and thousands of years without substantially altering it (that is to say, destroying it). That same rational person would have to ask why any sane individual would not choose to live that way if the chance were available, or aspire towards such an existence if the chance wasn't immediate.

That same rational person would then have to ask what's so "advanced" about a culture which generates authoritarianism and dictatorship as a social norm, which deprives its women, its ethnic minorities, its elders and its youth of any true social power, which engages in the most lethal warfare on a regular basis and has left perhaps a half billion mangled bodies in its wake during this century alone, which is eliminating entire species of plant and animal life forever and without real concern, and which has utterly devastated the environment of this continent in approximately two centuries. Finally, that same rational person would have to ask what sort of lunatic would *choose* to switch from the first way of life to the second.

The answer, of course, is probably even a lunatic wouldn't choose anything that crazy. The real question is why people trapped in the second way of life don't *really* start seeking ways to get over into the first one. The answer is, perhaps, simply that they don't know how. And, they're so used to pretending to have all the answers (that attitude seems to be inbred within the second way of life) that they're afraid to admit they no longer know how. So they—Christians, Capitalists, Communists, Fascists, the whole range of "ists" and "isms" making up Euro culture— demand that we Native People all become a part of their insanity and fear.

Our way of life was and is possible only because of the values and attitudes instilled in us by our spirituality, our spiritual traditions. The difference between Native spirituality here and the Christian form which dominates Europe can be measured in the difference between the two ways of life.

But things are not quite this simple. The European put down of Native peoples is more complex. They call us primitive, but as we've seen, there's no obvious rational reason for this. And Europeans pride themselves on their rationality. So there must be a less obvious reason. This seems to be that Europeans have decided, generally speaking, that our primitiveness lies in the fact that we (like most of the world) are "underdeveloped." Now, it's not immediately clear what is meant by this either. Clearly, Europeans generally don't know enough about the subtleties—or even the crudities—of our cultures to have any idea as to the state of our "development" in those terms. So the answer must lie in some superficial area which is immediately visible, even to a total outsider.

This leads me back to the "comrade's" observation that my people, the Lakota people, were a *stone age* culture before the whites came here. But how is that? Is there something stoney about our governmental forms or our medicine or our emotions, art, or food? What is this stone age by which Euros define our culture? Well, it seems that our weapons and tools were made of stone, a material utilized in its more or less natural state. Thus we are a primitive people. No more questions to ask about us in that. Thus too, are we underdeveloped. No further questions there either.

It can even be quantified. Let's see now, the stone age occurred in *Europe* about 10,000 years or so before Euros went sailing off to "discover" stone using peoples on the other side of the Atlantic. It follows, through some preoccupation or dementia, that the people stumbled upon by a group of thoroughly lost Italian and Spanish sailors must have been 10,000 years behind Europe; after all, they didn't even possess muskets and steel swords with which to civilize savages. Gee, what retards.

Now, none of these "enlightened" Europeans ever got around to asking the savages whether there might, in fact be a *reason* why the Natives fancied using stone tools and such. After all, no one could rightly expect an underdeveloped, primitive savage to *reason* about much of anything. Such an assessment, on purely material terms, was clearly borne out by the Aztec, Inca and Mayan (among other) cities "discovered" almost immediately by the conquistadores. And so, it has become a tradition in Europe to view virtually everyone else as underdeveloped, backward and retarded. Which isn't to say that Euros ever had much reason for such odd behavior, just that they were and are rather greedy folks on the whole, and possessed of the weapons (pure and simple) to enforce their peculiar standard of measure on anyone who happened to be nearby.

It's the peculiarity of the standard of measure here which strikes me as being most important. It's all a matter of the "will" and ability to accumulate material; the standard also indicates a need to constantly arrange and rearrange material. The standard of measure seems to me to be that the more compulsive a culture can become in terms of gathering up and rearranging material, the more "advanced" it is considered to be. The more relaxed, at peace, and willing to leave material things (beyond real needs) alone a culture can be shown to be, the more "backward" it is considered. Now, such "logic" is rather odd, to say the least.

A hundred years ago a great Lakota spiritual leader, *Tatonka Yatonka,* the Sitting Bull, observed of whites that, "the love of possessions is a disease with them." My hunch is that, as usual, the savage hit the nail squarely on the head. Of course, Sitting Bull didn't know much about the psychoanalytic theories of Sigmund Freud, and neither do I, but it would seem that Freud and the Bull were in total agreement on at least some things: that there is a certain neurotic behavior characterized by a driving compulsion to gather up material and play with it and that it's an obsessive preoccupation with purely physical accumulation and arrangement. The name of this particular disease or disorder of the mind, Freud termed *anal retention.*

Perhaps Freud considered this to be a disease indicating an "advanced" mental state. I'm not really sure about that. But it would seem quite possible, given the standard of measure it likes to foist off on other peoples, and which is really just the reflection of its own cultural value structure, that somewhere in the course of its "development" the whole of Europe got stuck in the adolescent and retentive stage.

Perhaps if some deep thinker can sit me down and prove to me that the Lakota were and are culturally deprived because of their marked inability to indulge in spectacular material displays like World War II, I would be prompted to change my analysis of all this. But I consider the probability of anyone really wanting to attempt to present such a case to be a bit low. Likewise, if someone could show me how plastic Barbie Dolls, TV Dinners, Porsche 911s, punk rock, double olympic sized swimming pools constructed for the officers in Saigon, Cam Rahn Bay and Danang, napalm and cluster bombs, lakes of asphalt called parking lots and all the rest of the vast array of lethal and useless European material *really* benefits my cultural essence one iota, I might reconsider. But again, I doubt very much that anyone wants to tackle such an absurdity.

I mean, *consider* the implications of a tradition which compels its people to march across half a continent, engage in a major war to steal the land from my people, engage in genocide in order to preserve their conquest, and all primarily so they can dig gold out of a small portion of that land, transport it back across the continent, and *bury* it again at Ft. Knox! The virulence of the disease Sitting Bull spoke of is truly staggering.

And, lest Marxists think they've somehow evaded this critique simply because capitalism held and holds power during the periods I'm talking about, let me remind you that it was a "hard core" Marxist who so smugly informed me that I needed to very carefully become "realistic," to *join* the insanity without "romantic" resistance, and get ready for the "new order" coming up. No matter what mud the capitalists might wish to sling at the memory of Karl Marx, they can never deny he was a good European: he transported the Puritan ideal of heaven in the next life through productive work in this one into an idealism proclaiming heaven is attainable on earth through the *same* productive work.

I've heard it said that Marx's greatest "achievement" was to completely secularize Christian dogma. I don't know if this evaluation is correct. However, I'm certain he accomplished this, and that it was a major theoretical turning point in European history. He set out to demolish the opium of Europe's people, and I'd calculate he succeeded. Whatever spirituality remained in Christendom died with Marx. The anal retentive complex which had always been sputtering in the Euro psyche became concretized as "dialectical materialism"; materialism has thus *become* the European religion.

The upshot of all this is that, as a non-European, an outsider, I have trouble differentiating between Marxists, Capitalists, and all the other "ists." Just like I've never really been able to unscramble all the theological fine points which distinguish the various denominations of the Christian religion. All Christians say essentially the same thing to me: "Become Christian." All the materialists have their own, essentially similar, message: "Get with the program, become a materialist." They are *all* proselytizers; that is, seeking to gain recruits, more recruits. All of them want me to change; none of them care to support who I am. A European is a European is a European.

Christians, Capitalists, Marxists; all any of them really want from me is my identity as a Lakota, as an "other." All any of them really want of the Lakota is their identity as a people, as something "other" than the understanding (or misunderstanding) of Europe. I, and my people, are just so much more *material* to be accumulated and rearranged into something we weren't and never wanted to be.

At this point, having thought the matter over, I arrived at a monumentally "romantic" conclusion. On a theoretical level, as well as a personal level, Marxism and I were necessarily going our separate ways. I may ultimately become fodder material for one another European power group vying for more things to play with, but not by *choice,* thanks. And as to the "unrealism" of my decision to attempt to participate in the continuation of Lakota traditions, values, and non-materialist spirituality, I will quote one of the Marxists who did (and still does, in a way) attract me, "Be realistic, demand the impossible." I believe Dany Cohn-Bendit said that. And anyway, the impossible, ain't.

Despite my disenchantment with Marxism and with the general potential for European culture to provide anything like solutions to the global problems it has created, I was intrigued when asked to prepare this paper. I decided to back up and study in a bit more depth, to read some of the Marxist literature beyond the "fundamentals" I'd earlier waded through. Much of what I attempted, although I thought I understood Marxism to be intended as a "working class" theory, was couched in a language which rendered it thoroughly unintelligible (much like Marx himself). I don't know that I understood all I read; I don't know that it's an issue one way or the other. Obfuscation is an aspect of intellectual "gamesmanship"; what I'm concerned with are practical realities. I doubt that I ever became proficient in "the meaning of Marcuse," if that matters to anyone.

Two of the books I read during this preparation period did grip my attention, however; at least in certain sections. These were *Unorthodox Marxism* by Michael Albert and Robin Hahnel (South End Press, Boston, 1978) and *Alienation* by Bertell Ollman (Cambridge University Press, 1971). The parts which really got me excited were the sections where the authors describe the Marxist idea of *dialectics*, which both books bring out in remarkably similar fashion, and the meaning of which I'd never been quite clear on before. As Albert and Hahnel in particular note, Marxists are often to be heard referring to dialectics this and dialectical that, but more often than not, they—never mind the rest of us "uninitiated" types—don't really seem to have a handle on what this somewhat mystical word is supposed to mean; it seems to usually be just another of the eternal string of left wing buzz words. So it was a revelation to read some reasonably articulate definition of the famous dialectic. I was also quite taken with some aspects of Ollman's alienation theory too, but I'll get to that later.

Now, if I may take the liberty to do so, I'd like to briefly lay out what it was that struck me about the above authors' descriptions of how dialectics work. All of them seem to agree that it is a *relational* means of conceiving reality. That is to say that any aspect of reality must be viewed as related, by virtue of existing at all, to all other aspects of reality. Nothing can be truly understood except in relation to everything else. Thus, the universe can be understood as a total of all its parts, but the understanding of any of the parts does not produce an understanding of the universe. In fact, unless the interaction of the universe is understood, a true understanding of any single part within it can never really be arrived at. Like I said, dialectics would seem to be—by design—a completely relational way of thinking; in other words, a view in which all things are relations.

Dialectics seems to be held out by Marxists as the foundation of all Marxian philosophy, the way of thinking which distinguishes Marxism from other European philosophies. Marxists pride themselves in being able to achieve a more total view of circumstances than can their opposition, which tends to think in terms of more simplistic linear systems, like cause and effect. Up to this point, I have to wholeheartedly agree with the Marxist theory, at least in principle. But I wonder how many Marxists have ever heard, much less understood, the word, *Metaku-yeayasi?*

As I understand it, Christians close their prayers with the word "amen," the meaning of which originally meant "all men," or some such. The term seems rather limited in its intended application (one might even term it "human chauvinist" in its implications) and clearly sexist in its structure, but that's the Christian church for you. The Lakota, on the other hand, close, open, and often punctuate their prayers with the word *Metakuyeayasi,* a generally accepted translation of which is "all relations." And anyone thinking "all relations" is referring simply to fathers, mothers, cousins and brothers, is less than ignorant of the Lakota. These human relations are, of course, included. But, in the same sense, so are the four legged animals, the animals which crawl and swim and fly, the plants, the mountains, lakes, plains, rivers, the sky and sun, stars, moon, the four directions... in short, everything. Everything in the universe is related within the tradition of Lakota spirituality; everything is relational, and can only be understood in that way.

The basis for this understanding on the part of traditional Lakota culture is its spirituality. The relationality of the universe is a spiritual proposition, a force so complex and so powerful that it creates a sense of wonder and impotence in any sane human who truly considers it. Only through the devotion of the better part of a lifetime of intensive study under the supervision of an array of seasoned teachers who have also devoted their lives to a lifetime of study can one hope to begin to fathom this complexity and power which we call *Tunkashila,* the Grandfather, the Universe, the Great Mystery. This is why our tribal elders are necessarily our spiritual leaders, our teachers: only they have had sufficient time to gain the knowledge which allows even a limited understanding of the Great Mystery of the Relations.

It may be a somewhat jolting announcement to make to doctrinaire Marxists who are convinced otherwise by the memorization of some "revolutionary" tract or other, but Lakota spirituality is—in perhaps the only translational terms comprehensible to Marxists—the pursuit of a true understanding of the dialectical nature of the universe. That, and to conform our lives to living relationally, as a relation among relations; *not* at the expense of our relations. Rather than being "an opiate" to the Lakota people, the traditional Lakota spirituality, our religion as it were, actually constitutes a stimulant, a social agent requiring a perpetual pursuit of dialectical knowledge and action. This, it seems to me, is what Marxists are always *saying* they're about. *Metakuyeayasi,* on the other hand, is the conceptual essence of Lakota spirituality, a spirituality which is the practical essence of Lakota life itself.

It also seems to me, the problem here is not merely one of a one-sided intercultural ignorance. Rather, as Albert and Hahnel point out in *Unorthodox Marxism,* even the "heavyweight" Marxist theorists seem at a loss to define the difference between how their "dialectics" works and how the more complex systems of linear logic work. I believe this is true because Marxism, at least in the form available in this country today, doesn't work through a dialectical system of thought at all. It *does* work through the same logical systems as the "bourgeois" theorists it says it opposes; it takes a linear, cause and effect, route to understanding problems and proposing solutions, rather than a truly relational approach.

So, when Marxists come upon a culture which functions on the basis of *truly* dialectical understanding and thought, they don't understand it, they don't recognize it, they condemn their own avowed means to reason as being "primitive" and "underdeveloped." As my Marxist acquaintances would say, the magnitude of the "contradiction" here is overwhelming. And so it goes. . . .

It seems entirely reasonable to me that, if Marxists had ever *really* been functioning on the basis of dialectics, they would have been interested in finding out enough about Lakota culture to discover whatever the exact relationship between the tradition and theirs might be. They didn't. But if they had, I'm confident they would (with some astonishment, no doubt) have discovered what I've noted above. Of course, since they have always been prone to dismiss Lakota culture as backward, *before* they investigated its true nature, there's no way they could make the subsequent discovery. Perhaps even if they had engaged in some serious attempts at investigation they would *still* not have understood the significance of what they were seeing, because I'm hardly convinced they yet understand or practice dialectical reasoning.

If Marxists had ever come close to comprehending the universe in anything remotely resembling a truly relational sense, it seems utterly inconceivable that they could engage in perpetuating the arrogance of logic through which Europe has assigned humanity a mystical place of inherent superiority among living things. It seems equally impossible that a relational world view could accomodate the rather stupid notion that the universe was somehow designed as the playground for human exploitation. Such examples could be continued at great length.

In any event, the question must be posed: if Marxism has been completely unable to discover the certain, rather obvious, commonality noted above between themselves and a Native tradition, what else has their "advanced learning" managed to miss? This is not an idle question. If Marxists truly believe dialectics is the most sophisticated "mode of reason" ever discovered by humanity (and, of course, this discovery is held to have been made in Europe—the way Europe "discovered" America), then they are hardly in a position to condemn a culture which functions on that basis as something to be "transcended" out of hand.

Rather than being condemned as "primitive", such cultures must be considered—if Marxist definition is not to be flatly self-contradictory—as "advanced" in terms of their "modes of reason." Europe pales to retardation by comparison. The simple fact is that the Lakota possessed a fully functional lifeway based in dialectical knowledge thousands of years before Marx, and it remains in matured effect while Marx's descendents are still attempting to actualize their dialectical rhetoric. We have *much* to teach our proto-dialectical friends.

V.

This leads me to the second point of real interest I discovered in reading the books I mentioned earlier. This is that a good deal of the current Marxist literature seems preoccupied with a social phenomenon called "alienation." I find that, according to Marxists, alienation represents an epidemic psychological disorder among members of modern "developed" industrial societies such as the United States and western Europe.

This situation, they attribute to the social conditions of "late capitalism"; a true cure to the disorder of alienation is the elimination of capitalism; steps leading to the elimination of alienation are in effect steps leading to the elimination of capitalism. In this sense, revolution becomes a matter of psychological health. As far as this goes, I have to agree. But, it seems anyone who wanted to could reach a similar conclusion concerning social/psychological conditions in eastern Europe, the USSR, etc. The people in those countries seem about as alienated in their lives as people in the capitalist societies. Some Marxist theorists have noted this factor and have developed a defense against such arguments. The degree of alienation experienced in the USSR and elsewhere, they say, corresponds to the degree to which the Soviets and others have abandoned Marxist ideals and substituted a modified form of "state capitalism" in their place. In other words, capitalism is still the problem.

This seems an odd and contorted argument at best. Exactly what is prescribed through Marxism which has been perverted in Russia is not really, or at least not convincingly explained. Marx called for centralization/rationalization of society, and the Soviets have centralized and rationalized. Marx called for elimination of all social classes except the working class or "proletariat." and the Soviets have eliminated whole social classes in pursuit of that objective. Complaints have arisen that the Soviets have established a massive bureaucracy, a police apparatus, huge military budget and standing army; Marx never called for these things. But then, he never said they shouldn't be established either, not when major capitalist powers still exist to confront the Marxist countries.

The more sophisticated Marxist theorists tend to dismiss the latter conditions noted above as being "aberrent" or byproducts of Lenin's "distortion" of Marxism. I'm not enough of a Marxist scholar to argue the finer points of "revisionism." but I do know that *every* Marxist revolution in history has been based on the Leninist version of Marx. That includes Mao's revolution in China, Castro's in Cuba, Ho Chi Minh's movement in Vietnam, Kim el Sung in Korea, etc. I've never heard of a revolution pulled off by the Frankfurt School, existential Marxism, phenomonological Marxism, structural Marxism, etc. The question of which brand is *really* Marxism is about as absurd as which denomination is *really* Christian; even Marx was pragmatic enough to allow validity to that group which showed ability to exercise *power.* And that group, among Marxists, is and has always been the Leninists.

So, if capitalism is not really the root of the problem socialist societies share with late capitalist societies, there must be something else, something shared in common. And that, it would seem to me, is industrialism. That, and the peculiar social forms generated by the industrial process itself. Centralization is a dynamic shared, of necessity, by any industrial/industrializing society. It is not capitalist *or* communist, it is simply an industrial byproduct. Rationalization is another factor; I don't believe assembly-line workers are alienated so much by the abstract notion of their "distancing" from their "product" or "profit" so much as they are alienated by the sheer physical misery of being trapped in a factory. Period. Yet rationalization is a necessity of industrialization, whether the factories be capitalist or communist.

The problem at hand here does not exist within the left/right paradigm which underpins all Marxist political analysis. Instead, it goes back directly to Marxism's rhetorical voicing of a "dialectical" position, while never having established a dialectical vision to match. If Marxism is to be forever forced into the constraints of its opponent's logic and assumptions, then *nobody* should wonder why the end result of Marxism is pretty much the same as the end result of capitalism: industrialization, alienation and human extinction. Alienation is just one of the aspects of a culture-wide anal-retentive neurosis which I referred to earlier and of which contemporary Marxism is itself a part.

Now, I want to double back again to my Lakota culture by way of making a contrast. As I noted in the preceding section, Lakota culture exists on the basis of a relational or dialectical world-view as thoroughly worked out as the linear view is in Europe. This is not a mode of thought we've come up with and are attempting to master, it is a mode we've practiced for thousands of years. You might say Lakota culture has dialectics down to a fine art. And, precisely because of this, questions of alienation have no meaning to us.

We, as a people (within the traditional cultural view, at any rate), view ourselves only in direct (natural) relation to everything else at all times. Thus, we *cannot* feel the sort of distance indicated in the notion of alienation, either between each other as people, or between ourselves and any aspect of the universe.

Alienation is an impossibility within traditional Lakota culture; we are prevented, by the way we view reality, from taking those steps which would, sooner or later, produce the condition of alienation. Thus, we are prevented, directly and concretely, from undertaking alienating and self-destructive steps such as industrialization. Lakota culture, in its traditional form, ends where the real possibility of alienation begins. The solution to alienation lies in dialectical vision *applied*.

If Marxism had ever developed the dialectical world-view it claims as its own, it could not help but arrive at a very similar understanding. To the extent that it has not, it remains fully a part of the process it opposes (in theory). Alienation is just one more indication of the failure of Marxism to develop the dialectical insights it itself offers as the only *correct* vision of humanity, insights held by "primitive" non-European cultures all along.

Until Marxism is prepared to discard its self-congratulatory and arrogant assumptions, stop proselytizing its "new" and misguided faith, and transcend the biases of its origins by *listening* to peoples already possessing the correct visions of humanity, it can do no more than fail. It has, to date, predetermined its own failure through its blindly stupid Eurochauvinism, a characteristic behavior not usually distinguishable to non-Europeans from any other caucasoid jingoism.

VI.

In closing, I feel the need to offer something in the way of positive commentary rather than simply leaving matters at the level of criticism. What I have in mind is to point to a means with which Marxists (and others, for that matter) might overcome some of the mental and theoretical problems I've tried to describe; might be able to get past the ethnocentrism of their theory and practice, might begin to attain an actual dialectical vision, might really begin to address the disease of alienation.

It seems that one of the more promising aspects of contemporary Marxism in the United States is a relatively new area called "Radical Therapy" or "RT". The basis of this, as I understand it, is that groups of Marxists gather around common interests and employ various techniques through which they hope collectively to overcome the oppressive "false consciousness" they associate with having lived their lives in capitalist society. Through this process they hope to establish more effective and penetrating social analysis, and thereby discover ways to reconcile their lives to their analytically generated course of action. This, they believe, will make them better Marxists, they will necessarily be better human beings since Marxism is the theory which seeks to overcome the conditions which lead to their need for therapy in the first place. This is simplified but, I think, true.

One of the primary therapeutic means employed to this end is (by whatever name or jargon it is described by the various practicing groups) the old Maoist technique called "criticism/self-criticism." This is where a group sharing a common theoretical view (in the Maoist case, cadres of communist troops and party members) gathers in order to straighten out its collective analysis and resulting performance. A particular member will be selected to receive "constructive criticism" of his/her thinking and activities. Upon completion of the group analysis, the selected member does not defend him/herself against the group critique; the group consensus view is given as inherently superior to "individualist" views. The selected member, rather than launching into self-serving polemics, *furthers* the group's observations/recommendations by engaging in self-criticism (again constructive) designed to reconcile the individual view to the group view, the individual line of action to the needs of the group, and so on. The function of all this is to produce the tightest, most effective possible cadres on the one hand, the most confident and securely developed people on the other. Through each individual, so the group; through the group, so—eventually—society. In rudimentary form, this *is* dialectical or relational (if only between people).

Criticism/self-criticism has been a very useful tool towards revolution for Leninists. It may become so for non-Leninist Marxists. In any event, the more or less continuous processing of thought against a collective sounding board and the conscious effort to live our lives in the best humanly possible way (always in direct conjunction with others) is inarguably to the good. People engaging in RT, at least in this form, are clearly attempting to put their bodies and minds where their mouths are, they are attempting to become the best possible human beings in the sense that they (through their theory) understand this.

Consider, now, the principle of the Lakota sweatlodge. If *Metakuyeayasi* is the conceptual mode underlying all Lakota spirituality, the sweatlodge might be viewed as *the* fundamental and consistent physical activity involved in what Marxists would call our "praxis." It is within the sweatlodge that groups of Lakotas reconcile their day to day living with the relational world-view. This occurs both in terms of mental outlook and growth, and in terms of the physical activities springing from this outlook. This also occurs both in terms of the group interaction involved and through individual efforts to achieve a reconciliation with the group (the people, ultimately) both physically and mentally. The sweat itself facilitates thought, introspection and realization. The sweatlodge, which the Lakota have possessed and used in this way for thousands of years, is not unlike the principle of criticism/self-criticism lately discovered by Marxism.

But, beyond the immediate similarities, there are important differences. First, and perhaps most obvious, is the fact that the Lakota have had *vastly* longer to perfect how such an activity might most effectively function. Second, and less immediately obvious, is that the Lakota employ this means to reconcile or seek harmony with *all* relations (rather than only with people) which reflects a more mature dialectical vision. Third, the sweatlodge is a guiding force among *all* traditional Lakotas, rather than an "innovative new idea" which its practitioners hope might "catch on." And finally, perhaps most importantly, the Lakota fully recognize the spiritual aspects of the sweatlodge experience; they possess no falsely arrogant notions of their own mental omnipotence; they call their spirituality *spirituality,* not *science.*

What I hope is made clear through this final cross-cultural comparison is that there is at least one practical tendency between "advanced" Marxist and "primitive" Lakota praxis, one which I believe would prove extremely rewarding to Marxists and Marxism *if* it were pursued to its full potential.

I believe it was Lenin who said something to the effect that "without revolutionary theory there can be no revolutionary practice." It stands to reason, then, that a crippled and visionless theory can yield only a crippled and visionless "revolution." What I suggest in this concluding section is not offered as a panacea, but a means—both tactical and strategic—to correct a defective theory which seems to me to be barring positive action. A *truly* revolutionary theory must be brought into being if there is to be revolutionary action.

Perhaps what is most immediately needed is simply for Radical Therapy people to begin asking the right questions, to attempt to at least consider whether there are not cultural blinders they need to discard. They might start with playing "devil's advocate" among themselves and *seriously* challenging the hallowed notion that productive abilities constitute *the* measure of human achievement. From that, they might proceed to question whether the ultimate hegemony of production relations is really *the* most desirable form of human social organization. If these two questions can be successfully dealt with, I believe it will become obviously necessary for RT groups to seek answers to why production has assumed such overriding importance in the traditional Marxian "dialectical" world-view, and how such a world-view differs—at a root level—from that fielded by capitalism. At this point, it seems to me that the nature of Marxism's *own* alienation will become clear to Radical Therapists. The stage will be set for a breakthrough. . . .

Radical Therapy will then be in a position, as a sociointellectual process, to *begin* to generate a theory capable of facing the test of global considerations. At that point, I foresee that the lack of prefabricated answers thus confronted by RT people will be rather traumatizing. They will be truly casting about for a way out of the void. They will be *spiritualized* by the overwhelming complexity and awesomeness of the questions before them.

The cultures and traditions of other peoples, which Europeans have historically chosen to deride and ignore, shall then emerge, revealed as brilliantly coherent and possessed of depths of understanding unknown to Europe. It will become clear that those aspects of comprehension only now dawning among Europeans have truly ancient applications elsewhere. Europe, after all, is the primitive culture, tragically arrested in the course of its development by an anal fixation; a pathetic bully, so to speak. Through RT, such a possibility exists. It is the point of departure to a "new age," a time when—like water seeking its own level—the dominance of European irrationalism is finally reconciled to its rightful relationships with the remaining cultures of humanity and takes its rational place within the relations of the universe. This is not to say that I am advocating that masses of non-Lakotas suddenly attempt—either literally or figuratively—to become Lakota. Or that they attempt to become Chinese, Tibetan, Bantu or anything else they are not and cannot be. Rather, it is to say that the Lakota and other non-European cultures claim no monopoly or copywrite on vision. They never did. It is entirely possible for Europeans, especially in the initially small groups implied by a structure such as Radical Therapy, to assimilate vision as a culturally beneficial characteristic. This is in much the same sense that the Lakota once assimilated the horse into their culture. Europeans must develop an antidote to their cultural chauvinism and blindness while retaining their identities as Europeans; just as we Lakota have had to adapt to vastly changing conditions while retaining *our* identities. It is no easy task.

Worse, in the situation addressed here, it may ultimately prove impossible. The real prerequisite to beginning, as with any other virulent mental disorder, is that the patient first *acknowledge* that a disorder exists, and that he/she *desires* to be cured. Admission of fundamental incorrectness in *anything* has never been demonstrated to be a European cultural characteristic. A way must be found out of such an impasse. *That* would be the single most therapeutic benefit RT could bestow upon its adherents.

And, as advanced peoples are wont to do, the Lakota will no doubt be willing to assist their neurotically retarded relations to achieve a more adult and wholesome outlook on reality. It may be assumed that other non-European cultures will do likewise. We must, as human beings, build upon our common strengths, not succumb to insanity and weakness. We have much to learn, much to do, as equal partners with the rest of creation. And we must do it together.

8

Marx Versus Marxism
Bill Tabb

On the Salt River Reservation abuting Phoenix, Arizona is an industrial park where young Pima Indians can learn urban occupations. "Industrial and commercial development offers the best possibility for making this reservation self-supporting" Hershel Andrews, a Pima Indian who is president of the Salt River Pima-Maricopa Indian Community tells the *Wall Street Journal.* Mr. Andrews likes to talk about "standing on your feet." That isn't easy, says the *Journal,* on a reservation that gets half its support money from the federal government . . . at last count, 38% of the more than one million U.S. Indians lived on incomes below the poverty line. "Among the reasons," says a 1976 government study, is "the scarcity of industrial or commerical jobs nearby."[1]

It's the old familiar story. Indians are poor because they won't move with the times. They need to get training and jobs in the modern world. The buffalo's gone and Indians have become lazy, drunken wards of the welfare system. But a few leaders are trying to help their people, explain the realities of life, help them compete in the modern world. Cliff Manuel, a Pima computer expert acknowledges the disappearance of tribal traditions. "But," he says, "we're surrounded. We must compete in all sectors with people in Phoenix. To do that, we must have Anglo educations and we must modernize. How do you do that and still retain old tribal traditions? That's the question," he says. "Maybe you can't turn back the clock."

Yes, friends there you have it, from the mouth of a genuine Pima Indian computer expert. Say, those people are sounding like real Americans. The *Wall Street Journal* welcomes all you minimum wage industrial reservation Indians to the American workforce, a little Third World profit center just miles from downtown Phoenix.

A counter perspective is offered in the Marxist tradition. "Imperialism, the penetration of Western capitalism into native cultures for purposes of exploiting their labor power and appropriating their raw materials represents uneven exchange forced on the colonized by the capitalists, usually through the use of force and economic blackmail." Marxists stand with the colonized peoples of the world: "Oppressed minorities at home and exploited workers everywhere against the system that oppresses us all".*

Such however was not the stance of the father of scientific socialism, Karl Marx. His Indian critics are quite right, I think. Marx believed the barbaric races should be civilized, made part of the capitalist system, turned into workers because then they could become proletarian revolutionaries and help bring about socialism.

In this essay, I argue that Marx took such a view, that Native Americans have every right to resent his position, and that too many Marxists today still accept what is a narrow and unsatisfactory analysis of indigenous cultures. I also argue that the Native Americans and other landbased peoples have much to teach Marxists if we are willing to listen, but also that Marxism (as I understand that evolving method of analysis and praxis) already accepts, in its most progressive variants, much of the Indian critique of industrialism and commodity production. The critique of the Native American contributors to this book may need not be a dismissal of Marxism, but can and should be incorporated by Marxists. Marxism as a methodology and as a revolutionary praxis would be the gainer if Marxists could be more open to such criticism. The name calling and cheap dismissals of other views on the part of some "left" contributors to this volume does not diminish the need to seek the intrinsic merit in the points of view.

*The quotes are meant to suggest the formulaic nature of the analysis.

Marx's Euro-Centrism

Marx's political economy was based on his study of Europe. He expected, in the words of the *Manifesto,* that European capitalism over time "draws all, even the most barbarian nations into civilization." The cheap prices of its commodities are the heavy artillery with which it batters down all Chinese walls, with which it forces the barbarian's intensely obstinate hatred of foreigners to capitulate. It compels all nations, on pain of extinction, to adopt the bourgeois mode of production, to become bourgeois themselves.

Indeed Marx and Engels generally rooted for the colonialist powers, believing that in the ultimate sense, and despite their hypocritical rationales of God and civilizing mission as a woefully inadequate cover for greed, colonialism did represent a state that non-western countries necessarily had to pass through. Marx did write:

> England has to fulfill a double mission in India: one destructive, the other regenerating the annihilation of old Asiatic society, and the laying of the material foundation of Western society in Asia.

Engels wrote,

> The conquest of Algeria is an important and fortunate fact for the progress of civilization.

Why wouldn't thoughtful Native Americans reject Marx? Marx, it seems probable, would have rejected *them,* calling them primitives and barbarians, backward and in need of colonizing by Europeans. Marx believed capitalism was driven to expand and encompass the whole world within its productive system, but that its very growth could not be sustained and as it ran out of room to expand it would find the conditions for its continued existence undermined. Without being able to expand further, it would turn in upon itself, become parasitic and undermine its ability to recreate itself. The drive to increase profits would lead it to irrational waste of resources, its ability to produce would exceed its capacity to create markets, costs would rise, increasingly more resources would be required to produce. He believed the gap between what was possible and what could be produced would widen as capitalism became overripe. Having created vast technological capacities, capitalism would itself ultimately stand in the way of their rational utilization.

In a world brought to an advanced stage in the development of the forces of production working people would see that what stood in the way of a better life was the irrational economic system which kept human potential from being realized. I think in this analysis Marx was correct. We see a single world economy emerging, pulling landbased peoples on every continent into the cash nexus. Commodities find their way everywhere forcing formerly self-sufficient people to enter the market in order to purchase items they come to see as necessary to their existence. For understanding this process of capitalist accumulation, Marxism is a most useful analytical tool.

At the same time there are a number of criticisms Native Americans in this volume make of traditional Marxism which I believe must be considered seriously. The first is the question of whether the problem is merely capitalism or whether it is also industrialism *per se*. Whether alienation, for example, is only a result of estrangement from ownership and control of the means of production or whether certain jobs are by their nature alienating and certain "efficient" ways of organizing work are intrinsically dehumanizing; whether factories in the Soviet Union do not have similarly alienating aspects to those in capitalist societies.

Lenin, in his desire to modernize, adopted almost too willingly Henry Ford's ideas on plant organization. One can say that the Soviet Union is not communist in the way Marx used the term, but there is still the issue of the way Marxists treat the relationship between the forces of production and the relations of production. Marx believed that overcoming basic scarcity was necessary before communism could develop. I think this is correct. But he underestimated both the extent to which capitalism could create artificial scarcity and that the degree to which it sought to increase production was *itself* destructive of the possibilities of healthy growth.[2]

Marx took land for granted. That industrialism fouled the air and water he was well aware. That the Enclosures, an early parallel to the seizure of rural lands by large agribusiness and mining corporations today, destroyed a people's way of life he understood. But he was basically optimistic about the long run effect of such changes in raising the overall standard of living. He could not know of the destructive powers of late capitalism and industrialism on the environment's ability to sustain itself.

Class and Land Based Struggles

Marxists have made too axiomatic a correlation between development of the forces of production and the potentiality of human freedom. While criticizing capitalist advertising with its "more is better" consumerism, Marxists have accepted the idea that capitalism *does* create the potential for human liberation by creating the possibility of material abundance, the basis for a just distribution and a transformed economy controlled by the direct producers. Upon this high material base, unalienated labor is seen to be possible.

Among Marxists today there is an increasing realization that technology is not neutral, something easily turned from bad (capitalist) to good (socialist) ends. Ends heavily influence means, as an old discussion has it, and assembly lines and typing pools just aren't much fun no matter how socially desirable the end product. Marxists must understand that when a ton of steel is produced so too are workers who are changed by the experience of their daily work in the mills. The toll the work itself takes must be calculated as part of the price of steel. The poisons emitted in the process, the health, safety, and psychological well-being of producers are all factors, or should be in a social calculation of what extent and type of production is desirable. I think it would be incorrect to say that there are no Marxists who think about such issues, and this is clearly to the good.

However, Marxism can be an insufficient tool of social analysis to the extent that it is reductionist. Economics *is* important. It *does* give shape to class issues, to politics, to culture. But it is also insufficient, as feminists rightly insist, to understand issues such as gender. Similarly, religion is not merely the sigh of oppressed people, their opium. Religion can, and in

Europe does, embody oppressive, authoritarian, and profoundly repressive values. But American Indian religions rooted in a oneness with nature can guide native peoples in a harmonious life-preserving pattern of behavior inspired by a spirituality that is *not* a reaction to oppression in a hierarchical class society.

As an economist, I find Marxism the most useful approach to understanding advanced capitalism, not because it has iron laws of history that replace the need for me to think and do historically specific research, but because of the relationality of its historical materialist and dialectical approach. This is my tradition. Frank Black Elk tells us, out of his tradition, a similar relational means of conceiving reality is called *Metakuyeayasi*. His spiritualism and my materialism intersect, so to speak.

The Indian view of nature as a living totality seems a more advanced formulation of the mechanical concept "spaceship earth" with which technically atuned men and women try to see through their limited understanding of feedback loops, a system that is both far more complex and infinitely simpler. That it is easier to resolve many of our technocratic problems by stopping their creation and reproduction than by looking for complex patch up solutions, seems an idea almost beyond the comprehension of the industrial world.

Because production comes first in contemporary Western society, solutions take the need to create the problems as a given. Stepping outside the system to see what really needs to be produced, what our real needs are and how best to meet those needs (rather than to feed the growth imperative for more commodities) seems almost beyond Western men and women functioning in a capitalist context. Our scientists and ecologists predict the end of abundance and the need for conservation, yet they do so within the context of trying to continue as many of the old patterns as possible. Native Americans and other landbased peoples have a great deal to teach the rest of us about alternatives that could increase our quality of living, if not the GNP.

Vine Deloria cogently questions: Why should Marx's central notions, such as "alienation", have meaning to indigenous peoples? These concepts are constructs derived from concrete experience in a particular historical setting, i.e., industrial capitalism. This is indeed a serious criticism of Marxism. To the extent Marxism claims universalism, it is false to non-Western experiences. Its generalizations truly have "little relevance to the tribal situation".

But Deloria has also asked of Western education that it adapt itself not to "the transformation of tribal cultures but the opening of the inner workings of white society to the understanding of tribal members." Marxism may not be of much practical use as a guide to tribal life, who really would expect that it would be? It was fashioned to understand capitalism as an economic system of exploitation and domination. If Native Americans wish to understand the process which oppresses and colonizes them, they may find Marxism helpful to that end.

Conversely, Marxist insights into capitalist development can be enriched by American Indian thinking about the destructive nature of industrialism. The 19th century optimism Marx had about developing the forces of production and then turning them to socially constructive ends appears somewhat superficial a century later. Such ideas of science, progress, and material plenty appear naive to present day Marxists too who understand what the degradation of work does to humans, what growth religion can be about, what crimes can be committed in the names of increasing GNP, completing the Five Year Plan. Similarly, we are less willing today to dismiss the role of myth and belief as powerful forces in society as were the rationalists of the 19th Century.

Marx was himself a product of 19th Century Western European capitalism. He developed a critical method for examining his society. His mind nonetheless was not that of an isolated intelligence, but that of an individual with a specific history in a concrete cultural context. The same constraints clearly apply to all subsequent Marxists in the European tradition. Native Americans and other oppressed groups, even while they grow up within the larger context of capitalist industrial society, have by the nature of their position and relative cultural autonomy an ability to see certain aspects of the dominant society from a different perspective.

The Strengths of Marxism

I have said some of Marx's Indian critics are right in their summary of his views. But there are a number of other points that must also be made. *First,* Marx in his writing understood that the universal system he attempted to build was not a useful analytic tool for studying non-western societies. Further, he understood the need to examine each particular cultural-historical setting and the futility of delivering *obiter dicta* of what an unstudied reality must be about. *Second,* the alternatives critics such as Russell Means appear to be offering are inadequate to their announced goals of saving landbased peoples. *Third,* Marxism is a useful analytic tool and political orientation for dealing with the main enemy at this time: an ever expanding global capitalism. I will discuss each of these three points.

It can be argued, as Shlomo Avineri has, that time and again Marx warns his disciples not to overlook the basically *European* horizons of his discussions of historical development. Marx warned not to "metamorphose my historical sketch of the genesis of capitalism in Western Europe into an historical-philosophic theory of a general path every people is fated to tread." *Das Kapital,* he said, "does not pretend to do more than trace the path by which, in Western Europe, the capitalist order of economy emerged from the womb of the feudal order of society."[3]

In this famous letter to the Editors of *Otechestvenniye Zapiski* of November, 1877, Marx further wrote, "Thus events strikingly analogous but taking place in different historical surroundings led to totally different results. By studying each of these forms of evolution separately and then comparing them one can easily find the clue to this phenomenon, but one will never arrive there by using as one's master key a general historical-philosophical theory, the supreme virtue of which consists in being super-historical."[4]

Marxists, surely even without such scriptural citation, should see the need for concrete investigations of particular cultures. For Marx himself such studies were not the central task, which was to investigate the nature of capitalism as an economic and social system. His conclusions as to the impact of the system on people remains a devastating critique and is in substantial agreement with that offered by some of the Native American writers in this volume.

Sitting Bull is widely quoted as having said of whites that "the love of possessions is a disease with them." Karl Marx's critique of capitalism was essentially similar. Money and the possession of things created the illusion that the wealthy were more intelligent, more beautiful, more cultured because they could buy the accoutrements of social acceptance. Yet their wealth came from others and the more they had, the less they were, he thought.

In the "Declaration of Dependence on the Land", drafted at and ratified by the 1980 Black Hills International Survival Gathering, was the statement, "the land has been desecrated because it has been treated as a commodity." Marx would have agreed. It was the basic distinction between use value and production to meet needs on the one hand and exchange value, production, or the market to expand capital and increase control over others, that was a central analytic element in Marx's model

If the direct producers controlled their labor power, the land, and capital, as well as the creation of labor, then production could not be exploitative. While Marx saw the oppression of men and women as workers in the capitalist system to be exploitative, he was less sensitive to abuses of the land. Writing at a time of the industrial revolution he saw the horrors done to people by the factory system, but he also knew of the harshness of rural life in England and saw the liberating potential of machinery. He was not altogether wrong in this hope. Science and technology *can* be liberating within a societal context of respect for nature and our fellow creatures.

While some land-based people can survive with less dependence on factory produced goods, it seems to me transforming industrial society rather than abandoning it is the more desirable option for most North Americans, few of whom live traditionalist lives. And I would think the majority of the world's population today require a relevant industrial society. The Indian traditionalist's preferences for autonomous development must be coordinated carefully with those of the majority who now inhabit lands which were once exclusively the Indians'. This, it seems to me, is the crux of the problem in Means' thesis.

It seems natural that traditionalist Native Americans want to be left alone by white society. If whites would just go away all would be well: "What do you whites want? Our land, the resources that we are stewards over. Whites pollute the air and water, wound the land with radioactivity and the scars of mining. Indians don't want power over whites. They would like never to see another white person who seems to bring only destruction in his or her short-sighted ignorance and greedy thirst to produce more and more. Whites want to possess, to accumulate. They do not know how to enjoy harmony with nature, with the forces of life that offer real contentment and purposeful existence." But is this a matter of skin color or of our economic and political system?

Thoughtful whites in increasing numbers share the Indian view of industrial society and its destructiveness of the environment, its spiritual bankruptcy, and its capacity to destroy the ecological possibility of the seventh generation from now knowing the beauty of nature. The question for them is building a revolutionary movement to challenge the existing order.

Means has an apocalyptic view of "revolution." He told the Gathering: "All European tradition, Marxism included, has conspired to defy the natural order of things. Mother Earth has been abused, the powers have been abused, and this cannot go on forever. No theory can alter that simple fact. Mother Earth will retaliate, the whole environment will retaliate, and the abusers will be eliminated. Things come full circle. Back to where i' started. That's revolution."

"It is the role of American Indian peoples, the role of al natural beings, to survive. A part of our survival is to resist. We resist, not to overthrow government or to take political power, but because it is natural to resist extermination, to survive. We don't want power over white institutions; we want white institutions to disappear. That's revolution."

What are the prospects that white institutions will "disappear?" Not likely, I think, unless Mother Earth does retaliate and the "Fire Next Time" destroys the vast majority of the human race. Russell takes heart in the likelihood that somewhere high in the Andes some Indians will survive to start again, or rather continue without the constraints of Europeans with their greed and destruction. Surely such a calamity is to be avoided rather than wished for and the question is how to avert such a fate.

Short of the Apocalypse, Means advocates an alternative economic system within the U.S. and resistance to industrial growth with its maximal production. It would seem useful to explore what such an alternative would look like and how we get from here to there. For many, appropriate technology, self-sufficiency and harmonious dealings with the ecological life of the planet are the answer. For some, such an alternative seems possible. Land self-sufficiency, the use of renewable energy sources, holistic health and survival skills were all shared.

But there was also a wide understanding, symbolized by the giant B-52s that drowned out speakers as they came to land at the air force base on the other side of the fence from the Gathering site, that it is difficult, indeed impossible to escape the system of violence, greed and capital accumulation that seeks to expand and take over everything on the planet. The system must be taken on and deflated if we are to have the possibility of living in harmony with nature. As the concluding document to the Gathering states:

> The need is not only to continue and escalate the attacks on the corporations, but to broaden and deepen struggles by creating an understanding of the inherent destructive power of technology. Those who remain in close and sacred contact with their land have this understanding. Control of land is the ultimate corporate control; failure to gain control of the land will spell the ultimate corporate doom. We must turn to those who live in harmony with the land for a focal point of the struggle for direction and understanding. When control of the use of land is held by the people who live on it, technology will be in the control of the people. This is a keystone to all of our survival.[5]

The analogy to Marx's view of control by the direct producers of their labor power is immediate. Present day Marxists should certainly be comfortable with the stress on landbased struggles in the light of the historic development of energy and resource struggles and the key role they play in capitalist development today. A key part of Marxism surely is to make analysis of the central contradictions of the historic epoch in which one lives.

Whether Marx would have joined any vanguard party which carried portraits of Stalin or Kim el Sung, Mao, or Che down Main Street America in 1981, I do not know. I rather doubt it. Late in his life when told what some of his erstwhile followers were up to he responded, "I am no Marxist." I do know in the context of Nineteenth Century England Marx did not favor conspiratorial vanguards, but mass based working people's associations. I do not think he would support imported ideological structures but might well have some interesting things to say about Eugene Victor Debs and Malcolm X.

One certainly cannot know what he would have thought of Russell Means' speech at The Survival Gathering. One presumes he would have said, "of course you want industrial society to leave you alone and to cease destroying the environment that supports landbased peoples. But capitalism won't do that. It is its nature to chew up workers and the very earth itself in pursuit of wealth. It is a system that must expand or it will die. You might as well rage against the wind for blowing or the moon for casting its light across the night sky. Only the working people united can overthrow this system based on greed. You say you are not a proletarian and don't want to be. It is not what you want but the choices capitalism gives you which are at issue. True, you can be a rebel. That may be personally gratifying, but is harmless enough to them. You must understand how capitalism works and creates a class conscious revolutionary movement to overthrow it. Only then can there be respect for nature and human beings' place within it."

Marxists have perhaps been too optimistic. Armed with the knowledge that in the last chapter the people's forces route the capitalists they can be insensitive to the irreparable damage uncontrolled industrialism can do. This can lead to a failure to see the centrality of control of resources and landbased struggles to the revolutionary process.

The struggles of Native Americans to protect their way of life, indeed to protect the Earth as a nurturer for future generations is an integral part of a number of interrelated struggles. These include on the one side the so far fairly successful efforts of the energy conglomerates to impose the high cost of ecologically and socially disastrous "solution" to the energy crisis upon the people of the world. The critique of highly centralized, expensive and destructive energy paths has long been made by Native Americans. Traditionalists have much to teach the rest of us about how to think of nature and resources in terms of our children's children seven generations into the future. This is not a romantic backward looking approach but is an example of sanity in a world so used to short-run thinking that we may be precluding possibilities of certain desirable futures through decisions now being made.

The Unity of the Struggle

Perhaps it is a comment on human nature, or at least on the ways of liberal white folks, that an increasing sensitivity to what this country did over the past three centuries—mass murder and stealing land from Native Americans—is not matched by an involvement in attempting to prevent present day genocide and theft of Indian lands.

The energy crisis of the last decade has opened a new chapter in the genocide practiced by the United States against Native Americans. Because seemingly worthless land, the reservations that Indians were granted, now is found to contain sixty percent of all domestic energy reserves, a new land grab is on. Ignoring the guarantees of the Fort Laramie Treaty of 1868, the U.S. Government and the energy corporations have declared the Black Hills of South Dakota a National Sacrifice Area. Not only Native Americans but small farmers and ranchers are to be driven from the land to develop coal and uranium.

At the Gathering, Winona LaDuke, a Chippewa member of Women of All Red Nations, quoted Lucie Keeswood, a Navajo activist resisting corporate takeovers of Indian lands in New Mexico: "Where will we be 20 to 25 years from now, when the coal has all been mined and the companies operating these gasification plants have all picked up and moved away? There will be nothing there. They will be working elsewhere and we will be sitting on top of a bunch of ashes with nothing to live on."

Susan Shetrom who, with her husband and seven year old daughter, lives three miles from the Three Mile Island nuclear facility, told the Gathering how she had totally trusted the government and the nuclear industry to act responsibly, had never attended a protest rally, but had come to see herself and others as victims of the nuclear industry's madness and greed. Her family now had twice the probability of getting cancer as before the accident, and her daughter's chance of bearing a healthy child had greatly diminished.

Activists at the Gathering understood that Susan Shetrom is unique only in that she lives so close to TMI. She and they realized that there is no safe place to move. It is not easy to find a community totally removed from the effects of the nuclear fuel cycle and impossible to find one not threatened by nuclear weapons.

The afterword to *The Keystone for Survival,* the Gathering generated statement, makes the same point. "The crimes of the Hooker Chemical Company at Love Canal are repeated in New Jersey, North Dakota, Los Angeles and elsewhere. The soldiers and Nevada citizens who were told to watch the atom bomb tests in the 50's sent their sons to Viet Nam to be sprayed with Agent Orange."[6]

Scientists, with their terrible hubris, have unleashed radioactive wastes they have no satisfactory way of containing; they produce carcinogenic and mutagenic chemicals and casually introduce them into the lives of unsuspecting millions; they trifle with the eco-sphere and start irreversible processes of unknowable dimensions. Present day Marxist critics of capitalism, of societies run by "experts", by a caste of corporate appointed initiates, can and do adopt many of the criticisms Native Americans make of industrialism into their critique of capitalism.

The cost of irresponsible forestry practices, the consequences of chemical intensive agriculture, of displacing a diversity of native seed varieties with a few hybrids were not issues Marx could have known about. The dumping of chemical and radioactive wastes, of strip mining, high voltage powerlines with their damaging electronic emissions are of course things he could not have foreseen. They are issues which should be important to contemporary Marxists. Not all Marxists may understand this, but then not all Native Americans do either. It would be a mistake to set up either "side" in this very artificial debate as either of one mind or as holding exclusive truth on their side. For example one of the Survival Gathering documents proclaims: "The Western industrial cycle of greed, profit and exploitation is fundamentally removed from any sacred tie to the Earth itself. The Oglala People believe this tie must be restored to break the destructive cycle and to show the way to live and survive in the world so as to preserve the land through the next seven generations."[7]

However, Native American activists must face the reality of their elected tribal governments selling out the traditional Indian way of life, having accepted energy development and exploitation of Indian lands. Coal gasification plants, synfuel processing and nuclear energy parks are being pushed on Native American peoples. Aquifers depleted of water used in mining will take centuries to replenish themselves. Strip-mined land may take as long to rehabilitate itself and radioactive waste may make areas uninhabitable.

Marxists are not surprised to see the U.S. Government and the energy corporations create a Council of Energy Resource Tribes with Indian leaders working to transfer energy rich lands from Indian control. The money is in exchange for the destruction of Native American landbased life and culture.

The Indian leaders quoted at the start of this paper who hope to bring education and training to compete in contemporary America to their people, and tribal leaders who are selling the coal and uranium on their reservations, giving permission for mining and building power plants, act with the authority of democratic election. They are representatives of their people chosen by their people. Native Americans have not succeeded any more than white radicals in mobilizing a majority or even massive minority of their people to oppose capitalist dominance. Nor can any one group in America alone defend itself and end the oppression and exploitation the system visits upon them.

Whatever the criticism those in the struggle may have of others who oppose the system, that criticism must be given in the context of the desirability of unity and the needs of the overall struggle. The points of contention debated in this book are not minor. I have suggested indeed that Marxists have much to learn from their Indian critics but also that the enemy is class domination and a system of exploitation that must be understood if it is to be successfully combated. Marxism is a crucial tool for understanding that system. The task is to join the strengths of the two traditions and to forge stronger alliances. Just as the American Indian Movement came into being because it is not just the Oglala people of the Pine Ridge reservation who are colonized and feeling the pressure of resource-hungry corporate America, but the Navajo, the Crow, the Hopi, the Northern Cheyenne and others, so too the struggle extends to the rest of the Americas and indeed the whole world. This point was made amply clear by speakers at the Gathering.

"General Miles, who led the slaughter at Wounded Knee in 1890, eight years later invaded Puerto Rico," Jose Alberto Alvarez, First Secretary of the Puerto Rican Socialist Party for North America, told the Gathering. He described the plight of the island under U.S. colonialism and especially of the struggles of the fishing and farming peoples of the island of Vieques (off the Puerto Rican coast) to force the U.S. Navy to stop using their island as a bombing range. Pierre Vuarin, from Lazac, France, where over a decade of struggle has transpired between farmers resisting relocation and NATO, told a similar story.

The Black Hills Alliance seeks to unite those theatened by the energy conglomerates' land and water grab plans—Indians, ranchers, farmers. It seeks alliances with anti-nuke activists, those who fight the dangers of nuclear weapons, those concerned with the fate of uranium miners whose very employment is death.

The Survival Gathering was an important event in our history. It brought diverse peoples together out of common concerns to learn from each other and to better work with each other. The essays in this book are a continuation of the Gathering. The dialogue it inspired must go on.

PART THREE

Where were you when we came close
  to the end?
When our land was being stolen, you just
  stood by.
When we were being massacred, you didn't
  even cry.
When they put us on reservations, you didn't
  lose any sleep.
When we were starving half to death,
  you had enough to eat.
When we had no voice, you never said a word.
When we cried out to you, you never
  even heard.
When our freedom was being denied, you never
  questioned why.
And when we needed help, somehow the
  well was always dry.
Where were you when we needed you, our friend?
Where were you when we needed you to bend?
Now you claim to be part Sioux or Cherokee.
But where were you when we came close to the end?

From a Song Sung By
Floyd Westerman

9

Reds Versus Redskins
Phil Heiple

On April 30, 1981, several of the contributors to this volume
had the opportunity to get together and exchange observations
on the Marxist/Indian debate. With Ward Churchill moderat-
ing, Vine Deloria, Jr., Russell Means, Bob Sipe, the audience,
and I had a highly stimulating time clarifying points of contact
and disagreement among us. I'd like to summarize what I think
these were, and their relationship to some of the practical political problems facing us in these times.

While Bob and I had certain disagreements, as did Deloria
and Means, lines of contention were clearly established on most
issues. On the question of what is to be done, the Marxists (Bob
and I) spoke of a radical reorganization of the social relations of
capitalism, while the Native Americans (Vine and Russell) called
for a qualitative change in the relationship between people and
environments. Where the Marxist point of view implied political
strategies ranging from decentralization to outright seizure of
power, the Native Americans suggested a radical separatism
which eroded the basis for existence of such power and where
traditional lifestyles are adopted on a limited and local scale.

As the Marxists criticized the Native Americans for a fatal underestimation of imperialist ease at corrupting and undermining traditional societies, the Native Americans responded with criticism of Marxism as being part of the corrupting tradition itself. The Marxists saw no hope for Native Americans: traditional societies were doomed long ago. The Native Americans saw no hope for Marxism: any participation in Western society, including internal criticism, only contributes to the suicide of humankind.

All this appears to leave very little for Marxists and Native Americans to talk about with any hope of agreement. But this is because the discussion thus far has focused mainly upon the differences between the perspectives, e.g.: where each sees the other going wrong, instead of their many and fruitful similarities. A survey of these similarities could go a long way toward minimizing the importance of differences and providing some basis for mutual understanding and cooperation.

As a sign of goodwill, Marxists and Native Americans could agree to disagree about a great number of things. Many positions in political theory are more a matter of personal taste and opinion than of logic and experience. "The lyrics don't matter as long as you like the beat," so to speak. By this I mean that the tone and temperament of a theory are as important as its elucidations. It seems to me that these subjective characteristics are what are most similar between Marxists and Native Americans, especially those militants exemplified by Russell Means and the American Indian Movement.

I think the main intersection is evidenced within the anger both sides share toward the destruction of human life and natural resources forged by Western imperialism. The differences stem from the diverging accounts of the origins and evolution of this destruction. Although both attribute it to practices and institutions originating in Europe, they differ sharply about the essential reasons behind it. Marxists view things in materialist terms, in how the objective conditions necessary for life were created and controlled by people with material access to those resources. Native Americans such as Means and Deloria argue that subjective factors—values and attitudes contemptuous of traditional lifestyle and "the natural order"—are the core problem.

Whichever reason is given, however, a number of political strategies remain the same. Both sides advocate civil disobedience and involvement in oppositional political movements. Both express a will toward greater personal involvement in and control over the means to survival. Both assert that identity and a sense of community are superior to "security" and a sense of power. And both sides loath and ridicule the symbols of commodity culture used to legitimate the system and engender popular support.

This strategic commonality should put Marxists and Native Americans side by side on most contemporary political issues. Nevertheless, there is considerable reason for Native American militants to remain suspicious of Marxism. Some of these, such as the Christian hue to Marxist tradition and practice, have been solidly advanced by Deloria and others. To this, I could add my own list of theoretical and practical problems relevant to the debate.

The main problem is the manner in which ethnic struggles and the "national question" have been handled within Marxist tradition. During the period within which they wrote, Marx and Engels saw the possibility for revolution only in large, centralized industrial states. They did not foresee problems of international alignment as barriers to change *within* states, and they therefore subordinated questions of ethnic struggle to questions of class conflict.

Hence, one finds Marx's scathing critique of the British domination of Ireland, as well as his view of the German domination of the Czechs as being a quite different matter: British colonization of the Irish had "advanced" the latter people to the point at which revolution was possible, while Czech independence from Germany would disrupt the economic organization prerequisite to successful proletarian revolution in central Europe. Likewise, Engels dismissed Slav yearnings for national independence on the grounds that subordination to the Germans was the best hope for spreading Western civilization and socialism in eastern Europe.

Yet, today, when one looks around the world, among the clearest and most dramatic examples of liberatory conflict are ethnic minorities involved in nationalist struggles. Some of these are the Basques, Catalans and Galicians in Spain, the Bretons in

France, the Quebequois, Metis and James Bay Cree in Canada, the Kurds in south-central Asia, Serbs and Croats in Yugoslavia, Palestinians in Israel, the Bahnar, Rhade and other "Montagnard" tribes in the highlands of Vietnam, the Greek and Turk Cypriots, Corsicans, Sardinians, Pathans, Baluchis, Eritreans, South Moluccans and, in the United States, Chicanos, Puerto Ricans, Blacks (especially Muslims) and Native Americans.

Contrary to Marx's expectations, the industrial proletariat in the advanced capitalist nations of the West (excepting perhaps France and Italy) has demonstrated a greater interest in aligning with state power than in opposing it. Further, socialist and Marxist states, while condemning the capitalist system, have been quite full of admiration for the productive forces that system has created. That such a situation should come to pass seems retrospectively predictable enough, given the conception of relations between humans and nature drawn by Marx in the *Communist Manifesto* and other writings.

In essence, this amounts to the notion of an inherent opposition between humanity and nature expressed through the quest to gain control over the forces of nature via the medium of labor and in order to convert these forces into economic products within an artificial or man-made world. This, in the Marxian—as well as capitalist—view represents, or at least has represented, "progress" for humanity.

On the basis of this tenet, one of Marxism's primary functions in the post-revolutionary society of the Soviet Union has been to transform a "backward" agrarian society into a massive industrial complex rivaling those evidenced in the late capitalist nations. To this can be added the imperialism and betrayal waged in the name of Marxism during the Twentieth Century: Kronstadt (1920), Spain (1939), Yugoslavia (1948), Berlin (1953), Hungary (1956), Indonesia (1965), Czechoslavakia and France (1968), Chile (1973), Kampuchea (1976-77), and France (again, in 1978). And then there are other frequently noted facts, such as that Hitler always termed himself a "socialist" while developing a state terrorism quite similar in many of its aspects to that constructed by Stalin, or that Mussolini emerged quite literally from the ranks of the Italian left. Today, there are rumblings of the Sandinistas imposing forced relocation upon the Indian tribes of the Nicaragua/Honduras border region while the Vietnamese conduct military operations against mountain tribes in both Vietnam and Laos.

To sum up, the complimentary attitudes toward nature and "natural peoples" expressed through both capitalist and Marxist doctrine, as well as the highly suspect performance/politics of the proletariat where industrialism has occurred, make for a very weak recommendation of Marxism as an emancipatory theory for ethnic/tribal nationalists—or anyone, for that matter.

This critique, however wide-ranging, is nonetheless far from exhaustive. It simply does not apply to most manifestations of Marxism in the West which represent considerable modifications ("revisions") of Marx's original theoretical model. Council communism, critical theory and phenomonological Marxism all hold positions on science, reason, nature and labor which are very different from traditional or "orthodox" Marxism. There are also ideologies of the left, such as anarchism and syndicalism, which can be (and often are) more critical of Marxism than either right-wing philosophy or criticism such as that extended by Deloria, Means, et. al.

A number of successes can and should be posted to Marxism's credit as well. The Russian Revolution of 1917 is probably the most important, followed by the Chinese Revolution in 1949, and almost every major revolution since: those in Cuba, Vietnam, Algeria, Angola, Zimbabwe, Nicaragua and elsewhere. Less dramatic are Marxism's organizing contributions to such struggles as the eight-hour workday, child labor laws, universal suffrage and the right of unions to picket and strike.

Of less importance perhaps, but still notably relevant is the Marxist impetus behind parliamentary oppositions within the governments of France, England, West Germany, Italy and Sweden. To some extent at least, they have proven successful in diminishing the brunt of capitalist imperial practice against the very colonial peoples represented in broad terms by the Native American contributors to this volume, as well as having achieved certain concrete gains for their own "mother country" populations.

Finally, and perhaps least important in this scheme of things, are the many artists whose aesthetic acumen and social sensibilities have been sharpened through a familiarity with Marxism and Marxist theory. A few of the better known include George Orwell, Kathe Kollewitz, Bunuel, Ernest Hemingway, John Dos Passos, Bertolt Brecht, Diego Rivera, Le Corbusier, Pablo Neruda, Aldous Huxley, William Faulkner, Pablo Picasso, Andre Breton, Jean Paul Sartre, Rita Mae Brown, Kandinsky, Paul Robeson, Richard Wright, Jane Fonda, Matisse, G.B. Shaw, and Joan Miro.

To completely discount such assets is to abandon the only tradition which has proven itself capable, however ambiguously, of resisting and defeating the forces of capitalism. While the radical stance of Native American activists in wishing to step outside of history to wage their struggle at the spiritual level has a trendy religious appeal, it seems to me that the only possible outcome of such a strategy would be the acceleration of their extinction. More than personal suicide, such a separatist line of action is precisely what representatives of the status quo want and need. The state, afterall, maintains itself primarily within the rule of "divide and conquer".

The common ground between Marxists and Native Americans must be further explored and built upon. Differences must be put in proper perspective and dealt with accordingly. For example, not only is the critique of Christian elements in Marxism rather weak when compared to other things worth complaining about, it is extraordinarily misplaced considering the overt attempts by politically-minded Christians (such as the so-called "moral majority") to control the economy and legislate morality. From an environmentalist viewpoint, the greater problem is not Marx's latent positivism, but the ideological licence claimed by Reaganites such as Interior Secretary Watt, who views himself as being on a mission sanctioned by no less the Jesus Christ himself: "My responsibility is to follow the scriptures, which call upon us to occupy the land until Jesus returns."

We must close ranks in the common interest and to confronts the common foe. When Deloria says "God is Red," Watt seems only to elaborate, "He is red, white, and blue."

Marxism and the
Native American
Ward Churchill

Battle has been joined, so to speak. A summary of the various arguments and observations offered in this book seems in order, biased though my assessment may seem (or be), for it is only through such review that we may seek answers to the question: "Where do we go from here?"

Elizabeth Lloyd has, in my opinion, done an excellent service in laying bare the theoretical bones of Marx's general theory of culture, a structure through which Marxian questions concerning issues of cultural differentiation might be resolved. In this, she is reinforced to some extent by Bill Tabb in his notation of Marx's admonition to his readers not to attempt to universalize conclusions drawn from the historical materialist examination of European cultural evolution. It may thus be rightly contended that the rudiments of a truly adequate system for the apprehension of cultures and their manifestations exist in Marx, and exist in a fashion remarkably clear of ethnocentrism. That Marx never fleshed out this basic theory is certainly no fault of anyone who has come along since, certainly not of the Marxist contributors to this volume.

But neither the framework nor even the fullblown rendering of such a theory is, nor could be, sufficient, merely by virtue of existence. What is, and always was, required is *practice derived from theory*: praxis, in the Marxist vernacular. This is precisely what is lacking in Marx and subsequently within Marxism. It is not enough to articulate an appropriate methodology when one abandons it at the next turn.

The notion that the pronounced economism of past Marxian theoretical practice is appropriate to elaboration of European conditions and fails to bear, in fact or intent, upon non-European conditions doesn't pass muster under even the most meagre scrutiny. The permeation of the Marxist cosmology with such concepts as "precapitalist" and/or "preindustrial" as well as a litter of jargon including "primitive" and "underdeveloped" has hardly been restricted in application—either by Marx or by Marxists. More than a century of Marxism, beginning with Marx, has indeed applied the standard of measure accruing from an intensive study of European cultural evolution, the antecedent phases of capitalism, to all other cultures. This is a mentality so embedded in most aspects of Marxist tradition that it can only be seen as integral to the whole, in practice if not necessarily in theory.

Thus Russell Means' critique of what has essentially been Lenin's grafting of Bakuninism on to the corpus of Marxism—as represented through a series of twentieth century revolutions and resultant "socialist orders"—need not be restricted entirely to the Leninist line of thinking. Economism is a strand which runs, with various degrees of overt expression, through virtually all the Marxist thinking in this volume. Means is perhaps preoccupied with Leninist expression insofar as it has evidenced itself most clearly in historical terms. His analysis nonetheless is considerably broader in its implications. The temporal insinuations of Marxism *vis a vis* all that is not European engulf the theoretics springing from Frankfurt, for example, to at least as great an extent as the "cruder" offerings of Leninist doctrine. Citations from critical theory contain references to the supposed virtues of "early societies," yet no attempt is ever made to address the obvious question of what, exactly, is "early" about non-industrialized societies which exist here and now, in 1983. Critical theory, in this sense at least, is perhaps the direct equivalent within Marxism of the "liberal sophistry" of the fascist/capitalist "moral majority" trend.

Still, it is certainly correct that Leninist adherents can be crude, at least at this juncture. Little could better fill that description that the "sly" announcement that "Russell Means wants to eat shit" (by "looking for the second harvest") when he dares to challenge the scripture of the Revolutionary Communist Party faith. Despite (or perhaps because of) the vehemence of its response, the party offered little with which to address the substantive issues raised by Means' critique. They did, on the other hand, do us all the service of trotting out virtually the full range of banalities, misinformation and outright absurdities concerning Indians lodged in Americana and holding currency on the left. Hopefully, Dora-Lee Larson and I were able to clarify matters in many of these areas.

Bob Sipe enters the fray with an exposition of the principal tenets of critical theory and extends a thorough case as to its analytical potential as a mode through which Native Americans may better understand the inner workings of the dominant culture surrounding them. It seems to me, however, that his argument loses force in at least two significant ways: a) his critical apprehension of advanced capitalist negativity does not seem particularly different from that advanced by Means; only his "solutions" are different. b) And, as Vine Deloria Jr. points out, compellingly, I think—the solutions hardly correspond to needs generated through the American Indian heritage and experience. Thus, although Sipe's recipe for the nature of the new society may be applicable to the European heritage, for Indians it is a matter of attempting to drive round pegs into square holes—at any cost.

This, it seems to me, is a central theme common to all the Indian contributors to this volume. The Marxist analysis of capitalism is a good beginning , at least in large part: it is held in common and even expanded upon by a number of Native American militants and traditionalists. As Phil Heiple points out, where Indians and Marxists part company lies within the realm of conclusions to be drawn from analyses of what is wrong with the capitalist process; with a vision of an alternative society. Beyond redistribution of the products of capitalism itself, Indian critics see little differentiation between the two supposedly contending modes. And redistribution of the proceeds accruing from a systematic rape of the earth is, at best, an irrelevancy to American Indian tradition.

Confronted with such argumentation, Marxists seem to have little with which to reply other than to insist that deindustrialization is "impractical" (so say the capitalists, as well). Beyond this, they simply begin to repeat—as if by rote—their arguments toward the humanization of society through worker control of the means of production and concomitant redistribution of the wealth produced. At best, Marxists such as Tabb acknowledge the substance of Indian criticism through agreement that technological solutions to the environmental impact of industry are not only crucial but must be supplemented by a reevaluation of society's priorities in relation to the natural world. More commonly, it is assumed that under socialism the technological problems will take care of themselves.

The Indians in this volume have suggested (or demanded) something rather different than application of the proverbial technological fix. Rhetorically at least, much of Marxism agrees much more profoundly with Dupont ("Better Living Through Chemistry") Chemicals and Philips ("we can make a well-head blend with any environment") Petroleum than with any of the Indian contributors. Small wonder then that Means refers to "continuity rather than revolution" as the Marxist credo, and calls both capitalism and Marxism just the "same old song" of Europe.

Such a situation may seem paradoxical. That avowed revolutionaries might allow such obvious commonality between themselves and their "opposition" presents a riddle. It may be explained through another theme, one which runs with amazing consistency through all the Marxist writing in this volume: The forces of capitalism are as inevitable and natural a circumstance as earthquake and glaciation, as primeval as life. In sum, they are byproducts of "human nature," the "scientific laws" of human development, as Marx once put it.

That capitalism is a system composed of a myriad of *human* decisions, and glaciation is not, is a distinction which seems to escape them. In elevating a humanly determined system to the status of a "natural law" they have predetermined their inability to determine what alternatives are actually viable; the choice has been made by the very system they ostensibly oppose. To quote Engels, as cited by the RCP in underpinning to polemic against

Means, "The forces operating in society work exactly like the forces operating in nature..." Even Tabb, who seems to reject the "inevitable natural law" interpretation, can find no better analogy for the futility of denying the inevitability of industrialism. "You might as well rage against the wind for blowing or the moon for casting its light across the night sky."

From first to last, Marxists insist upon the specific inevitability of industrialization and capitalism as sanctification of their "science" in the same fashion that biologists approach theirs: through assertion of unassailable physical *fact*. From this perspective, Marxists can no more step outside their preconceptions of order to seriously entertain other considerations than a responsible biologist could reasonably engage in professional discourse on the aeronautical characteristics of the blue whale.

This is no doubt understandable, given the assumed validity of the perspective in question. The problem is that the validity is *only* assumed, never proven. For all Karl Marx's elaborate attempts to establish his theory as an "objective" or even physical science, he was unsuccessful, partly because he limited his data essentially to a single cultural context. That the examples of other cultures could well have served to refute the "iron laws" of societal evolution into capitalism seems hardly arguable, since only Europe has ever followed that particular trajectory. But to truly allow for this disparity from culture to culture would necessarily have removed the aura of objective fact from his pronouncements, leaving instead the mist of social science subjectivity.

It was thus left to those who came after Marx to uphold his scientism through the exclusion of all examples, all data which would diminish and impugn the Marxian hypothesis, constructing instead ever more insular layers of "proof" and reinforcement. Such phenomena are, of course, not without precedent in the realm of pseudo-science. Consider the Piltdown hoax, or the more recent flocking of the US anthropological community to validate the fabrications of Carlos Castaneda. These two examples were debunked in a quarter-century and less than a decade respectively, while Marxism has lasted nearly a century and a half. All of Castaneda's supporters have disappeared now, except for a few who rallied to his "insights" like true religious zealots. Adherents to Marxism, under its many factional guises, burgeon with the passage of time. We are confronted with something rather more than a false lead in the area of science. False leads can generally be dispensed with through the extension of contradicting data and the logic of informed argument. Marxism is a self-contained system, allowing consideration only of data which serve to perpetuate it; logic and evidence are of no use in confronting it. Since Marx, the Marxian question has always been "how?", but never "whether?" The latter approach is magically but no less inevitably diverted back into the former through sheer reiteration of scriptural "fact." This is the foundation of no known science. Rather, it is the assertion of will, of faith and of pure religiousity. The RCP's Bob Avakian is thus little more (or less) than a Marxist equivalent to Oral Roberts, Sipe and Tabb equivalents to Chardin.

Marxism is predicated upon capitalism for its very existence, and it believes in the same things at base. It can only continue, never truly renounce its industrial heritage, for to do so would represent its own negation. Hence, it must insist on the ultimate negation of all that is non-industrial as the final signification of its sanctity, its "scientific" correctness. That this flies directly in the face of any conceivably "liberatory" ethic is irrelevant to true believers. Species suicide may well be the result of the "iron laws of history" and a small price to pay for final validation. That Russell Means rejects this as an alternative route to liberating his people from the death-grip of imperialism should come as no surprise.

Nor should Deloria's observation that Marxism reduces to little more than "materialist missionarism." He is, after all, a trained theologian. He recognizes missionary zeal when he meets or reads it, regardless of its anti-religious trappings. And as might be expected, the Marxist counter-arguments seem weak. For example, the contention that Deloria and other Indians "look to the past" for illustrations of Native American differentiation are both inaccurate and irrelevant. First, traditional Indian cultures—contrary to Euro mythology of the "vanishing redman"—continue to exist with an amazing vitality and continuity on a number of reservations. Hence, "past" is hardly an appropriate term to apply to the substance of Deloria's examples.

Second, Deloria never argues for the recreation of the specific physical context of the nineteenth century, but to a further reliance upon the *values* and *worldview* of a cultural reality which has long demonstrated its ability to eliminate social alienation in ways only speculated upon by Marxists. Analyses of contemporary Indian traditionalism as somehow "past" dovetail neatly with references to contemporary non-industrial cultures as "early."

Such semantic gambits are intended to mask (though they do a poor job of it) a cultural chauvinism and arrogance built into the Marxist outlook which is addressed by Frank Black Elk when he picks up Deloria's comparison of Marxism to missionarism. Black Elk, however, makes his approach in primarily concrete rather than theoretical terms, calling on his own life experiences to punctuate his points. A veritable one-two punch is thus afforded between theory and practice which should give pause to thinking Marxists, but one which is neatly sidestepped by the other contributors. For example, while Tabb focuses with some enthusiasm on Black Elk's stated perceptions of at least potential commonality between Lakota tradition and that of Marxism, he homes precisely upon the aspect of Black Elk's essay which serves, however tenuously, to validate the principles of Marxist doctrine.

And with the exception of Tabb, the Marxist contributors insist that the elaborate texture of Marxism represents a necessary and "overarching" reality to which Indians and their insights must inevitably be subordinated. The first priority is for Native Americans to become intimately acquainted with this implicitly more "advanced" perspective, so that they will be in a position to assist in the perfection of Marxism. Marxists uniformly maintain that theirs is the "superior" system, all the while picking off pieces of "Indian-ness" with which to enrich their outlook. Sipe discovers that Indians may well be living a "prefiguration" of the coming socialist order, a way out of the "oedipal" tangle of capitalist socialization. Tabb and Sipe acknowledge that "Indians have much to tell us" about matters such as ecology, evironment, and "appropriate technology." One might add, about agriculture, pharmacology and a few other things as well, if Marxists were "astute enough to listen." But there are many ways to listen.

(The reader will forgive me if I recall that it was the major formulative aspect of this book—an aspect expressed to all contributors along the way—that it was Marxism which was to respond to critique by defining its utility and potential to Indians, *not* the other way around. It seems dubious at this point that many Indians have been or are likely to be swayed by the Marxist articulations here. The Marxists, on the other hand, seem to have gleaned a lot of potential from the Indian view, if only for deployment within Marxism...which is what the Indians have insisted thoroughout. This should tell someone something.)

The positive contributions available within indigenous traditions which might be made, contributions which should surprise no one except Euro-supremicists, are not at issue here. The point is whether Marxism is intent upon a symbiotic or even a reciprocal relationship with non-European cultures and traditions. Truly, we find even the more "sympathetic" Marxist contributors to this volume skimming off the "high points" of Indian culture for potential incorporation into *their* system. And what do they offer in exchange? Only the "superiority" of an analytical system which is at best substantially similar to that already utilized by the Indian, and a set of conclusions, the outcome of which would necessarily be the dissolution of Indian culture. One hears echoes of the crusaders pirating the concept of the vaulted arch from the "heathen" Moors and incorporating it into European architecture. European systems and institutions have always enriched themselves with the knowledge and at the expense of non-Europeans. It is a method Martin Carnoy calls "cultural imperialism."

Empire, whether it be physical or intellectual, must be defended. Hence, one finds even the most clear-thinking Marxists resorting to all manner of strange and wonderful arguments as a means of defending the sanctity and hegemony of their theoretical domain. Witness Bill Tabb warning Indians that their traditional culture cannot prevail insofar as their "elected" leaders cooperate with the federal government. Aside from the observable fact that this is precisely the same rationale utilized by the Bureau of Indian Affairs to impose *its* "superior" vision and management upon Indians, what does this mean?

Tabb maintains that Indians must "face the reality of their own elected officials selling out the traditional Indian way of life." Conversely, the BIA holds that Indians must face the fact that traditionalism sells out "progress." Does Tabb concur? Clearly, his version of progress would differ from that projected in BIA scenarios, but the suggestion is that traditionalism is a "write-off" either way, whether its passing is assisted or lamented. And this hinges, neatly, on the fact that *elected* officials are involved.

As Tabb should know, this democratic jargon is extremely misleading. The system of so-called elected officials never derived from traditional culture, nor does it in any way represent traditionals. It was in fact imposed from Washington, essentially by fiat, through the "Indian Reorganization Act of 1934." The traditionals did not and generally do not vote in the elections for the simple reason that voting was not and is not a part of *their* traditional form of governing themselves. The tribal councils referred to are the appurtenances of colonial rule, and are thus designed to sell out traditionalism at every turn. How such a system works should present no particular mystery to anyone at all knowledgable in the methodology of colonialist rule—like Tabb.

The sell-out by "elected officials" has never precluded Marxists from advocating the development of autonomous local resistance struggles. To put it another way, would Marxists have been inclined to advise the Castro brothers and Che Guevarra that the struggle for liberation in Cuba was hopeless because Batista was an obvious US puppet? Would they have sought to explain to Ho and Giap that the unification struggle in Vietnam should be considered as vain because the elected officials of the South had sold out to US interests? What would their advice have been to Fanon during the latter's preparation of manuscripts concerning the anti-colonial struggle in Algeria?

The situational analyses in these cases rack up rather differently than that usually afforded to Indian activists. Why? Surely the acutely negative objective conditions facing the other dissidents were at times comparable to those facing Indians in this country to-day. Yet the left is known to have frequently and loudly proclaimed that those who were so badly outgunned eventually won out in each case, won with active moral support from Marxists and people of conscience abroad. Such support is frequently denied Indian resistence fighters through precisely Tabb's formulation, which somehow proves that *their* cause is much more hopeless than the rest.

Of course, each struggle at some level or another is emphatically different from the others. On the other hand, each of the non-Indian struggles is the same insofar as they share a doctrinal adherence to the principles of Marxism. Should Russell Means and John Trudell suddenly announce a newfound faith in Marxist scripture, one is forced to wonder whether Marxists might equally suddenly discover a way to overcome the reality of the sell-out of tribal officials. At that moment, might the left find some corner within the Marxist analysis for a prospering of Indian traditionalism?

These correspondences between the arguments advanced by Tabb and orthodox Marxist positions give rise to questions about the "missionarism" attributed by Deloria and others to Marxist theory and practice. Tabb has done and continues to do work with Indian-focused organizations such as the Black Hills Alliance. His work, noted in his essay, relative to the 1980 Black Hills International Survival Gathering was commendable; his services are valuable, his explanations of the intricacies of advanced capitalist processes gladly accepted and put to use. But this does not deny the appropriateness of the question which must be asked of *any* Marxist: Does he or she come *ultimately* to join an extant and ongoing struggle conducted by local people, or do they come to transform that struggle into a reflection and validation of their own faith? Are they ultimately supporters or recruiters? Fighters of this struggle or missionaries of another? Such questions perhaps carry with them no immediacy— Marxists, after all, are not presently in power in the United States. But as Means rightly insists, in the longer view these issues will emerge as crucial considerations.

This dynamic is explicit in Sipe, who calls upon Native Americans to develop a "class consciousness" as a means to associate themselves with the broader mass of common oppression and common interest across the nation. While Sipe presumably means more than just economic class, the terminology minimizes the vast differences between the oppression of the Indian and the proletariat under capitalism. American Indians have no class in any conventional sense; insofar as they have become proletarians (usually unemployed) they have already been torn from their traditional cultures—a condition that Sipe and Heiple, for example, want to encourage, as it provides potential supporters for *their* cause.

Where is it written in Marxist scripture that the colonized, as a matter of "first priority," must identify with the working class of the colonizing power? Fanon has been stood on his head. Did not Sartre argue convincingly enough that the task of Marxism (and the left in general) was to convince the working class of France that their class interests lay *with the colonized* of Algeria? In the US, this flow is magically reversed: the "black skin, white masks" of Fanon's thesis are to be imposed by the "liberatory" doctrine of Marxism itself.

Many Marxists even go beyond Sipe's position to ridicule Native American Third World "pretensions." In this view, the colonial equation is predicated upon the existence, occupation and adequate defense of a defined (or at least definable) homeland, a contention which would no doubt cause a certain consternation among Palestinians. Since the American Indian cannot be counted upon to successfully defend reservation areas against all-out military assault by the United States, the whole consideration of engagement in purely anti-colonial struggle is dismissed as absurd. In effect: "Indians should give up this delusional nonsense of retaining their cultures and homelands, getting on with the *important* business of merging with the interests expressed by everyone else among the opposition." Of course, there is a word for this line of thinking and action: assimilation. Its result is cultural genocide. Abandonment of their landbase is not an option for Native Americans, either in fact or in theory. The result would simply be "auto-genocide."

These are points which are bound to induce something less than enthusiastic trust and confidence among Indians concerning the "alternatives, benefits and solutions" available to them through contemporary Marxist thinking. To the contrary, it seems almost as if the Marxist contributors to this book had decided among themselves to validate Russell Means' "harsh" assessment that Marxism is identical in its implications for indigenous peoples as is capitalism, intentions notwithstanding. Certainly, they have proceeded to bear him out through all manner of contradictory and convoluted logic. When seeming opposites become ideologically fused, a whole results. In a sense, the Indian critique of Marxism likens its relationship to capitalism as a sort of parallel to the relationship of the democratic and republican parties within the United States. Between democrats and republicans ideological distinctions certainly exist and are the source of bitter controversy. To a Marxist, such distinctions are insubstantial, idle chatter, the contestants represent basically the same thing regardless of style and inflection. So too, to traditionalist Native Americans, are the finely wrought differentiations betwen Marxists and capitalists.

To a democrat or republican, the terms of the game are clearly understood and representative of the "realistic" choices available. It must seem inconceivable to either that another individual might reasonably step outside the game altogether and thereby determine other viable options, options which truly transcend the so-called "left-right dichotomy" within US electoral politics. Yet any Marxist can testify that one may take such a step and, indeed, be the better for it. Once taken, the step beyond the electoral system opens new vistas of opportunity, releases the shackles of narrowly defined political constraints, and so on. The choice between democrat and republican seems trivial or irrelevant to the Marxist, and the Marxist is no doubt right in this summation.

Yet, as democrats and republicans cannot allow that their perspective might be usefully transcended, neither can Marxists. The idea that there are other views on this planet which go well beyond the limits afforded through their system is as alien to them as it is to their capitalist counterparts. And as Milton Friedman and William F. Buckley resort to all manner of spurious "technique" to defend their chosen doctrine from transcendence, so too do Marxists. As defensive polemic takes hold, the openness necessary for theoretical development atrophies, and the basis for broadening the range of understanding disappears. Doctrine becomes dogma, regardless of the sophistication and permutations of its articulation. So it is with Marxism, and so it has been for some time.

Perpetual incantation of the catechism of Marxist virtue does no more to favorably resolve the situation than do similar pronouncements on the part of exponents of "free market" doctrine. As Means observed, Marxism and capitalism are two sides of the same coin. He then went on to describe the fundamental attributes he perceived the contenders holding in common. None of the Marxist rejoinders refuted, or really attempted to refute, any point of that list. Yet each in turn professed to be appalled at his conclusion, insisting he was wrong despite tacitly acknowledging his correctness through the lack of refutation.

The two sides of the coin are thus demonstrably fused, although one half still demands to be considered as operating independently of the other. The coin may well believe this, but observers need not follow suit. A term is necessary to denote the phenomenon; Means employs "Euro" (a generic term, like "Indian"). It is perhaps not the best possible word choice (is "Indian"? "Native American"? "Amerindian"?), but it is at least accurate insofar as it ascribes the origins of the outlooks that Indians find both synonomous and reprehensible—capitalism, Marxism and missionarism—to Europe, cultural transplantations from that continent to this. Until Marxism can extricate itself from its commonality in existence with capitalism it can never be other than "Euro," a part of the same cultural coin.

Nonetheless Means maintains that "Euro" is a mindset, a worldview, not an innate characteristic which accompanies white skin. As was noted earlier, the "system," whether defined as Marxist or capitalist or Euro, is composed of human actions, human decisions. Only those devoutly religious in their zeal would ascribe its existence to an act of god, something not to be transcended through conscious counter-action. For them, there may well be no hope; regrettably this neurosis encompasses all who hold their human system to have been enacted as a primeval force, Marxists or not.

That one need not be genetically, or even culturally for that matter, non-European in order to transcend the binary options of the Marxist/capitalist coin is demonstrated by the recent phenomenon of "post-Marxist" theory. This process of "immanent critique" (identical in name and practice to the methods employed by Karl Marx in transcending Feuerbach) represents Marxists themselves overcoming the inherent contradictions of their system which has long left that doctrine hopelessly theological and ethnocentric in its basic assumptions. Perhaps the exemplary exponent of this practice is the French writer Jean Baudrillard whose book, *The Mirror of Production,* should be read by all, especially Marxists, who have been given even brief pause by the Indian critique offered in the present volume. This holds particularly true for Baudrillard's essay "Marxist Anthropology and the Domination of Nature." The reader will find that despite a rather tortuous language and occasionally circuitous route, Baudrillard arrives at many of the same conclusions as Means, Deloria and myself, and for virtually the same reasons. For example:

> Radical in its *logical* analysis of capital,, Marxist theory nonetheless maintains an *anthropological* consensus with the options of Western rationalism in its definitive form acquired in eighteenth century bourgeois thought. Science, technology, progress, history— in these ideas we have an entire civilization that comprehends itelf as producing its own development and takes its dialectical force towards completing humanity in terms of totality and happiness. Nor did Marx invent the concepts of genesis, development and finality. He changed nothing basic regarding the *idea* of man *producing* himself in his infinite determination, and continually surpassing himself toward his own end.

This, despite an entirely different sort of background and heritage from any Native American author.

The Indian arguments are thus no more innately Indian than "Euro-consciousness" is innately the property of those possessing caucasian genes. They are shared in large part by at least a few European theorists. This, it would seem to me, represents something of a breakthrough, if only a small one at present. But to paraphrase Marcuse, it is from such small breakthroughs that the overcoming of false consciousness can occur. The route currently being explored by American Indian activists (and other Third or Fourth Worlders) from one cultural perspective and, from another by Baudrillard and other post-Marxists, suggests itself as an obvious course to be pursued beyond the discussion contained in this book.

This is, however, a more or less purely theoretical direction. Many people, Marxists and Indians alike, are not particularly inclined toward the rarified atmosphere of fullblown abstraction. More direct sorts of activity are required to allow for constructive participation by all those of Marxian bent who wish to test the reality behind the Indian words contributed to this dialogue.

Here I whole heartedly concur with the line of activity undertaken by Bill Tabb in his association with the Black Hills Alliance. I also completely agree with his evaluation of the 1980 Black Hills International Survival Gathering, sponsored in large part by the Alliance, as a singularly important event. I would suggest, however, that generalized support for and participation in Alliance activities not be restricted to major and spectacular demonstrations such as the Gathering. There is day to day struggle being waged. Marxists can learn the realities of this struggle through direct participation on a consistent basis.

Prior to undertaking such a line of action, a bit of factual orientation (as opposed to theory) seems imperative. This is multifaceted and could easily become a carreer occupation, so little is really known by the bulk of the American left about the Indian experience in America, but I will attempt to assemble a rudimentary "crash course" which will allow up front perspective. First, everyone needs "historical grounding," so a copy of Francis Jennings' *The Invasion of America* and Dee Brown's *Bury My Heart at Wounded Knee* are in order. A number of leftists have read the latter, but a rereading never hurts. The problem is, however, that few leftists ever go beyond this rather minimal historical perspective in attempting to truly understand things Indian.

A second historical orientation is needed, and in a rather less glamorous vein. This concerns the evolution of Indian policy from 1776 through the present. Here *Indian Treaties: Two Centuries of Dishonor* by the American Indian Historical Society and Vine Deloria's *Of Utmost Good Faith* represent a good start. For a particularly contemporary twist, Deloria's *Behind the Trail of Broken Treaties* would be helpful, as would Roxanne Dunbar Ortiz' *The Great Sioux Nation.* As to achieving a grasp of events within the Indian movement itself, *Voices From Wounded Knee: 1973* by the people of Akwesasne is critical. They also put out a paper, *Akwesasne Notes*, which is probably the premier tabloid publication of the Indian opposition, and back issues are sold (covering a full decade of activity) in bundles at a nominal rate. They are well worth it. A reading of Bruce Johannsen and Roberto Maestes' *Wasi'chu: The Continuing Indian Wars* and Rex Wyler's *Blood of the Land* will round out the package.

It seems that most non-Indians, for whatever reasons, wish a grounding in "Indian spirituality" before approaching Native American settings. This is well nigh impossible, particularly through such standards as *Black Elk Speaks, Lame Deer: Seeker of Visions and The Sacred Pipe*, all of which attempt (unsuccessfully) to convey literal content to the uninitiated. I will recommend only Vine Deloria's *God is Red* and *The Metaphysics of Modern Existence* to offer appropriate insights, as well as to explain why detailed *knowledge* is impossible in this connection on the basis of literature. At this point, the nature of Indian issues should be emerging.

Next, a visual exercise is in order. Acquire a standard Bureau of Indian Affairs map indicating the location and boundaries of all current reservation areas. It comes in black and white, so color in the reservations with a red magic marker or colored pencil. Pin it to your wall. Practice looking at the scale of the landbase involved, not as federal trust areas akin to national parks, but as sovereign territories guaranteed in perpetuity by internationally binding treaty agreements between the United States government and the various Indian tribes. Consider the implications of these nations lying *within* the borders of the United States itself; they are *internal* colonies presently engaged to varying extents in anti-colonial struggle.

Two things should have occurred at this point for persons who approach the project with an open mind. First, the potential for oppositional action, centering upon tangibles such as landbase rather than abstractions on the order of "class interest" and (worse) "repressive desublimation" should be starkly evident. Concomitantly, the threat to the stability of the status quo should be readily apparent. A whole body of anti-colonial theory should spring to the mind of any well-read leftist and serve to underscore this point. Preliminary factual orientation should now be complete.

One is now ready to begin the approach to direct action per se, but as a novice, not an "expert." These readings and exercises have barely scratched the surface of what must be learned. The particulars of struggle, in America as much as anywhere in the world, are intrinsically the product of local conditions and local people. The latter are the experts. Initially at least, information flow is likely to be one way; "they" will inform you as to the meaning, content and importance of various actions and phenomena. There is very little of relevance you may initially impart, no doubt a bitter psychological pill for a member of a tradition predicated upon "explaining the world to itself."

Only through learning the specifics of the local struggle can one hope to "fit it into the broader picture" without intellectually forcing it, *a priori*, into the constraints of preconception and stereotype. Often, the "broader picture" itself is changed for the better in the process. This is an entirely valid methodology seemingly long forgotten by the American left, at least where Indians are concerned. Such a prescription does nothing of itself to deny the analytical utility of Marxism in understanding the internal dynamics of capitalism (which Marxists seem so defensive about). It does, on the other hand, preclude Marxism's *automatic* assignment to itself of "most favored theoretical status," from overriding ("overarching") the reality with which it purports to deal. Or, to put it another way, it allows Marxism— finally—to remain true to Marx's own methodological structure, as spelled out by Elisabeth Lloyd.

Perhaps through the simple expedient of taking Marx at his word within his methodological postulations, Marxists can overcome the long stasis of ethnocentrism deriving from confusion of the tenets of general theory and the specific byproducts of his investigation of particulars. It can be argued, after all, that Marx designed his system to transcend *itself*. If there is any merit at all to that point, Marxists have long since failed the promise of their first thinker. Baudrillard is generations overdue.

Such a move would do much to start the removal of the intellectual baggage currently impeding or preventing fruitful intercultural dialogue, understanding and joint action. And it would do more: in recognizing the Eurocentrism of the assumption of economic determinism, Marxism could open itself up to the full range of socio-cultural realities operant within the European paradigm itself. Thus could Marxists at long last begin to *fully* investigate the meanings and functions of such things as kinship structures, sex roles, and aging, long subordinated—in their guise of mere "superstructural" elements—to the tyranny of the economic base.

This prospect should be encouraging, indeed stimulating, to those seeking true understanding of and solutions to the vast complexity of interpenetrating problems facing us all. At minimum, the proposition should hold nothing fearful to anyone with an open and reasonably inquiring mind. In such an endeavor, those such as American Indians, who harken from markedly different patterns of socio-cultural experience, should prove admirable allies if accepted for whom and what they are, rather than what they are needed to be by the requirements of one or another theoretical predetermination.

In any event, a first locus of action is necessary. In this, I would immediately recommend (and anticipate Tabb's agreement) that the place to begin such participation is with the Black Hills Alliance, in whatever form of activity is deemed desirable by the locals. They may well recommend certain types of activity within your own home area: work for the Leonard Peltier or Dick Marshall legal defense efforts, for example. At times, lobbying efforts are extremely important in certain areas. Participation in information dissemination efforts is always important on a fully national basis, and so on. They will probably attempt to put you in contact with groups associated with the Alliance functioning in your area, invite you to visit their Rapid City, South Dakota offices, or both.

Another possibility, depending largely upon the circumstances of your contact, is that they recommend you lend your support—in a variety of ways—to *Wakinyan Zi Tiospaye*

(Yellow Thunder Camp), a reoccupation of usurped treaty land in the Black Hills region of South Dakota undertaken by Dakota AIM and Oglala Lakota tribal elders on April 4, 1981. This, for a number of reasons, is a watershed anti-colonial action within the contemporary United States. It directly confronts the nature and history of violation of the 1868 Fort Laramie Treaty (you'll have already learned the basics of this while reading *The Great Sioux Nation*). Few clearer bases for such action exist. The issues are so crystalline that they are immediately understandable to most people and thus represent an excellent general organizing tool.

My reason for recommending that one begin with the Black Hills Alliance rather than with Yellow Thunder itself is twofold. First, the Alliance is unique in that it incorporates a "United Front" approach juxtaposing white ranchers, militant miners, Indian activists and non-Indian radicals. This it seems to me offers an excellent "entry vehicle" for anyone wishing to undertake a transition from an essentially non-Indian to a primarily Indian activist context. Yellow Thunder *is* emphatically Indian, although people of all races and cultures participate and are welcomed as relatives.

Second, Yellow Thunder is an ongoing occupation community. It is isolated. Support logistics can present a tremendous problem. Hence, it is not always appropriate or even possible for additional people to take up residence, even for short periods. Initial contact with the Alliance, which is in constant communication with the Yellow Thunder people, allows for a necessary control and screening mechanism as well as for assignment and coordination of useful support activities in other locations.

For those who still cannot reconcile themselves to a line of action which allows for unchallenged Indian leadership of Indian struggles and supports struggles for Indian self-determination at face value, free of a residual clutter of "class struggle" and the like, there remains a substantial basis for supportive participation. Consider that every inch of stolen ground recovered, every bit of control over resources regained, every iota of political autonomy achieved by anti-colonialist Native Americans comes directly from the imperial integrity of the US itself.

If the agendas of AIM, the International Treaty Council and other oppositional Indian groups were fulfilled, if the treaty obligations of the United States to the various tribes *which are on the books right now* were met, the landbase of the 48 contiguous states'would be diminished by approximately one third. Further, identified US energy resource reserves would be reduced by two thirds. Significant reserves of minerals including gold, silver, iron, molybdenum, magnesium, bauxite and sulfur would also pass from US control. Any hard-nosed Marxist revolutionary should be able to detect the absolutely critical nature of the issues. By any definition, the mere potential for even a partial dissolution of the US landbase should be a high priority consideration for *anyone* concerned with destabilizing the status quo.

Of course "the Indian can't go it alone." The Indian never asked to. Native Americans are being forced to attempt to do so by a persistent demand from all quarters that they stop being Indian as a precondition to assistance. The Indian can do little to change this, but those doing the demanding can. Assistance and support without preconditions are entirely within the grasp of Marxists and progressives in general. The left in this country is in the process of missing a critical and unique opportunity to forge a truly *American* radicalism based first on those conditions which are most peculiar to America, one with a chance of cutting the US power structure deeply. By allowing American Indian struggles to be conducted in effective isolation while Marxism concerns itself with "more important matters" such as how to assert its "natural primacy" and hegemony over all liberatory strategies, the left is consigning itself to more of the repeated cycles of oblivion which has marked its history in the United States.

I share with various Marxist authors in this book a belief that the Native American has much to teach Marxism. I differ in that I don't hold that the way for this to occur is for Indians to become Marxists, but that through wide-eyed participation in Indian liberation struggles on Indian terms Marxists will learn much about themselves with which to alter and enrich their own doctrines and traditions. I rely upon direct action and experience to overcome the defects of theory and massive ignorance of the first Americans which currently pervades contemporary US Marxist thinking, and I extend a basic human faith that such new found knowledge can be put to use in better assisting the process of decolonizing the Indian nations. I call *this* common ground.

If Yellow Thunder and the other active liberation struggles of Native America are defeated while the left stands idly by debating "correct lines" and "social priorities," a crucial opportunity to draw a line on the capitalist process in America will have been lost, perhaps forever. In view of the emergence of outright American neo-fascism—as represented by the "New Right" and "Moral Majority"—none of us can afford to pass such opportunities by, least of all on points of polemical pride.

A generalized and consistent left support for Native American causes *could* be enough to tip the scale toward limited wins in issues of land/resource rights and sovereignty. These wins can and should be rallying point for *all* oppositional people. Bill Tabb has said, "Let the debate continue." I would only add, "and let the action begin."

NOTES AND BIBLIOGRAPHIES

Notes For
The Same Old Song In Sad Refrain
by Ward Churchill and Dora Lee Larson

1. The language related to the *Insurgent Sociologist* request for manuscripts comes from correspondence to Ward Churchill generated by Eugene (Ore.) editorial collective member, Rebecca McGovern. The request was reiterated on several occasions, verbally. The language concerning the rejection was made by a regular *IS* consultant reader and editorial collective member at large who preferred (of course) to remain anonymous but who is known to be a white jr. college sociology teacher in Minnesota.

2. It could be asserted with equal validity that Means was applying the teachings of his *elders' elders*. See, by way of readily accessible examples, *Black Elk Speaks,* John G. Neihard (transcription), University of Nebraska Press, Lincoln, 1961 and *The Sacred Pipe,* Joseph Epes Brown (transcription), University of Oklahoma Press, Norman, 1953.

3. See *The Mirror of Production,* Jean Baudrillard, TELOS Press, St. Louis, 1977.

4. Leakey is more generally noted for his discovery of skeletal material of *Momo habilis* ("handy man") in Africa during the 1960's in "Zinjanthropus", a large variety of Australopithecine at Olduvi Gorge (East Kenya). These discoveries of "prehuman" types has led to a considerable revision of the theoretics concerning human evolution. His final discoveries at Calico Hills, in conjunction with Ms. Ruth deEtte Simpson, could have even more far-reaching consequences in rearranging notions of evolutionary chronology and geography. See "Archeological Excavations in the Calico Mountains, California: Preliminary Report", L. S. B. Leakey, R. E. Simpson, and T. Clements, *Science,* V160, March 1, 1968. Also see *Leakey's Luck,* Sonia Cole, Harcourt Brace Jovanovick, New York, 1975.

5. There are, of course, exceptions to this position on the part of Native Americans; non-migration is not a monolithic belief. For example, in his book *They Came Here First,* D'Arcy McNickle accepted the 12,000 year Bering Strait land bridge position fully. Archeological data, however, disputes McNickel's contention as readily as anyone else's. It seems probable that the Eskimos and certain Athabascan groups *did* cross the Strait from Asia during the period in question; an interesting proposition in this connection, and one which seems to be gaining some degree of currency, is that these groups represent a *return* migration rather than a simple influx of population for reasons unknown.

6. Goodman has a book, *American Genesis: The American Indian and the Origins of Modern Man* (Summit Books, New York, 1980) which covers not only his own work in the Flagstaff area, but the whole of the data underpinning reverse migration theory. The bulk of the data in this section derives from that book.

7. For an articulation of how these demographic calculations have been derived over the past century, see *The Invasion of America*, Francis Jennings, (W. W. Norton, New York, 1975). Also see Wilber Jacobs testimony on Native American demography as presented at the 1976 Sioux Sovereignty Hearings and published in *The Great Sioux Nation: Sitting in Judgement on America*, Roxanne Dunbar Ortiz, Moon Books, New York/San Francisco, 1977.

8. See Roxanne Dunbar Ortiz' testimony on indigenous agricultural economies in *The Great Sioux Nation*, op. cit.

9. For a brilliant and closely reasoned articulation of the implications of the second law of thermal dynamics in the socio-industrial context, see *Entropy: A New World View*, Jeremy Rifkin with Ted Howard, New York: Viking Press, 1980.

10. See *Selections From V. I. Lenin and J. V. Stalin on the National Colonial Question*, Calcutta Book House, Calcutta, India, 1970.

Bibliography for
The Same Old Song In Sad Refrain
By Ward Churchill and Dora Lee Larson

Baudrillard, Jean, *The Mirror of Production,* St. Louis, Missouri: TELOS Press, 1977.

Brown, Joseph Epes, (Transcription), *The Sacred Pipe: Black Elk's Account of the Seven Rites of the Oglala Sioux,* Norman, Oklahoma: University of Oklahoma Press, 1953.

Cole, Sonia, *Leakey's Luck,* New York: Harcourt Brace Jovanovick, 1975.

Goodman, Dr. Jeffrey, *American Genesis: The American Indian and the Origins of Modern Man,* New York: Summit Books, 1980.

Jennings, Francis, *The Invasion of America: Indians, Colonists and the Cant of Conquest,* New York: W. W. Norton Co., 1975.

Leakey, L. S. B., R. E. Simpson, and T. Clemments, "Archeological Excavations in the Calico Mountains, California: Preliminary Report," *Science,* V160, March 1, 1968.

Lenin, V. I., and J. V. Stalin, *Selections From V. I. Lenin and J. V. Stalin on the National Colonial Question,* Calcutta Book House, Calcutta, India, 1970.

McNickle, D'Arcy, *They Came Here First: The Epic of the American Indian,* New York: Harper and Row, 1949.

Neihard, John G., (Transcription), *Black Elk Speaks: Being the Life Story of a Holy Man of the Oglala Sioux,* Lincoln, Nebraska: University of Nebraska Press, 1961.

Ortiz, Dr. Roxanne Dunbar, *The Great Sioux Nation: Sitting in Judgement on America,* New York and San Francisco: International Treaty Council/Moon Books, 1977.

Rifkin, Jeremy with Ted Howard, *Entropy: A New World View,* New York: Viking Press, 1980.

Notes For
Marx's General Cultural Theoretics
By Elisabeth Lloyd

1. See Bertell Ollman, "With Words That Appear Like Bats," *Alienation,* 2nd Edition, Cambridge University Press, 1976.

2. This is essentially Lenin's articulation of triadic dialectical characteristics, as expressed in his *Karl Marx,* Foreign Language Press, Peking, 1976.

3. For a fuller and quite lucid examination of dialectical ontology and epistemology, see Michael Albert and Robin Hahnel, *Unorthodox Marxism,* South End Press, Boston, 1979.

4. The quotation from Althusser is gleaned from the glossary of his *For Marx,* Vintage Books, New York, 1969.

5. Albert and Hahnel, op. cit., p. 53.

6. *Introduction to the Critique of Political Economy,* Vintage Books, New York, 1973, p. 302.

7. Ibid., p. 300.

8. Ibid., p. 294.

9. *The Communist Manifesto,* Washington Square Press, New York, 1967, p. 36.

10. *Grundrisse,* Vintage Books, New York, 1973, p. 600.

11. *Introduction to the Critique of Political Economy,* p. 292.

12. Ibid., p. 278

13. Ibid., p. 276

14. Ibid., p. 291. Also: the "totality of social life" which Marx seeks to explain is, as he tells us on another occasion, "the reciprocal action of the various sides on one anther," *The German Ideology,* International Publishers, New York, 1939, p. 28.

15. Paul La Fargue is quoted from "Reminiscences of Marx," *Reminiscences of Marx and Engels,* Moscow, no date, p. 78.

16. Many of the formulations in this section are borrowed from the work of Bertell Ollman.

17. *Grundrisse.* p. 176.

18. Ibid., p. 600.

19. *Marx and Engels: Selected Correspondence.* ed. and trans. Dona Torr, London, 1940, p. 7.

20. *The Holy Family,* International Publishers, New York, 1949, p. 163.

21. *Introduction to the Critique of Political Economy,* p. 268.

22. *The Economic and Philosophic Manuscripts of 1844,* International Publishers, New York, 1973, p. 75.

23. Ibid.

24. *The German Ideology*, p. 7.
25. *Economic and Philosophic Manuscripts of 1844*, p. 72; *Grundrisse*, p. 505.
26. Ollman, op. cit., p. 23.
27. *Marx and Engels: Selected Correspondence*, p. 447.
28. *Capital, Vol. III*, New World Publishers, New York, 1967.
29. *Poverty of Philosophy*, Moscow, no date, p. 195; and *Letters to Kugleman*, London, 1941. p. 19.
30. *The Economic and Philosophic Manuscripts of 1844*, p. 105.

Bibliography for
Marx's General Cultural Theoretics
By Elisabeth Lloyd

Albert, Michael; and Hahnel, Robin, *Unorthodox Marxism*, South End Press, Boston, 1979.

Althusser, Louis, *For Marx*, Vintage Books, New York, 1969.

Engels, Freidrick, *The Dialectics of Nature*, International Publishers, New York, 1940.

LaFargue, Paul, *Reminiscences of Marx and Engels*, Moscow, no date.

Lenin, V. I., *Karl Marx*, Foreign Language Press, Peking, 1967.

Mao Tsetung, *Selected Readings From the Works of Mao*, Foreign Language Press, Peking, 1971.

Marx, Karl, *Capital, Vol. III*, New World Publisher, New York, 1967.

Marx, Karl; and Engels, Freidrick, *(The) Communist Manifesto*, Washington Square Press, New York, 1967.

Marx, Karl, *(The) Economic and Philosophic Manuscripts of 1844*, International Publishers, New York, 1973.

Marx, Karl, *(The) German Ideology*, International Publishers, New York, 1934.

Marx, Karl, *(The) Grundrisse*, Vintage Books, New York, 1973.

Marx, Karl; and Engels, Freidrick, *(The) Holy Family*, International Publisher, New York, 1940.

Marx, Karl, *Letters to Klugeman*, London, 1941.

Marx, Karl; and Engels, Freidrick, *Marx and Engels: Selected Correspondence*, ed. and trans. by Dona Torr,.London, 1940.

Marx, Karl, *(The) Poverty of Philosophy*, Moscow, no date.

Ollman, Bertell, *Alienation*, 2nd edition, Cambridge University Press, 1976.

Notes For
Culture and Personhood
By Bob Sipe

1. Diamond, Stanley, "The Search for the Primitive," *The Concept of the Primitive,* Ashley Montague, ed., The Free Press, New York, 1968, p. 144.
2. Arato, Andrew and Eike Gebhardt, eds., *The Essential Frankfurt School Reader,* Urizen Books, New York, 1978, p. 185.
3. Marx, Karl, *Capital, Vol. 1,* Progress Publishers, Moscow, 1965, p. 183.
4. Markhovic, Mihailo, *From Affluence to Praxis,* University of Michigan Press, Ann Arbor, 1974, p. 66.
5. Horkeimer, Max, *Eclipse of Reason,* Seabury Press (a Continuum Book), New York, 1972, p. 270.
6. *Ibid.,* pp. 267-268.
7. Shroyer, Trent, *The Critique of Domination,* George Braziller, New York, 1973, pp. 30-31.
8. Jay, Martin, *The Dialectical Imagination,* Little Brown and Company, Boston, 1973, pp. 82-83.
9. *The Critique of Domination,* op. cit. p. 30.
10. Terkel, Studs, *Working,* Random House (Pantheon Books), New York, 1972.
11. Reich, Wilhelm, *Sex-Pol: Essays, 1929-1934,* Random House (Vintage Books), New York, 1972, p. 358.
12. *Capital,* op. cit., p. 72.
13. Berger, P., and S. Pullberg, "The Concept of Reification," *The New Left Review, 35,* London, 1966, p. 61.
14. *Ibid.*
15. *The Essential Frankfurt School Reader,* op. cit., p. 191.
16. Lukacs, George, *History and Class Consciousness: Studies in Marxist Dialectics,* Rodney Livingstone, trans., MIT Press, Cambridge, Ma., 1971.
17. *Ibid.,* p. 84.
18. *Ibid.,* p. 87.
19. *Ibid.,* p. 88.
20. *Ibid.,* p. 90.
21. Marcuse, Herbert, *One Dimensional Man,* Beacon Press, Boston, 1964, p. 12.
22. *Sex-Pol,* op. cit., pp. 234-235.
23. *One Dimensional Man,* op. cit. p. 77.
24. *Ibid.,* p. 30.

25. *Ibid.,* p. 71.
26. *Ibid.,* p. 57.
27. *Ibid.*
28. Freud, Sigmund, "Charachter and Anal Eroticism," *The Standard Edition of the Complete Works of Sigmund Freud, Vol. IX,* Hogarth Press, London, 1957, p. 198.
29. Reiche, Reimut, *Sexuality and Class Struggle,* Praeger Publishers, New York, 1971, p. 25.
30. "Character and Anal Erotoicism," op. cit., p. 201.
31. Marcuse, Herbert, *An Essay on Liberation,* Beacon Press, Boston, 1969, p. 47.
32. Aronowitz, Stanley, *False Promises: The Shaping of American Working Class Consciousness,* McGraw Hill, New York, 1973, pp. 74-75.
33. *An Essay on Liberation,* op. cit., p. 14.
34. *Sexuality and Class Struggle,* op. cit., pp. 135-136.
35. Laing, R. D., *The Divided Self,* Random House (Pantheon Books), New York, 1969, pp. 40-68.
36. Fromm, Eric, *Beyond the Chains of Illusion,* Simon and Schuster, New York, 1962, p. 56.
37. *Ibid.,* p. 140.
38. *An Essay on Liberation,* op. cit., p. 51.
39. "The Search for the Primitive," op. cit., pp. 124-126.

Bibliography for
Culture and Personhood
By Bob Sipe

Arata, Andrew and Eike Gebhardt, eds. *The Essential Franfurt School Reader.* New York: Urizen Books, 1978.

Aronowitz, Stanley. *False Promises, The Shaping of American Working Class Consciousness.* New York: McGraw-Hill, 1973.

Baran, Paul and Paul Sweezy. *Monopoly Capital, An Essay on the American Economic and Social Order.* New York: Monthly Review Press, 1966.

Baritz, Loren. *The Servants of Power: A History of the Use of Social Science in American Industry.* New York: John Wiley & Sons, 1965.

Blauner, Robert. *Aienation and Freedom, the Factory Worker and His Industry.* Chicago: University of Chicago Press, 1964.

Boadella, David. *Wilhelm Reich, The Evolution of His Work.* Chicago: Henry Regnery Co., 1974.

Braverman, Harry. *Labor and Monopoly Capital, The Degradation of Work in the Twentieth Century.* New York: Monthly Review Press, 1974.

Bright, James R. *Automation and Management.* Boston: Harvard University Press, 1958.

Brown, Bruce. *Marx, Freud and the Critique of Everyday Life.* New York: Monthly Review Press, 1973.

Crozier, Michel. *The World of the Office Worker.* Chicago & London: University of Chicago Press, 1971.

Edwards, Richard C.; Reich, Michael; and Weisskropf, Thomas E. *The Capitalist System, A Radical Analysis of American Society.* Englewood Cliffs, N.J.; Prentice-Hall, 1972.

Freud, Sigmund. *Civilization and Its Discontents.* New York: W. W. Norton and Co., 1961.

Freud, Sigmund. *Group Psychology and the Analysis of the Ego.* New York: Bantam Books, 1960.

Freud, Sigmund. *The Ego and the Id.* New York: W. W. Norton & Co., 1960.

Freud, Sigmund. *Three Contributions to the Theory of Sex.* New York: E. P. Dutton & Co., 1962.

Friedan, Betty. *The Feminine Mystique.* New York: Dell Pub. Co., 1963.

Fromm, Erich. *Beyond the Chains of Illusion.* New York: Simon and Schuster, 1962.

Fromm, Erich. *Crisis of Psychoanalysis, Essays on Marx, Freud and Social Psycholgoy.* New York: Holt, Rinehart, and Winston, 1970.

Fromm, Erich. *Escape from Freedom.* New York: Avon Books, 1941.

Fromm, Erich. *Man For Himself.* New York: Greenwich, Conn: Fawcett Pub., 1947.

Gerth, Hans and C. Wright Mills. *Characte and Social Structure.* New York: Harcourt Brace and World, Inc. (A Harbinger Book), 1953.

Gilbreth, Lillian. *The Psychology of Management. The Writings of the Gilbreths.* Edited by William R. Spriegel and Clark E. Meyers. Homewood, Ill: R. D. Irwin, 1953.

Greenstein, Fred I. *Personality and Politics, Problems of Evidence, Influence, and Conceptualization.* Chicago: Markham Pub. Co., 1969.

Horkheimer, Max. *Critical Theory.* New York: Seabury Press (A Continuum Book), 1969.

Horkheimer, Max. *Eclipse of Reason.* New York: Seabury Press, (A Continuum Book), 1974.

Israel, Joachim. *Alienation, from Marx to Modern Sociology.* Boston: Allyn and Bacon, Inc., 1971.

Jay, Martin. *The Dialectical Imagination.* Boston: Little, Brown & Co., 1973.

Laing, R. D. *The Divided Self.* New York: Random House (Pantheon Books), 1969.

Lens, Sidney. *The Labor Wars.* Garden City, N.Y.: Doubleday & Co. (Anchor Books), 1974.

Lowen, Alexander. *Bioenergetics.* New York: Coward, McCann & Geoghagen, Inc., 1975.

Lukacs, George. *History and Class Consciousness, Studies in Marxist Dialectics.* trans. by Rodney Livingstone. Cambridge, Mass: The MIT Press, 1971.

Marcuse, Herbert. *An Essay on Liberation.* Boston: Beacon Press, 1969.

Marcuse, Herbert. *Eros and Civilization.* New York: Random House (Vintage Books), 1955.

Marcuse, Herbert. *Negations.* Boston: Beacon Press, 1968.

Marcuse, Herbert. *One-Dimensional Man.* Boston: Beacon Press, 1964.

Markovic, Mihailo. *From Affluence to Praxis.* Ann Arbor, Mich.: University of Michigan Press, 1974.

Marx, Karl. *Capital,* Vols. I-III Moscow: Progress Publishers, 1965.

Marx, Karl and Frederick Engels. *Selected Works,* Vols. I-III. Moscow: Progress Publishers, 1969.   •

Maslow, Abraham. *Toward A Psychology of Being.* Princeton, N.J.: D. Van Nostrand Co., 1962.

McLean, Alan. *Mental Health and Work Organizations.* Chicago: Rand McNally & Co., 1970.

Pollard, Sidney. *The Genesis of Modern Management: A Study of the Industrial Revolution in Great Britain.* Cambridge, Mass.: Harvard University Press, 1965.

Reich, Wilhelm. *Function of the Orgasm.* New York: Farrar, Straus, and Giroux (Noonday Press), 1971.

Reich, Wilhelm. *Sex-Pol Essays,* 1929-1934. New York: Random House (Vintage Books), 1972.

Reich, Reimut. *Sexuality and Class Struggle.* New York: Praeger Publishers, 1971.

Sartre, Jean Paul. *Search for a Method.* New York: Alfred A. Knopf (Vintage Books), 1968.

Schiller, Herbert. *Mass Communication and American Empire.* Boston: Beacon Press, 1971.

Schiller, Herbert. *The Mind Managers.* Boston: Beacon Press, 1973.

Schroyer, Trent. *The Critique of Domination.* New York: George Braziller, 1973.

Shepard, Jon M. *Automation and Alienation: A Study of Office and Factory Workers.* Cambridge, Mass: Harvard Univ. Press, 1971.

Taylor, Frederick W. *The Principles of Scientific Management.* New York: Harper & Row, 1967.

Taylor, Frederick W. *Scientific Management.* New York and London: Harper, 1947. This single volume contains: *Shop Management* (1903); *Principles of Scientific Management* (1911); and a public document, *Hearings Before Special Committee of the House of Representatives to Investigate the Taylor and other Systems of Shop Management* (1912).

Thompson, E. P. *The Making of the English Working Class.* New York: Random House, 1963.

Zaretsky, Eli. *Capitalism. the Family, and Personal Life.* Santa Cruz, California: Loaded Press, 1974; (originally printed in *Socialist Revolution.* Jan.-June, 1973).

Adorno, Theodore, "Sociology and Psychology," *New Left Review,* 46, 1967, pp.

Berger, P. and S. Pullberg, "The Concept of Reification," *New Left Review,* 35, 1966, pp. 56-71.

Diamond, Stanley, "The Search for the Primitive," *The Concept of the Primitive.* Edited by Ashley Montague, New York: The Free Press, 1968.

Freud, Sigmund, "Character and Anal Eroticism," *The Standard Edition of the Complete Psychological Works of Sigmund Freud,* Vol. IX, London: Hogarth Press, 1975, pp. 169-175.

Freud, Sigmund, " 'Civilized' Sexual Morality and Modern Nervous Illness," *The Standard Edition of the Complete Psychological Works of Sigmund Freud,* Vol. IX, London: Hogarth Press, 1957, pp. 181-204.

Grannis, Joseph C., "The School as a Model of Society," *The Learning of Political Behavior,* Edited by Norman Adler and Charles Harrington, Glenview, Ill.: Scott Foresman & Co., 1970, pp. 139-148.

Marglin, Stephen A., "What The Bosses Do; The Origin and Function of Hierarchy in Capitalist Production, Parts I & II," *Review of Radical Political Economics,* Summer 1974, pp. 60-112; Spring 1975, pp. 20-37.

Portes, Alejandros, "On the Interpretation of Class Consciousness," *American Journal of Sociology,* Vol. 77, No. 2, Sept. 1971, pp. 228-244.

Rothschild, Emma, "GM in More Trouble," *New York Review of Books,* March 23, 1972, pp. 19-23.

Smith, M. Brewster, "A Map for the Analysis of Personality and Politics," *Journal of Social Issues,* Vol. XXIV, No. 3, 1

bibs, sipe bibliography

Notes for
Circling The Same Old Rock
by Vine Deloria Jr.
1. Schaff, Adam, *Marxism and the Human Individual*, p. 134.
2. Marcuse, Herbert, *Reason and Revolution*, p. 74.
3. *Ibid.* p. 319.
4. *Ibid.* p. 75.
5. Schaff, p. 73.
6. *Ibid.* p. 69.
7. *Ibid.* p. 100.
8. Marcuse, p. 77.
9. Fromm, Erich, *Marx's Concept of Man*, p. 47.
10. Schaff, p. 106.
11. *Ibid.* p. 112.
12. Marx, Karl, *Economic & Philosophical Manuscripts*, in *Marx's Concept of Man*, Erich Fromm, p. 97.
13. Marx, Karl, *Private Property and Labor*, in Fromm, Erich, *Marx's Concept of Man*, p. 129.
14. Marcuse, p. 246.
15. Schaff, p. 66.
16. Marcuse, p. 60.
17. *Ibid.* p. 187.
18. Schaff, p. 43.
19. *Ibid.* p. 128.
20. *Ibid.* p. 132.
21. *Ibid.* p. 229.
22. *Ibid.* p. 205.
23. Marcuse, p. 239.
24. *Ibid.* p. 112.
25. Fromm, p. 66.
26. *Ibid.* p. 3.
27. Marx, Karl, *Private Property and Labor*, in Fromm, Erich, *Marx's Concept of Man*, p. 127.
28. Schaff, p. 222.
29. Schaff, p. 218.
30. *Ibid.*.
31. Northrup, F.S.C. *The Taming of the Nations*, p. 189.
32. *Ibid.* p. 192.
33. Bellah, Robert, *Beyond Belief*, "Religious Evolution," p. 22.
34. *Ibid.* p. 45.
35. Fromm, p. 36.

218   Marxism and Native Americans

**Bibliography for
Circling The Same Old Rock
By Vine Deloria Jr.**

Bellah, Robert, *Beyond Belief,* New York: Harper & Row, 1970.

Fromm, Erich, *Marx's Concept of Man,* New York: Frederick Ungar Publishing Co., 1961 (Containing several of Karl Marx's shorter works including: *Private Property and Labor* and *Economic and Philosophical Manuscripts*)

Marcuse, Herbert, *Reason and Revolution,* Boston: Beacon Press, 1960.

Northrup, F. S. C. *The Taming of the Nations,* New York: Macmillan, 1954.

Schaff, Adam, *Marxism and the Human Individual,* New York: McGraw-Hill Paperbacks, 1970.

Notes For
Marx Versus Marxism
By Bill Tabb

1. Ray Vicker, "The Industrial Reservation; Plan Seeks to Blend Indians into Urban Society Without Sacrificing Identity as Tribe Members," *Wall Street Journal*, May 21, 1981, p. 56.

2. See William E. Connolly, "The Politics of Industrialization," *Democracy*, July 1981, pp. 20-21; and Andre-Gorz, *Ecology as Politics*, Boston: South End Press, 1980, for ecologically "with it" Marxist perspectives.

3. See Shlomo Avineri, ed., *Karl Marx on Colonialism and Modernization*, Garden City, N.Y.: Anchor Books, 1969, p. 6.

4. *Ibid.* p. 470.

5. Black Hills Alliance, *The Keystone to Survival*, Rapid City, South Dakota, Black Hills Alliance, P.O. Box 2508, 1981, p. 103.

6. *Ibid.* p. 107.

7. *Ibid.* p. 57.

ABOUT THE CONTRIBUTORS

Frank Black Elk, Ogala Lakota, is head of Colorado Aim and founder of the Society of Native Indigenous Peoples. He lives and works in Denver.

Ward Churchill, Creek/Cherokee, is director of Planning, Research and Development for Educational Opportunity Programs at the University of Colorado/Boulder, and is co-director of the Institute for Natural Progress. He is a member of the American Indian Movement.

Vine Deloria Jr., Hunkpapa Lakota, is a professor of American Indian studies, political science, and the history of law at the University of Arizona. He is author of a number of books, including *Custer Died for Your Sins; We Talk, You Listen; God Is Red;* and *The Metaphysics of Modern Existence.*

Phil Heiple is an applied cultural activist/critic working as a disc jockey (specializing in reggae music) with radio station KDYP in Santa Barbara, Ca. He is also a freelance journalist and graphic artist.

Winona Laduke, Anishinabe, was a member of the founding group of Women of All Red Nations. She is currently director of the Anishinabe Oral History Project on Minnesota's White Earth Chippewa Reservation where she lives and works. She is a co-director of the Institute for Natural Progress.

Elisabeth Lloyd is a doctoral candidate in philosophy at Princeton University.

Russell Means, Oglala Lakota, was a co-founder (with Dennis Banks) of the American Indian Movement in 1968. Since then, he has played a major role in events such as the 1972 AIM take-over of the Bureau of Indian Affairs building in Washington D.C., the 1973 occupation of Wounded Knee, and the 1980 establishment of Yellow Thunder Camp in South Dakota's Black Hills. He is currently a candidate for the presidency of the Pine Ridge (Oglala) Reservation government in South Dakota.

William K. Tabb teaches economics at Queens College, CUNY. He is author of *The Long Default: New York City and the Urban Fiscal Crisis* as well as a number of scholarly and popular economics articles.

Robert B. Sipe teaches political and psychological theory at Sangamon State University. He was founder of the Redland Radical Therapy Collective in Springfield, Il., where he has lived the past dozen years. Sipe is an editor of and frequent contributor to the quarterly journal, *Issues in Radical Therapy.*